THE REMINISCENCES OF
Rear Admiral Doniphan B. Shelton
U.S. Navy (Retired)

INTERVIEWED BY
Paul Stillwell

U.S. Naval Institute • Annapolis, Maryland

Copyright © 2003

Preface

This oral history originated in an unusual manner. In 1999 Admiral Shelton called the Naval Institute to inquire about ordering a copy of the oral history of a fellow aviator, Rear Admiral James D. "Jig Dog" Ramage. During the course of the conversation, I mentioned that I recalled he had come from Missouri. It turned out that both of us had attended the same junior high school and high school in Springfield, Missouri. Though he was more than 20 years ahead of me, some of the same teachers were in the high school for both of us. Because of the common background, Admiral Shelton invited me to come visit him the next time I was in California. What I heard about his naval career during the informal visit was so interesting that I invited him to record his stories on tape, and he agreed. The result is the oral history that follows.

The path to a commission for Shelton involved shipboard service as an enlisted man, Naval Academy prep school, then a three-year wartime course at the academy. He served through the end of World War II in the cruiser St. Louis and then found his true calling as a fighter pilot. During the 1940s night fighter operations were in their infancy in the U.S. Navy. Don Shelton was one of the pioneers in development of what has become a valuable asset. He recounts some of the difficulties in the night operations being accepted on board aircraft carriers, which had up to then conducted flight operations almost exclusively in daytime. In the U.S. Navy of the 21st century, night carrier operations are accepted as challenging but routine. Don Shelton had a substantial role in bringing them to that condition.

In other parts of the oral history, the admiral tells of tours of duty as fighter pilot in the Korean War, as a test pilot, the problems involved in trying to bring the F7U Cutlass fight into the fleet, commanding a squadron and air group, and his role as commanding officer of two ships during the Vietnam War. Ashore he served in the Pentagon, was a student at the Armed Forces Staff College and Naval War College, and made a significant contribution as commander of the naval base at Subic Bay in the Philippines. In the latter billet he eliminated a difficult racial problem and then served as host for thousands of South Vietnamese refugees who poured through Subic in 1975 after their nation had fallen.

George Van, a former naval officer, did the initial transcription of the interview tapes. Both Admiral Burke and I have edited the transcript in the interests of accuracy, smoothness, and clarity. In addition, I have inserted footnotes to provide further information for readers who use the volume.

Ms. Ann Hassinger of the Naval Institute's history division has made a significant contribution through her diligence in the overall process of printing, proofreading, and overseeing the binding of the completed volumes.

Paul Stillwell
Director, History Division
U.S. Naval Institute
April 2003

REAR ADMIRAL DONIPHAN B. SHELTON
UNITED STATES NAVY (RETIRED)

Doniphan Brown Shelton was born in Kansas City, Missouri, on 22 May 1921, son of Robert Ferrell and Mary Maud (Brown) Shelton. He graduated from high school in Springfield, Missouri, and on 6 August 1939 enlisted in the U.S. Navy. He attended boot camp at the Naval Training Station, San Diego, California, from August to October 1939, then joined the USS New Mexico (BB-40). In April 1940 he transferred to the USS California (BB-44) and in October of that year was detached for instruction at the Naval Academy Preparatory Class, Naval Operating Base, Norfolk, Virginia. He entered the U.S. Naval Academy, Annapolis, Maryland, in 1941. Graduated and commissioned ensign with the class of 1945 on 7 June 1944, he subsequently advanced in rank to that of rear admiral, to date from 6 November 1971.

Following graduation from the Naval Academy in 1944, he joined the USS St. Louis (CL-49) and was on board that cruiser during the Battle of Leyte Gulf. On 27 November 1944, four out of six kamikazes scored direct hits on the St. Louis, causing extensive damage. He is entitled to the ribbon for, and facsimile of the Navy Unit Commendation awarded that light cruiser. Detached from the St. Louis in October 1945, he next had flight training at the Naval Air Stations Dallas, Texas; Corpus Christi, Texas; Pensacola, Florida; and Banana River, Florida.

Designated naval aviator on 6 February 1947, he was assigned in July of that year to Fighting Squadron One Easy, based at the Naval Air Station, North Island, Coronado, California. In August 1948 he transferred to Night Composite Squadron One at the Naval Air Station, Barbers Point, Oahu, Hawaii. From November 1949 to July 1951 he served as F6F-5N/F4U-5N night fighter team leader, instrument instructor, and flight officer of Composite Squadron Three. In that assignment he participated in operations in the Korean area of hostilities and is entitled to three stars on the ribbon and facsimiles of the Navy Unit Commendations awarded the USS Philippine Sea (CV-47), USS Princeton (CV-37), and USS Valley Forge (CV-45), as well as the Air Medal.

In July 1951 he reported for test pilot training at the Naval Test Pilot School, Naval Air Test Center, Patuxent River, Maryland. He remained at Patuxent, serving from February 1952 to December 1953 as project test pilot in the Service Test Division, after which he had duty in connection with Project Cutlass (F7U-3) at the Naval Air Station, Miramar, California. During the period October 1954 to February 1956 he was team leader of the F7U-3 Transitional Training Unit (forerunner of the present RAG squadrons) with Composite Squadron Three. He then was assigned as executive officer of Fighter Squadron 124, the first West Coast F3H Demon squadron.

He reported for instruction at the Armed Forces Staff College, Norfolk, Virginia, in January 1958 and in June of that year returned to the Naval Test Pilot School to serve as administrative/flight instructor until February 1961. Following assignment as prospective commanding officer with Fighter Squadron 121 (replacement air group), he assumed command of Fighter Squadron 92 (F3H Demons) in July 1961. He was detached from command of that squadron in July 1962 for instruction at the Naval War College, Newport, Rhode Island.

He was assigned in August 1963 to Combat Readiness Air Wing 12, as prospective Commander Carrier Air Wing 19 and assumed command of the latter in March 1964. In April 1965 he reported as National Command Matters Officer in the Command Policy Section, Office of the Chief of Naval Operations, Navy Department, Washington, D.C. He became head of that section in May 1966 and for meritorious service was awarded the Navy Commendation Medal.

In June 1967 he assumed command of the USS Paricutin (AE-18) and in July 1968 became the third commanding officer of the USS Tripoli (LPH-10). In that duty he was awarded the Legion of Merit with combat V. While under his command, the Tripoli was awarded the Navy Unit Commendation for joint amphibious assault operation Bold Mariner. Detached from the Tripoli in August 1969, he next headed the Aircraft and Weapons Requirements Branch, Office of the Deputy Chief of Naval Operations (Air), Navy Department. He was awarded a gold star in lieu of the second Legion of Merit.

Assigned to the office of the Chief of Naval Operations, he served as deputy director of the Politico-Military Policy Division from July 1971 to April 1972, then as director and from November 1971 had additional duty as special assistant for Pan American affairs. In February 1973 he assumed command of the Naval Base, Subic Bay, Luzon, Republic of the Philippines, and in April of that year was assigned additional duty as Commander Naval Forces Philippines and Commander in Chief Pacific's representative in the Philippines. He was awarded the Distinguished Service Medal for exceptionally meritorious service.

In August 1975 Rear Admiral Shelton was reassigned as Deputy Director, Research, Development, Test and Evaluation (OP-98B) in the Office of the Chief of Naval Operations, Navy Department, Washington, D.C. His final tour of active duty, from August 1977 to September 1979, was a director for plans (J-5) on the staff of Commander in Chief Pacific. Upon retirement from active duty on 1 October 1979 he was awarded a gold star in lieu of the second Distinguished Service Medal.

In addition to the Distinguished Service Medal (two awards), Legion of Merit with gold star and combat V, Air Medal, Navy Commendation Medal and the Navy Unit Commendation ribbon with five stars, Admiral Shelton is authorized to wear the Asiatic-Pacific Campaign Medal (three stars); the World War II Victory Medal; the Navy Occupation Service Medal, Asia Clasp; the China Service Medal; National Defense Service Medal with bronze star; the Korean Service Medal with bronze star; United Nations Service Medal; Vietnam Service Medal with silver star; Humanitarian Service Medal; Philippines Legion of Merit (Degree of Commander); Korean Order of National Security Merit (Cheonsu Medal); Vietnam Cross of Gallantry; the Republic of Vietnam Campaign Medal; and the Philippine Liberation Ribbon with one bronze star. He also has the Korean Presidential Unit Citation Badge.

Admiral Shelton is married to the former Peggy Terrell. They have two daughters, Deborah Irene and Donna Mary.

Authorization

The U.S. Naval Institute is hereby authorized to make available to individuals, libraries, and other repositories of its choosing the tapes and/or transcripts of two oral history interviews concerning the life and naval career of the undersigned. The Naval Institute may also, at its discretion, use the material in electronic/digital format, including posting on the Internet. The interviews were recorded on 10 and 11 February 2000, in collaboration with Paul Stillwell for the U.S. Naval Institute.

The undersigned does hereby release and assign to the U.S. Naval Institute the rights and title to these interviews, with the exception that the undersigned retains the right to use the material for whatever purposes he deems appropriate. The copyright in both the oral and transcribed versions shall be the sole property of the U.S. Naval Institute. The tape recordings of the interviews are and will remain the property of the U.S. Naval Institute.

Signed and sealed this 3rd day of April 2000.

Doniphan B. Shelton
Rear Admiral, U.S. Navy (Retired)

Interview Number 1 with Rear Admiral Doniphan B. Shelton, U.S. Navy (Retired)

Date: Thursday, 10 February 2000

Place: Admiral Shelton's home in Del Mar, California

Interviewer: Paul Stillwell

Paul Stillwell: Admiral, it was a genuine pleasure to meet you a couple of days ago and to reminisce about our respective growing-up years in Springfield, Missouri. Now I'm delighted that you have agreed to do an oral history also. Could you please start by telling something about your parents and those early years in Springfield?

Admiral Shelton: Well, thank you. I, too, was pleased to meet somebody from Springfield that had gone somewhere and done something. I think that your job back there at the Naval Institute is really a fine job, and I appreciate this opportunity to get a little of my experiences and thoughts on paper. I was born on 22 May 1921 in Kansas City, Missouri, only because my mother happened to be visiting up there at the time in Excelsior Springs, where my father's family all came from. But I grew up in Springfield, Missouri, and I consider Springfield my hometown. My father was Robert Ferrell Shelton. The Ferrells are all up around Excelsior Springs, and his mother was a Ferrell. They lived a couple of farms over from the James brothers' farm, which was in Kearney.

Paul Stillwell: That would be Jesse and Frank James?

Admiral Shelton: Jesse and Frank, that's right.[*] As a matter of fact, my grandfather knew them both pretty well and, maybe not so surprising, kind of liked them. Many people back there in that part of Missouri did like the James brothers. My mother's maiden name was Mary Maude Brown. Her mother and father lived in Springfield, and they came from the Grey family—G-R-E-Y, I think it is, not G-R-A-Y—from

---

[*] Jesse James (1847-1882), who was born in Clay County, Missouri, was a criminal who joined his older brother Frank in robbing banks and trains in Missouri and nearby states. During the Civil War the brothers were part of Confederate guerrilla groups.

somewhere back in Virginia and eventually, of course, from Europe. So basically Scotch, Irish, and French is the heritage on both sides there.

Paul Stillwell: I think you told me that you inherited your first name from your grandfather.

Admiral Shelton: That's true. My grandfather on my father's side was named Doniphan Scott Shelton, and he, as I said, lived in Excelsior Springs. He was a fellow haberdasher and friend of Harry Truman.* This fellow Doniphan was what we would call a reserve today. He led a band of Missouri reservists down into Mexico in the Mexican War and did a pretty good job. He came back, ran for the Senate, was elected, but didn't care for Andrew Jackson, so he got out of Washington and went back to Missouri.† I really don't know what he did for a career once he came back to Missouri, but evidently he was fairly successful.

There is a Doniphan, Missouri, down around Cape Girardeau, and there is a Doniphan County in Kansas. So that was Doniphan, and I very seldom get anybody that finally finds out what my name really is that doesn't want to know where it came from. So there it is. The biggest problem I have is that everybody wants to say my name is Donald, and I try to steer them away from that.

I went to three schools in Springfield: Bailey Elementary, Pipkin Junior High School, which was only a couple of blocks from the old ballpark at that time, and Central High School, which is still there. It's not being used very much but still there. It was then the only high school in town, so that's where I went.

When I started school, I lived on Chestnut Street in Springfield, which is now a throughway right through the middle of the city, going from west to east or east to west. The old house that we lived in is long gone but was right across the street from what is now the main post office in Springfield. We lived there until I started junior high, when we moved to 963 North Grant. From there I went to Pipkin for junior high, and also from North Grant I went to senior high school.

---
* In the years shortly after World War I, Harry S. Truman was co-owner of a clothing store in Kansas City, Missouri. He later served as President of the United States from 1945 to 1953.
† Andrew Jackson, a hero of the War of 1812, served as President of the United States from 1829 to 1837.

Almost all of my early learning was in music. There was a man in Springfield, Missouri, named Doctor R. Ritchie Robertson, who had come over from Scotland. He set up a music program in Springfield, and he was the director of music for all the Springfield schools. That started not in grade school exactly, but by the time you were in junior high, if you were interested in music, you became a member. If you were a boy, you could also be a member of the Boy Scouts' band that had three levels—the beginners, the intermediate, and the concert band. Doctor Robertson had the band under his command, if you want to put it that way. He was a great musician himself, and he was a great disciplinarian.

Paul Stillwell: How much talent did you bring along with your interest in music?

Admiral Shelton: Well, as it turns out, I brought a fair amount of talent. I didn't know about it when I started, but both my brother and I started on the trumpet. Actually, he played the trumpet, I played the cornet, and there is a little difference between the two instruments, mostly in the mellowness of the tone of the cornet. I started out when I was about in the fifth or sixth grade, I guess, maybe a little bit before that. By the time I was 11 years old I wasn't really eligible for the Boy Scouts, 12 being the age, but Doctor Robertson managed to let me get in anyway, and I had a hard time finding a uniform that could be cut down for me to wear. It was a great experience, and he did a great job for all the young people in the city of Springfield.

I think one of the things that I remember most about him was that during the Depression, and it was a Great Depression, he was almost solely able to raise the money to take the Boy Scouts band to the Chicago World's Fair in 1933.* It was billed as the largest Boy Scouts band in the world, and I'm sure it was. We had a great time, and as I've already mentioned to you before, we managed to see Gypsy Rose Lee and a couple of others up there that were pretty interesting.†

---

* Following the crash of the New York Stock Exchange in late October 1929, the United States was plunged into the Great Depression, from which it did not recover until the nation geared up for World War II at the beginning of the 1940s. The Depression was marked by high unemployment and many business failures.
† Gypsy Rose Lee was a noted strip-tease artist of the period.

Paul Stillwell: What sort of work did your father do, and did the Depression have an effect on that?

Admiral Shelton: Yes, the Depression had a great effect on what my father was able to do. He did not graduate from high school, as many men did not back in those days. I remember him most as being in charge of a dining car on the Frisco Railroad, a Fred Harvey dining car from Kansas City to Birmingham, Alabama.* We lived in Springfield at that time, and then we moved to Kansas City for a couple of years, because that's where he ran to and from all the time, but basically that's what he did.

Before that he had gone out to Pleasanton, Kansas, and had developed 50 head of Jersey cattle for a dairy. I never knew anything about that. My brother and sister were both born in Pleasanton, Kansas, but I came along after they had moved to Springfield, so I never knew much about Pleasanton. From that and the Fred Harvey thing he sort of got into the restaurant business, and he ran a Fred Harvey restaurant in Springfield for a while. Then he built his own small restaurant near the new KWTO/KGBX radio station and did all right there, but basically during the Depression he had a very hard time.

He didn't have much of the education that a lot of the other people did have that survived the Depression in good shape. He was not a man that could go out and labor, so he had hard time finding work that he could work at and make any money. He ended up during the Depression working as a WPA supervisor, and he supervised building one of the parks in Springfield there.† It didn't bring him in much money, but it kept him pretty busy.

Paul Stillwell: You ate steadily, but no luxuries I take it.

Admiral Shelton: Ate steadily but no luxuries. The eating was based on our garden and a once-a-week trip to Harrison's Grocery Store down on Boonville. We had either ham or

---

* The St. Louis and San Francisco Railroad was commonly known as the Frisco. It has since been swallowed in a corporate merger and no longer operates as an independent entity. The Frisco Railroad Museum is in Admiral Shelton's hometown of Springfield, Missouri.
† WPA—Works Progress Administration, a Depression-relief agency that sometimes created various public works projects in order to stimulate employment.

a round of beef or something like that, and that was the meat for the week, maybe for the month sometimes. So life was not very great in those days from a money standpoint, but we had a lot of family ability and willingness to solve daily problems. One of the good things going for us, my mother was a graduate of Drury College, and she had been a valedictorian at Central High, which is where I went later.[*] Then she was summa cum laude at Drury College. She brought with her those values to the family, and so what my dad could not make up for in those kinds of values, my mother certainly did, and she tried to inculcate those into all three of us kids.

Paul Stillwell: The value and importance of education.

Admiral Shelton: Absolutely. Sometimes it took, and sometimes it didn't, but she tried hard all the time. Much of any success I have had I certainly owe to her.

Paul Stillwell: How much was religion a factor in the family as you were growing up?

Admiral Shelton: A pretty big factor. My grandmother on my mother's side was Presbyterian. My grandfather on my mother's side was Catholic. We grew up as Presbyterians, and we all went to the old First and Calvary Presbyterian Church there out on Dollison Avenue in Springfield.

Paul Stillwell: Near the Southwest Teachers College.

Admiral Shelton: Near Southwest Teachers College and almost absconded by the college at this point.[†] But I think that part of the religion we got. We—sister, brother, myself—went every Sunday, and we took our nickel and put in the collection, except for one time when we stopped back by to buy a hamburger with the nickel that we were supposed to put in the collection box. My dad found out about that, and that's probably the only whipping that my dad ever gave me with a cherry limb, which was limber and hurt.

---

[*] The interviewer graduated from Central High School and Drury College in the 1960s.
[†] The school is now known as Southwest Missouri State University.

Paul Stillwell: So that was the only time that happened.

Admiral Shelton: That was the only time that happened. I knew better than to do it again. We didn't have much money, but we had a lot of other good things going for us.

Paul Stillwell: What did you do for recreation?

Admiral Shelton: Recreation was mostly street hockey and rubber-gun fights. For street hockey you'd go out and find a limb that looked something like a hockey stick. Then you'd take one of the old Pet milk cans, and you stomp on it till it becomes a puck. And you get out in the middle of the street. There wasn't much traffic on Chestnut in those days, and so we played street hockey. Played a lot of softball, and later on when I got into junior high and high school I played quite a bit of hardball, but I never did excel to the point of being on any of the good teams around there.

Paul Stillwell: How much awareness was there of current events as time passed, the rise of the dictators in Europe and so forth?

Admiral Shelton: Well, not a whole lot. The Midwest was the Midwest, and the news was slow traveling to the Midwest. You have to remember it was mostly by voice or by radio in those days. We had newspapers, but the newspapers mostly reported on local stuff.

Paul Stillwell: I see.

Admiral Shelton: The Midwest in those days was not too vastly interested in what was going on in the rest of the world. That did play a part as I got towards graduation in high school. I graduated in 1939, and, of course, that's about when we started getting serious about getting into the war in Europe.

Paul Stillwell: And the Middle America was really isolationist at that time. There was a Springfieldian named O. K. Armstrong that was known as prominent in that movement.

Admiral Shelton: That's right. O. K. Armstrong I remember quite well. At the time when I graduated, as I said, I'd grown up in the music world, and I was pretty good at it. I had an opportunity for a scholarship to the University of Illinois, which in those days was one of the very best music schools in the country. I also had an opportunity to join the U.S. Navy band in Washington, which I had decided not to do. Most of my friends back there were all musicians, and they went their way in the music world. But I decided that with the war looking like it was coming on that I ought to be doing something else.

I had gotten interested in the Naval Academy, because there was a fellow named Louis King who was in the class of '40 out of the Naval Academy.* He dated and later married the sister of a girl that I didn't really date but that was one of my good friends in high school. So I got to know about Louis King and his way of getting to the Naval Academy. He enlisted in the Navy, spent his two years or so as an enlisted man, and then went into the Naval Academy. About that same time there were a number of movies that came out, several of them with Robert Young in them about Annapolis.

Paul Stillwell: One called Navy Blue and Gold had James Stewart in it.†

Admiral Shelton: Yes, and there were a couple of them on West Point, too, but they didn't quite register with me like the ones on Annapolis did. So I began to look into that when I was about a sophomore or maybe a junior in high school, which was kind of late to be looking into it, to tell you the truth. I decided that's the route that I wanted to go. About that time a Life magazine came out, and it had a big picture of Al Bergman from Kankakee, Illinois, on the front cover. I thought, "Man, that's great." They had a big spread on the inside and all of the views of the campus there, if you want to call it a campus—the yard at the Naval Academy. I began to think pretty seriously that that's the

---

* Midshipman Louis N. King, USN, who eventually became a brigadier general in the Marine Corps.
† The 1937 movie Navy Blue and Gold featured James Stewart and Robert Young as Naval Academy midshipmen and Lionel Barrymore as a Navy captain.

route that I wanted to take. I didn't know what I wanted to do once I graduated from the Naval Academy, if I were going to be that fortunate, but that came later on.

Paul Stillwell: Dewey Short was a legend there as the congressman. Did you have any connection with his office?

Admiral Shelton: I tried but was not successful with Dewey Short.* The other congressman was named Reuben T. Wood, and I had more success with him.† I did manage to get a third alternate appointment from Congressman Wood.

I started looking into what I needed to do to pass the exams, and it was a pretty big list of things. I went to my math teacher in high school—her name was Gideon I believe, Gideon or Gibson, Gideon. I said, "You know, this exam is pretty well slanted towards math." History and English I didn't have a problem with, but I did with the math. I hadn't been too good in plane geometry at that time, and so I knew I was going to have a problem with that. Well, she tried to tutor me, but she finally said, "Don, I'll tutor you all you want, but you're going to have trouble with this exam." And she was right. I took the exam, and I passed everything except math. As I recall, I had a 2.1 in math, and that wasn't good enough since I needed a 2.5. So that opportunity went out the window as far as going into the academy right from high school.

Hindsight's always pretty good, and maybe that was a good thing, because I really wasn't prepared for the kind of academics that I would face at the Naval Academy. In spite of my mother's good tutoring, I did not have the study habits that help you in a situation like that. As I mentioned, I'd known about Louis King enlisting in the Navy to go, and I looked into that. I thought that if I enlisted in the Navy I'd have a fair shot at going to the academy in a year or two, so that's what I decided to do.

Paul Stillwell: Was there any competition for slots in enlisting during that period?

---

* Dewey J. Short, a Republican, served in the U.S. House of Representatives from 4 March 1929 to 3 March 1931 and from 3 January 1935 to 3 January 1957.
† Reuben T. Wood, a Democrat, served in the U.S. House of Representatives from 4 March 1933 to 3 January 1941.

Admiral Shelton: No. They were glad enough to have me, and I enlisted right there for six years, although enlistments had been for four years until just a couple of years earlier. I signed up at the post office in Springfield, which in those days was on Boonville Avenue, not far from the courthouse.

Paul Stillwell: It was at the corner of Central.

Admiral Shelton: Central.

Paul Stillwell: That's where I registered for the draft in 1962. [Laughter]

Admiral Shelton: You and a good many others. Yes.

Then I went to St. Louis for the physical, and then we all went by train from St. Louis. In those days there wasn't a choice. You either were sent to Lake Michigan, near Chicago, Illinois, for the boot camp there, or you were sent out here to San Diego for the boot camp here.[*] I was lucky enough to get to San Diego. I enlisted on the seventh of August, which was my brother's birthday, and I got out here on the tenth of August, which was my dad's birthday. Then I went to boot camp.

Paul Stillwell: Probably the longest trip you'd ever made in your life.

Admiral Shelton: Oh, yes, yes. You know, going back to the Midwest, Chicago had been the furthest I'd ever been from Springfield and probably one of the very few times other than going to Wichita or Pittsburg, Kansas, a couple of times for music contests. I also went to Champaign, Illinois, for a national high school band week at the University of Illinois. Otherwise, I'd never been out of the state of Missouri, and I wasn't that much different from a lot of other people in those days. So, yes, it was a long journey. We trained to Los Angeles. Caught another train coming down to San Diego, and even in those days I can still remember coming through Del Mar and thinking what a really nice place that looks like. I don't know that I decided right then I was going to live there

---

[*] "Boot" is a slang term for a newly enlisted sailor or Marine. Recruit training is known as boot camp.

someday or not, but certainly it was kind of in the back of my mind, and it certainly looked like a fine place to think about.

Paul Stillwell: It caught your attention.

Admiral Shelton: It caught my attention. And so did boot camp. We had two chiefs. One of them was a fire controlman and the other was a—I don't really remember what the other one was, but the one that was senior to us was a chief named Foulke, so it's not hard to imagine how we bandied his name about.

Paul Stillwell: [Laughter] You're right.

Admiral Shelton: He was good. He was good. He was tough, as most drill instructors are, but he was very fair, and the company that we were in we managed to get the flag for the best company going through at that time.

Paul Stillwell: Well, please tell me a little about what boot camp life was like, the discipline, the content of the training.

Admiral Shelton: It was discipline, marching, washing your own clothes. You learned how to make a tie-tie on your clothes when you hung them on the line to dry so that there were no French ends showing as you they used to say. Then it was all about every Friday morning laying out your seabag in a certain way with all of your uniforms folded and tied a certain way so that they would fit in the seabag properly. The idea was that when you were going to leave and were going to pick up your seabag and put it on your shoulder, why, you had all your clothes, all your belongings right in that seabag, and they all had a place to fit.

Paul Stillwell: Tied them up with clothes stops.*

---

* A clothes stop is a small cotton lanyard used for fastening parts of a uniform to a line after washing or for securing uniform items that are rolled up.

Admiral Shelton: Tied them up with clothes stops and no French ends. If by any chance when you hung them all up and the inspector came along and he didn't like the way you'd hung them on the line, he had a good, sharp pocketknife, and he would cut all the clothes stops. So the clothes would fall to the ground, and he would stomp all over them and get them good and dirty, and then you had a chance to wash them all again. So you learned a lot of things.

Paul Stillwell: Chance? That's kind of a euphemism. It was more than a chance. It was an obligation.

Admiral Shelton: Yes, and I'm sure that there were a few intentional times there. I'm sure of that. But it all served a good purpose. And if you weren't marching right, they had a habit of coming up behind you with a swagger stick and rapping on your piece, your rifle, and telling you to get it where it ought to be.

Paul Stillwell: Would you say any of this discipline was unfair?

Admiral Shelton: No. As a matter of fact, I thought it was all very fair. I didn't really have a problem with it. I was probably too scared to have a problem with it. [Laughter] But I didn't have a problem. I was also very naïve. You know, I was 18 and coming from the Midwest, like I said I had, I didn't have very many viewpoints on anything, other than to try to get through there successfully and to make a mark so that I could try for the Naval Academy.

In those days if you wanted to try for the Naval Academy when you enlisted, you signed a little card or something that said, "Yes, I want to try for the Naval Academy." That piece of writing accompanied you to the boot camp, where you took an exam while you were there. And if you passed English and math, et cetera, et cetera, with good enough marks, they would send you to one of the larger ships, either a battleship or a cruiser preferably over a destroyer or anything like that, because the battleships and cruisers had more officers, more space, more room to study and a better atmosphere as far as studying is concerned.

Paul Stillwell: Was that preparatory exam less rigorous than the one that you had not passed previously?

Admiral Shelton: I would say it was probably a little less rigorous, because it was based mostly on what you could have expected to have learned in high school, as compared to what you were expected to know to pass the entrance exam to the Naval Academy, and that's a different horse totally.

Paul Stillwell: What do you remember about the camaraderie with your shipmates in boot camp?

Admiral Shelton: They were pretty good. I particularly remember a fellow named Watson, and he was from the South someplace, I don't know where, but he and I were pretty good buddies. Of course, I've always been short, so I was at the back end of that platoon, just like I was always at the back end of all the platoons at the Naval Academy too. Sand blowers, as they called them at the Naval Academy. I don't remember too many of them, but we had quite a few of them. There was a fellow named A. C. Lewis from Topeka, Kansas, that I got to know quite well.* He and I both ended up going to the USS New Mexico, which was a battleship. Beautiful battleship, beautiful ship.

Paul Stillwell: Was there any provision for you to go to the Naval Academy Prep School?

Admiral Shelton: Yes, that was the whole book. When you took this set of exams in boot camp, if you passed those, then that cleared you to take another set of exams later on to go to prep school, and prep school convened normally about the first of October every year. So sometime late in the spring or early summer, there would be a fleet-wide set of

---

* Midshipman Albert Clayton Lewis, USN.

exams that you could take to qualify to go to prep school. That was the way it was set up. I was supposed to go aboard the New Mexico, and I was supposed to be able to study while on board there for the exams to go to prep school. And basically that's what happened. I finished boot camp about the first of October, maybe a little bit before that.

Paul Stillwell: It's just after the war had started in Europe.

Admiral Shelton: Just after the war had started in Europe.[*] So I can remember in boot camp reading the newspapers, and it seemed that the newspapers in San Diego were so much more wide about broadcasting the news. "Here we go. We're going to get into a war," than the newspapers back in Springfield had indicated. So I kind of said, "Well, maybe this is the right decision after all." Because about that time all my buddies that I was still corresponding with back in Springfield that were musicians—they all enlisted or were drafted to go in the Army band or one of the service bands. Not necessarily the ones in Washington, but they needed a lot of bands in those days, and the services paid a lot more attention to having a good band around for various occasions than they seem to now, which I think is too bad. But they did. So most of my music buddies back in Springfield all went in one kind of a service band or the other, and they all stayed there during the war.

Paul Stillwell: Did you get liberty in San Diego while you were in boot camp?

Admiral Shelton: Got liberty one time in San Diego, and that was after graduation. I'd never had a beer in my life. I didn't have one then. I can remember going down on Broadway and finding a place that had chocolate sodas or something like that, and that's what I did and went to the movie and came back to the base. [Laughter] I didn't want to do anything that was going to scotch my chances. I didn't want to get put on report the only time I was on liberty and be picked up by the shore patrol and brought back to the base. So I really was a pretty clean liver on that first liberty there.

---

[*] World War II began on 1 September 1939, when German ground forces invaded Poland. Two days later Great Britain and France declared war on Germany. U.S. neutrality laws prevented the United States from taking part in the hostilities prior to the Japanese attack on Pearl Harbor in December 1941.

Paul Stillwell: Probably felt like a man let out of jail.

Admiral Shelton: Really did, but it wasn't so bad. We had a lot of good times in the boot camp. We marched and marched and marched and marched and marched, and we did a lot of things over and over and over again until we had it right. But, all in all, I'd hate to say that I thoroughly enjoyed it, but I didn't have any animosity towards the system. I thought it was pretty good, and it seemed to me that it was certainly designed to put a sailor aboard ship and the kind of a sailor that they wanted. And, as I said, I was looking ahead to go to the Naval Academy, so I was happy to do anything they wanted me to do.

Paul Stillwell: Well, that boot camp experience teaches you teamwork and cooperation with your fellow sailors.

Admiral Shelton: Yes. It also taught me that the tall guys are always up front except when they take a picture. [Laughter] Then the short guys get to sit in the middle in the front. That carries on fairly much. You look at almost any military organization and the platoon leaders, the company commanders, all that sort of thing, more often—not so much lately. I've noticed lately in the last few years in the Naval Academy there are some short guys or girls out in front, but basically back in those days the tall, muscular, athletic, good-looking guys were the ones out in front.

Paul Stillwell: What was the curriculum in boot camp? What subjects did you cover?

Admiral Shelton: They didn't cover anything except tying knots and seamanship, sailing, watch standing, that sort of thing.

Paul Stillwell: Marksmanship?

Admiral Shelton: No. Well, a little bit. Not much. In those days old Camp Mathews was right out here where UCSD is now, and they brought us up there for about a day or two days of getting acquainted with the rifle and shooting a rifle and a pistol, but that was about it.* Our biggest acquaintance with the rifle was carrying it around on our shoulder when we were marching. But they did take us up to Camp Mathews for two or three days, and we got to shoot and learn what that was about. But most of it was devoted to deck seamanship, standing watches, what you were expected to be able to do. You had to learn how to holystone, which nobody has ever heard of these days.† But once you got aboard ship the decks were teak. And the only way you got teak clean was every Friday on field day, starting at 4:00 o'clock in the morning, you got out your broomstick and half of a sand brick, and you holystoned the deck with water and salt, saltwater.

Paul Stillwell: Was the Bluejackets' Manual used in your training?‡

Admiral Shelton: Yes, I should have covered that, because everything that you did was in the Bluejackets' Manual, and so you were responsible for reading that section of the Bluejackets' Manual that you were going to be doing that day or the next day or whenever. So, yes, all of it was in there, all the seamanship, all the watch standing, how to tie knots, how to handle lines. All that sort of thing is all in there, as well as knowledge about the different classes of ships and all that sort of thing. It's a good book.

Paul Stillwell: Did you acquire a growing sense of confidence as you went through this process?

Admiral Shelton: [Chuckle] I don't know whether I did or not. I think I did, but that kind of confidence can get knocked down a little bit when you think you've done a pretty good job and some first class petty officer comes along and tells you, "You stink." [Chuckle]

---

* UCSD—University of California at San Diego.
† Holystoning refers to the practice of cleaning a ship's wooden decks by scraping them with bricks pushed back and forth across the planks by means of wooden handles. It is a laborious operation.
‡ The Bluejackets' Manual, which has been published by the U.S. Naval Institute in various editions over the years, has long been considered the "bible" for Navy enlisted men. It is a basic textbook and reference volume on a wide variety of naval subjects. Formerly these topics were addressed in chapters designated by letters from A to N.

Paul Stillwell: Those might not have been his exact words.

Admiral Shelton: No, those weren't his exact words, but he let you know that he wasn't too happy with whatever it was that you were doing at that time. And that did come into play on the New Mexico.* I mentioned to you the other day that the New Mexico, of course, was based in Long Beach along with the other battleships and cruisers in those days, and it was due to come down to San Diego in about two weeks after I graduated. So there was a draft of us of about, oh, I don't know, 20 or 25 sailors I guess that were waiting for the New Mexico. During that time, we all took our turn spreading horse manure on the grass areas there at the NTC, which were principally around the quarters areas.† So I always tell my two daughters that the reason that grass is so green is because of all of the horse manure that I spread down there during those two weeks, and I spread a lot of it. [Laughter] But when we did get on the New Mexico, of course, we were cruising around out here at San Clemente and basically right off the West Coast most of the time. I was in the fourth division, which had the after part of the main deck on the port side.

Paul Stillwell: Was that also aligned with the number-four turret?

Admiral Shelton: Yes, not necessarily though. The turrets were really numbered forward to aft, and so were the deck areas, but they started with one, two, starboard and port up forward and then three and four back aft. So I was in the fourth division, which was a deck division, not a gunnery division or somebody down in the bowels of the ship or anything like that. But it was a deck division, and that was good. I didn't mind that.

As soon a I got on board, my division officer recognized that I was on there to study for the Naval Academy, and he and another division officer, he being Francis John Fitzpatrick, who still lives in Annapolis. He was the class of '39, and the other fellow

---

* USS New Mexico (BB-40) was commissioned 20 May 1918. She was modernized at the Philadelphia Navy Yard from March 1931 to January 1933. Among the most noticeable changes was the replacement of her cage masts with a tower bridge. As modernized, her standard displacement was 33,420 tons. She was 624 feet long and 106 feet in the beam, and maximum draft of 31 feet. Her top speed was 22 knots. She was armed with 12 14-inch guns, 12 5-inch broadside guns, and 12 5-inch antiaircraft guns.
† NTC—Naval Training Center.

was Norm Doudiet, who was also out of class of '39, and they were both fresh-caught ensigns out of the Naval Academy.*

They were very good about sitting me and Ace Lewis down and some of the others that were trying to get there and saying, "Here's what you have to do, and here's how you have to learn how to study, and here's what you've got to know." So they gave us lessons and we all did the lessons, et cetera, et cetera, so they were really very good.

The one guy in the division that really didn't give a rat's ass whether I got to the Naval Academy or not was the first class petty officer. His name was Smith, Smitty, and he was a typical first class boatswain's mate. He had the square hat down over his nose, the dead cigar in his mouth, and a coffee cup whenever and wherever he wanted it. I wouldn't say he didn't like me, but he didn't care whether I got to the Naval Academy or not.

Paul Stillwell: Did he haze you?

Admiral Shelton: He didn't make it easy on me. I can remember that he got mad at me one time and he said, "Okay, Shelton, your job before you get any more liberty is to take that motor launch over there, liberty launch, and clean it down and sand it and repaint it before you go ashore."

Paul Stillwell: That's a big job.

Admiral Shelton: That's a very big job, and it took me roughly a week and a half to get that done. There was a third class coxswain in the division named Kayo, and Kayo was a little more amenable. He kind of helped me every once in a while. During that week and a half or so when I was trying to get that motor launch to Smitty's specs, he gave me a little help here and there. But, anyway, I said, "Well, you know, there's two sides to this thing. We'll see what happens." So Smitty's office, if you want to say that, was just inside the quarterdeck area there, where the break in the main deck was up to the forecastle deck. He had a little cubbyhole back in there which was his master-at-arms

---

* Ensign Norman W. Doudiet, USN.

shack. And that master-at-arms shack had two portholes in it.* And out there off of San Clemente there's a lot of times when those battleships roll a little bit. So when they went to sea and steaming around out there, they normally closed all those portholes and dogged them down tight. Well, Smitty wasn't around one day when we were rolling a little bit, and I got in there and I undogged those two portholes. [Chuckle]

Paul Stillwell: This was your revenge?

Admiral Shelton: That was my revenge. It flooded him out, and I mean it really flooded him out. Even myself I was kind of amazed at the catastrophe that I had caused. I guess he always thought that I did it, but he never could prove it. [Laughter] And I never did tell him. [Laughter] So we kind of managed to stay squared away. He had the upper hand. There's no question about that. So I tried to not tantalize him and to do my job and not give him any reason to bang me on the head. But he was good for me. He was an old-time sailor, and he was a good sailor. He knew what that deck division was all about, and he knew what he wanted me to do. So I tried my best to fit into that mold—at least for him.

Paul Stillwell: Now, some of those senior petty officers were cruel. I guess you wouldn't describe him as that.

Admiral Shelton: I could never call him cruel, but I could say that he was pretty tough. You know sailors in those days, senior sailors, and I don't know whether I should really put it this way or not, but most of them had kind of come up the hard way. They didn't have the best education in the world. They had enlisted in the Navy for a variety of reasons and maybe least of all the reason that they really wanted to be a sailor. It was only after they got in the Navy and found themselves a niche and got promoted to a certain level of authority that they perhaps began to enjoy it. But still I would have to say that he was good. He knew his stuff. You knew if you wanted him to solve a mathematics equation, you could forget it, but if you wanted to know anything about how

---

* The master-at-arms is essentially a shipboard policeman.

that deck was supposed to operate he could tell you. And not only could he tell you, but you could tell and show you how you were going to operate.

Paul Stillwell: Another point is that for many of those senior enlisted men the Navy was their whole life. There was no outside interest.

Admiral Shelton: That's right. Most of the sailors in those days saved up their leave for their whole first hitch, which was normally four years, and so they would have 120 days' leave coming when it was time to ship over. Most of them would take that 120 days' leave and go out and have one hell of a good time on the money they'd saved, come back, and reenlist.

Paul Stillwell: And start over.

Admiral Shelton: Start all over. [Laughter] That's right, start all over, and Smitty was one of those.

Paul Stillwell: But not many were married, so they lived and worked in the same place.

Admiral Shelton: In those days you know, what the hell, I was making 36 bucks a month as a seaman second on the New Mexico.* Now, I don't know how you're going to support a wife on 36 bucks a month—and not even a very aggressive girlfriend for that matter. [Laughter] So not many of them were married and for good reason. They couldn't afford it. That's all changed today, and I'm not sure that it's for the better. I think the Marine Commandant had a pretty good line on that. He almost got his head chopped off, but he said that he didn't think that the junior Marine should get married until they had enough money to support a wife, and unfortunately that's not the way it is

---

* When an individual enlisted he was classified as an apprentice seaman; when he was advanced in rate following boot camp he became a seaman second class, known as "seaman second" or "seaman deuce."

these days.* But back in those days they didn't worry about wives. They didn't want a wife most of them, and they didn't have money enough to afford one if they did.

Paul Stillwell: You talked the other day about the messing and berthing arrangements on the New Mexico.

Admiral Shelton: Yes. Just inside, right where Smitty's master-at-arms compartment was, that was also the living compartment for everybody else in that division, spread out, of course, in a little bigger area there. Along the side of the ship there, inside, was the area where you could stow your hammock. When you got up in the morning you had to tie up your hammock and stow it in the hammock stowage area there. All the mess tables were stored up against the overhead. They were collapsible tables that took two men, one on each end, to lift down out of the hangers in the overhead and bring down to the deck.

Then whoever was the messcook would bring the food when you had breakfast, lunch or dinner, whatever. When you had a meal, the messcooks would go to the galley, which was a couple or three levels up above, so they had to bring everything down in tureens, down the ladders, down to the living compartment and then distribute it, et cetera, et cetera. Not an easy job, particularly if there was a little rolling or anything like that.

When you were going to sleep at night, the hammocks were all swung in that same area, and the junior people's hammocks were all swung so that they were right up against the overhead, in other words right up against the bottom of those mess tables. So the junior people always liked to tell the messcooks, "Be sure and clean those tables really good, because we don't like the smell of them when we get up there in our hammocks at night and have to smell them while we're trying to go to sleep." All the senior people swung their hammock down below, and so you had an exercise in knowing

---

* On 11 August 1993 the Marine Corps announced a new policy, that it would phase out the recruiting of married men and women, so that all by 1995 all new recruits would be single. The announcement was a political embarrassment for President Bill Clinton, and the policy was withdrawn within a few hours. On 12 August General Carl E. Mundy, Jr., Commandant of the Marine Corps apologized and explained that he had approved the new policy without seeking the advice of senior civilians in the chain of command.

how to get up to your hammock, which was about six feet in the air, something like that; maybe it was a little more. So you had to know how to get up there and slide over into your hammock and settle down without having the hammock dump you over on the other side when you were trying to get in. So you learned that pretty fast.

Paul Stillwell: You had to have those things strung pretty taut too.

Admiral Shelton: Absolutely. Yes. The men down below, the seniors, weren't quite so particular about having them strung taut, but they didn't want you sagging down in their face, so you had to string yours pretty tight.

Paul Stillwell: Then every morning you had to wrap them up and put them in the hammock nettings.

Admiral Shelton: You had to take them down, fold them, strap them up, I forget what the terminology was now, but you had to put them all together and put them over there in the hammock stowage area.

There was no proliferation of heads around the ship.* All the crew's heads were all the way forward in the battleship, and they had a tile floor up there. All the urinals, all the heads, all the showers—everything was up there in that area. When you were going to wash your clothes or take a shower, you had a bucket that was stowed there in your living compartment. It had your name on it or a number on a brass tag that was your number. You were responsible for keeping that bucket not only to use but to keep clean and shining like a silver dollar.

So when you wanted to take a bath or wash clothes, you grabbed a bar of saltwater soap, took your clothes, took your bucket, go forward all the way to the bow, where the head was, and all that sort of thing and shower area. You washed yourself and your clothes with saltwater and saltwater soap. Then when you got through, you got one bucket of fresh water to rinse off yourself and your clothes. And then your clothes you brought back, and there was an area in the living compartment there where you could

---

* "Head" is the shipboard term for a bathroom.

string those up. Not everybody washed clothes at the same time, because there wasn't that much room for all the clothes to be hung, so you kind of had to learn when your part of the schedule was and stick with that. So life was not all that simple on a battleship, but it was pretty good. I enjoyed my time on there.

Paul Stillwell: What do you remember about some of the ship's operations while you were on board?

Admiral Shelton: Well, of course, as I said the, battleships and the cruisers were all berthed in Long Beach, and they had what they called Battleship Row and Cruiser Row. So when you went on liberty you rode the motor launches in to Long Beach, and then you could do whatever you wanted to do on liberty. As far as operations are concerned, mostly we'd go out around San Clemente, and at least in those times we would participate in gunnery exercises for the most part. I didn't have much to do, because I was not based in a turret. To tell you the truth, I really didn't have much to do as a new seaman second on board except to stay out of the way.

Paul Stillwell: What do you remember about the gunnery practices?

Admiral Shelton: Oh, I can remember how big a blast it was when those guns went off. We also had some antiaircraft exercises once in a while, and I can still remember standing too close—without anybody telling me that I shouldn't—to a 5-inch antiaircraft gun. I'm surprised that I have any hearing left these days because I really was standing too close to it. But it didn't take me long to remove myself a little further away. So mostly in the fall, why, that's what we did.

We went in and out of Long Beach Harbor. Mostly we'd go out Monday morning and come back in Thursday evening or Friday morning but usually Thursday evening because Friday morning nearly always was field day and that was a 4:00 o'clock reveille. As I've said, you would holystone the decks, clean everything up including the decks in the living compartment and everything else, shine your bucket, do all those good things. Then, about 6:30, they'd finally get around to having breakfast, and breakfast was always the same thing. It was pork and beans and eggs over either medium or hard depending on how they came out. That was breakfast every Friday morning.

Paul Stillwell: You'd be pretty hungry by the time breakfast came around.

Admiral Shelton: When I was a kid in Springfield, I cannot ever remember really having eggs for breakfast, so when I had gotten up at 4:00 o'clock and done the field day bit I was personally happy to have as many eggs as I could get my hands on. [Laughter] Yes, you learned a lot of things. Just in general I was a finicky eater when I was a kid. I didn't like almost anything. I didn't like tomatoes and I didn't like lettuce and I didn't like hardly anything except hamburgers if I was fortunate enough to have some of that. But I learned to eat a lot of things when I came in the Navy. And I learned that all of it can be pretty good, and I changed my eating habits pretty remarkably. [Laughter]

Anyway, that was kind of the routine for the remainder of the fall. Then sometime early January or middle of January we sailed up to Bremerton, Washington, as it turned out, to get the radar installed on the topmast there—big, old bed-springs type of thing.* On the way up there, we got into a lot of swells up off of Oregon, which can be pretty heavy. The 50-foot motor launches were all swung on davits up and swung in, oh, up by the galley deck, so they were probably a good 50 or 60 feet above the water. We were rolling so much that those 50-foot motor launches all got swept off of the davits and disappeared in the ocean. So when we got to Bremerton we didn't have any of those 50-foot motor launches left. I thought it was really remarkable. It's a real demonstration of the force of those waves first of all, and it shows you what the ocean can do with even a big ship like a battleship. As I recall, we rolled something like 41 degrees port and starboard. I'm not sure this is accurate, but later I was told that 45 degrees was about the limit that that ship was built to roll, so maybe we came closer to rolling over than we thought. I don't know, but I didn't hear anybody that really sounded worried on the ship.

Paul Stillwell: What was the sensation inside when she was rolling that much?

---

* Puget Sound Navy Yard, Bremerton, Washington.

Admiral Shelton: Oh, man, you hung onto anything you could hang onto, and you tried to make sure that everything stayed tied down, secured as well as you could do it, because anything that wasn't secured was going to take a roll across the decks. And, of course, they didn't let anybody topside, because anything topside was going to be washed off into the ocean pretty promptly. So the only people outside really were up on the bridge, and the New Mexico had an open bridge in those days, so there were some people up in the open up there, but they could hang on pretty good up there too. But everybody basically hung on during those big rolls from side to side.

Paul Stillwell: Did you get any new antiaircraft guns during that yard period?

Admiral Shelton: Not that I remember. That's a good question. I think we may have. We went from one type of 5-inch to another 5-inch. The old 5-inch/25 I think we went to, but I really can't remember that too well.

Paul Stillwell: Were you given any explanation of what the radar was?

Admiral Shelton: No, a big secret. Nobody would talk to you about it. You weren't supposed to ask any questions about it, and I think the gunnery officer and the captain and the exec and a few other officers were probably the only ones that knew anything about it. But at my level I certainly did not know anything about it.

Paul Stillwell: You probably had some curiosity then.

Admiral Shelton: I did. I didn't know what it was. I'd never heard of radar in the first place. R-A-D-A-R was not a word that I was familiar with, and so I didn't know what it was. I suspected there was some kind of communications gear, but I didn't know what. Found out though. We left Bremerton in about a month and a half or so and steamed out to Hawaii. That was when the Pacific Fleet moved to Hawaii at the direction of, I guess, the President at that time. No, couldn't have been the President. CNO.

Paul Stillwell: Well, I think it was the President. I think that's where the impetus came from.*

Admiral Shelton: That's where it ended up, but I know there was a lot of argument about moving the fleet out there, and it took a pretty high-level decision to make it happen. But we steamed out there, and we went to Lahaina Roads there at Maui.† We just stayed offshore there and did at least one big exercise that I can remember. I think there were two scheduled, but I don't think the second one ever happened.

Paul Stillwell: Did you get any sense during the exercise what was going on with the opposing fleets?

Admiral Shelton: No, I didn't. I'm sure there were officers on there whose duty it was to know what was going on that did know, but no. There again, they told you over the speaker system what you were supposed to do and when you went to general quarters or whatever you were going to do. But they did not go out of their way to explain the whole exercise or say, "This is what we're engaged in, and this is why we're doing it," or any of that kind of thing. At least not at my level.

Paul Stillwell: We really didn't talk too much about liberty in the Long Beach area. What were some of the attractions?

Admiral Shelton: I very rarely stayed in Long Beach. I had a cousin that lived in Glendale, and I would go up there sometimes. Other times they had the old red trolleys that ran from Long Beach to Los Angeles. For 50 cents you could buy a round-trip ticket to Los Angeles and still have money enough left to go to one of the theaters for a good show or one of the big bands. In those days a lot of the big bands were playing in the

---

* Fleet Problem XXI took place in the Hawaiian area in the spring of 1940. When it was completed, President Franklin D. Roosevelt directed that the fleet remain at Pearl Harbor rather than return to its bases on the West Coast. The idea was that leaving the fleet in Hawaii would serve as a deterrent to Japanese aggression in the Far East.
† Lahaina Roads is an area off the Hawaiian island of Maui. The U.S. Fleet often used it as an exercise area and anchorage in the years prior to World War II.

theaters, and so probably for a dollar and a half you could have a hell of a liberty. I still wasn't a beer drinker or any other kind of a drinker at that point, so that's mostly what I did. Ride the launch in, go to L.A. or go up to my cousin's house in Glendale, come back and ride the motor launch back out to the New Mexico.

Paul Stillwell: And usually the ride back to the ship was rowdier than the one away from it.

Admiral Shelton: Absolutely. I didn't drink, but there were a lot of them that did, and they usually had had a pretty good time on liberty. And, of course, the New Mex was on the outer row of the battleship row, and that was a pretty good ride from the dock to out there. I don't know how far that is, but I suspect it's probably about a mile or a mile and a half, something like that.

Paul Stillwell: I've heard that in the fog each ship would ring its hull number on the bell to guide the coxswain back to his ship.

Admiral Shelton: That may be true. I never knew how he got there, but I always had confidence in the coxswain that he knew how to get there. So that was essentially my liberty time. When we were in Hawaii we didn't get any liberty that I can remember. We stayed right there. About that time the New Mexico had a band, and while we were in Bremerton I played in the ship's dance band. A little later on, that's also about the time that I took the exams for prep school, which I didn't know how I'd done of course. But about that same time the bandmaster found out that I had played cornet, so he wanted me to play with the band—not just the dance band. This eventually led to not a decision on my part but a decision on his part that he wanted me to join the band, and, unbeknownst to me, he got approval to transfer me from the deck division to the band.

Also about that same time the band was moved from the New Mexico to the USS California, another battleship.[*] I never knew exactly why that transfer happened either,

---

[*] USS California (BB-44) was commissioned 10 August 1921. She had a standard displacement of 32,000 tons, was 624 feet long and 97 feet in the beam. Her top speed was 21 knots. She was armed with 12 14-inch guns, 14 5-inch guns, and two 21-inch torpedo tubes.

but anyway I ended up going to the California with the ship's band, still waiting to hear what was going to happen with the Naval Academy bit.

Paul Stillwell: Was that in the summer of 1940 that you moved?

Admiral Shelton: That was in the summer of 1940; that's right.

Paul Stillwell: She was a flagship. She had Commander Battle Force on board.

Admiral Shelton: That's right. She was the head shed of battleships in the Pacific Fleet and of everything else I guess. There was a fellow on there that was the exec named Robert B. Carney, who later was CNO.[*] I remember I wasn't on there very long, and about that same time I got the news from Reuben T. Wood back in Missouri that he had given me a first alternate appointment. So I actually had two ways of getting to the prep school and two ways to get to the academy because an appointment automatically guaranteed that you would go to prep school. All you had to do was go fill out a chit and show that you had the appointment and you'd go to prep school. I think I went to prep school basically on the basis of the appointment rather than waiting to hear what happened with the exam.

Paul Stillwell: How long did you spend on board California?

Admiral Shelton: I'm not sure exactly when I went on there, but I got off of there in about September, so I'd been on there maybe two months or three months at the most.

Paul Stillwell: Any impressions from that time? Any differences from New Mexico that you have noticed?

---

[*] Commander Robert B. Carney, USN. As a four-star admiral he was Chief of Naval Operations from 1953 to 1955. His oral history is in the Columbia University collection.

Admiral Shelton: Biggest difference I noticed that you were on the battleship of the head shed, and everything was more prim, more proper, and more clean.

Paul Stillwell: If that's possible.

Admiral Shelton: If that's possible. We did not have an admiral on the New Mexico, but we did have on the California, and I didn't even know who it was at the time. But when I left the California to go to prep school I do remember that it was on an inspection day, probably Friday morning, and my division officer had told me, "Now, just get dressed in your blues. Get your bag together and all that kind of stuff, and we're going to put you in this little space here. You just stay right in there until this whole thing is over, and then you can get off the ship and go." Well, I was standing there as he told me inside this little space, and it was probably, I don't know, some storage space of some kind. Then the exec opened the door.

Paul Stillwell: This would be Commander Carney.

Admiral Shelton: Commander Carney, who said, "What the hell are you doing in here?"

I said, "I'm waiting for this inspection to be over so I can leave the ship and go to prep school."

He said, "Good luck," and walked out. So that was my meeting with then-Commander Carney and later CNO.

Paul Stillwell: His son-in-law just died a couple of months ago, Joe Taussig.[*]

Admiral Shelton: Yes, right. I did not know him. I was familiar with his reputation at the academy, but I did not know him out in the fleet. Great guy, I guess, as far as I know. So anyway I went to prep school and started there about the first of October.

Paul Stillwell: Where was it?

---

[*] Captain Joseph K. Taussig, Jr., USN, who was married to Carney's daughter Betty.

Admiral Shelton: In those days it was at the old NOB, Norfolk, right inside the main gate.* There was a set of buildings there. That was the barracks. The school itself was down on the main drag not too far from the old airport there. So that's really kind of where I got a little bit of a chance to see the airplanes take off and land. We'd had airplanes on the aft deck there on both battleships, of course, and so I was always interested in watching them getting catapulted. Then they'd make what in those days they called a Cast recovery, where the ship made a big slick and they would taxi up and get caught in a net and hoisted aboard. So that interested me quite a bit.†

But when I went to prep school the landing pattern for most of the fighters landing there at NOB came right by the window of the prep school. I can remember that very distinctly. In those days they were almost all F4F-3s.‡ I enjoyed watching them land. When I was a kid in Springfield, Roscoe Turner had come through there on one of his barnstorming tours with a Curtiss Condor, and I'd gotten a ride with him. And I had gotten to see Lindbergh.§ So those things kind of all added up, and that's kind of when my interest in aviation started really to jell.

I remember at prep school we had another taskmaster; his name was Lloyd. Chief Lloyd was a no-nonsense-whatsoever chief, and for good reason. He had a bunch of guys there—about 130 of us, I guess—I forget whether it was 100 or 110 that could go in from the Navy at that time. I think it was 100. And his only task in life was to get us to school regularly, get us up and get us going, make sure we studied, and he did that with a lot of authority. He was good, no nonsense. He didn't take any nonsense from any of us. Nobody got away with anything. If you wanted to get away with anything, you weren't going to stay in that prep school very long because he had a dedicated purpose. He felt that his purpose was to see that everyone of those 130 or however many there were did their very best to get into the academy.

---

* NOB—Naval Operating Base.
† "Cast," which represented a letter in the phonetic alphabet of the time, designated a recovery method whereby the airplane landed on the water, rode up on a sea sled, and was lifted aboard by a crane on the ship's fantail.
‡ Grumman F4F Wildcat fighters first entered fleet squadrons in late 1940. The F4F-4 was 28 feet, 9 inches long; wingspan of 38 feet; gross weight of 7,952 pounds; and top speed of 318 miles per hour.
§ Charles A. Lindbergh became a national hero when he made the first solo flight across the Atlantic Ocean in May 1927.

Paul Stillwell: That was good. I mean, it wasn't trying to weed people out then.

Admiral Shelton: No, no, no. Not trying to weed them out at all. He had a different view than Smitty had had about the whole thing. So his whole viewpoint was to keep you healthy, do your exercises, do the running and everything that you were supposed to do to stay in shape, all this kind of stuff, and get you to school and get you back from school and try to get you to pass those exams.

Paul Stillwell: What would a day be like a prep school?

Admiral Shelton: Well, you'd get up about 6:00 o'clock or 5:30, and you'd go to breakfast, chow, and then you were generally at school I think about 7:30 or a quarter of 8:00, and you spent all day at school.

Paul Stillwell: What subjects did you cover?

Admiral Shelton: All the entrance exams, which were chemistry, plane and solid geometry, algebra, history, English. I don't know whether I've forgotten anything or not, but it was a full course. And the instructors there were all reservists.

Paul Stillwell: Officers?

Admiral Shelton: Officers. For instance, the English teacher was a jaygee, and he had come down from Boston College.* The algebra teacher was a little reservist from somewhere in Georgia. They had gotten reserve commissions. I don't think any of them had ever spent really any time in the Navy, but they knew the subject. And they knew what you had to know to pass those exams, and, believe me, they really put it to you.

Paul Stillwell: So they were really teaching to the exam.

---

* Jaygee—lieutenant (junior grade).

Admiral Shelton: Basically that's correct. They were teaching to the exam, but in doing that, you learned a lot of math, and you learned a lot of history, and you learned how to study. The entrance exams back in those days had a fairly consistent format to them. For instance, on the history exam I know that you could almost count 100% on having to draw a map of the United States and put in the Louisiana Purchase and all that kind of thing and fill in all the states and name all the states, et cetera, et cetera. It was a pretty good exercise in knowledge of that kind of thing.

Paul Stillwell: So these were not multiple-choice exams.

Admiral Shelton: Oh, no, no multiple choice. There was nothing like that. You had to put it on paper, and it had to be out of your head, and it had to be substantive.

Paul Stillwell: So a lot of memory work involved?

Admiral Shelton: Absolutely. A lot of memory, particularly in history and English. Chemistry was a big memory thing. I'd never taken chemistry in high school, so chemistry was a really dark subject for me, and I really had to study to feel like I had any confidence in the entrance exam because we didn't have any labs. We weren't doing any of the tests or anything like that. It was strictly a book learning chemistry situation where you had to know whatever it was.

Paul Stillwell: That's tough, starting from scratch.

Admiral Shelton: Yes, it was for me. By all measure, the chemistry was the hardest subject for me to study. I can't say that it got any easier when I got to the academy—that and electricity. You know, to get ahead of myself, we got a degree in electrical engineering back in those days. They didn't have a degree in marine engineering. And to this day if there's any subject that I really don't know a whole lot about it's electricity.
[Laughter]

But at the prep school we got a little bit of liberty. About every two weeks we'd get liberty in Norfolk. In those days Norfolk was not a very good sailors' town anyway. They literally had some of those old signs that you remember hearing about that said, "Sailors and dogs keep out." And they meant it.

Paul Stillwell: Granby and East Main was an area that was a sailors' hangout.

Admiral Shelton: Yes, and only because that's the only place they could go and be welcome, so to speak.

Paul Stillwell: Mostly bars.

Admiral Shelton: Mostly bars. There were a lot of whorehouses down there, too, but mostly bars. The reason the sailors went down there was because they basically weren't too welcome in the residential areas unless they happened to know somebody.

Paul Stillwell: So it was basically playing to the stereotype.

Admiral Shelton: Yes, that's right. Playing to the stereotype sailor. And so I didn't really spend a whole lot of time down in Norfolk. There were a lot of things to do on the base. We kind of got used to picking our buddies there, and so I picked a guy named William (None) Wade from Massachusetts. And A. C. Lewis was there, Ace Lewis, and a guy named Miller, Jughead Miller. That was about it. The four of us kind of did things around the base. Went into town maybe on rare occasions or whatever but didn't spend time down in Norfolk.

I did have one experience early on at prep school that might be of interest. Back then, Navy Day was 27 October, as I recall, and someone in Washington called the prep school to have one of the student sailors come to Washington to be interviewed on the Navy Day radio program. I never knew why, but I was chosen. I went to Washington with orders to report to Arthur Godfrey at his office in the old Warner Building on

Pennsylvania Avenue, close by the Willard Hotel. You may remember that Arthur Godfrey was a huge radio personality and a big, big supporter of the Navy.

Anyway, he gave me tickets to the theater where Helen O'Connell was singing with Ray Eberle's big-time band. That was great! I also was directed to report to Admiral Ernest J. King in his office in the old Navy Department Building on Constitution Avenue.[*] A little nervous, I was ushered into Admiral King's office. I can't say we chatted, but he did ask why I was there, where I was from, a few more questions, then said, "Good luck, young man." Then I was ushered out. At the time I'm not sure it sunk in on me just who he was, but I was impressed. As scheduled, I was interviewed on the Navy Day radio program by Arthur Godfrey, who did the program in the sail loft at the Washington Navy Yard. I might add that in those days there was a weekly Navy Band concert broadcast from the sail loft. All in all, a very interesting weekend.

Paul Stillwell: Did you encounter examples of racial segregation in Norfolk?

Admiral Shelton: I probably did, but I don't really remember. I really don't. If you ask me about Springfield, I can tell you more about racial segregation there than I can in Norfolk at that time.

Paul Stillwell: Well, please do. We didn't really talk about that in the Springfield context.

Admiral Shelton: Well, Springfield was right on the Mason-Dixon Line, of course, and it was a north-and-south town. The black people had their own schools. They were run by the same H. P. Study who was superintendent of all the schools in Springfield. As far as I remember, we never had any athletic activities with those schools. But at the same time they had all the equipment that we had: bats, gloves, balls, et cetera, et cetera. The same good schools, the same good education opportunity, teachers. For the life of me I don't

---

[*] Rear Admiral Ernest J. King, USN, was then a member of the Navy's General Board. In early 1941 he became Commander in Chief Atlantic Fleet as a four-star admiral, and in December 1941 he became Commander in Chief U.S. Fleet.

know whether those black schools had any white teachers in them or not. They may have. I really don't know.

Paul Stillwell: There were two different societies in the city.

Admiral Shelton: Two different societies, and I hate to say this, but I was not aware that there was a big problem there like any semblance of that sort of thing is today. But in Springfield in those days there really was no problem. I don't remember any problems, and I don't remember that anybody felt put upon particularly.

Paul Stillwell: There was not a stimulus for you to get involved in that separate society.

Admiral Shelton: No.

Paul Stillwell: And I'm sure they didn't get much coverage in the local media.

Admiral Shelton: I do remember that one time when we were still living on Chestnut Street there in Springfield, so I had to be not more than about 10 or 11, something like that, 12. I do remember I was out in the front yard one day, and my dad said something about the black people. He used a different word. And I can remember to this day that I turned and I said, "What the hell is wrong?" I didn't say "What the hell is wrong?" to my dad, but that was pretty much my voice. I said, "What's wrong with those guys?" you know.

My dad said, "Well, you'll learn someday that there's a difference between you and them." And I've never forgotten that. I didn't agree with him at the time, and I don't agree with him now. But he was brought up that way. Excelsior Springs was that much further north, and that's the way the north people were brought up. Springfield on the other hand, as far as I know, had the first national cemetery with both North and South people buried in it.

Paul Stillwell: Right.

Admiral Shelton: And I think that includes blacks as well as anybody else.

Paul Stillwell: Well, I remember even coming up in Springfield some 20 years after you, and you would not see pictures of black people in the society pages, for example.

Admiral Shelton: No, that's right. I never thought of it that way, but you're right. On the other hand, I do remember that the best place to get barbecue was at a place owned by a black man. It was called Washington's Barbecue Pit over on Washington Street, which was not too far from where we lived and only about three blocks from the high school. Everybody—blacks, whites, whatever—went to Washington's Barbecue Pit to get barbecue. And it was good.

Paul Stillwell: I remember going there myself.

Admiral Shelton: Yes. But to get back to Norfolk, gee, I'm sure there must have been that at the time, but I wasn't really conscious of it. It probably would have had to hit me in the face, you know, like a baseball bat for me to be conscious of it at that time, because my entire focus was on passing the entrance exam. So I wasn't looking around for any other diversions or anything like that.

Paul Stillwell: When you were in the prep school were you treated as a higher status than you had been in boot camp?

Admiral Shelton: Only because we'd been in the Navy a couple of years I guess, and some of them had been in a little longer than that. And Chief Lloyd was a competent leader and barracks master. We had some senior guys in that prep school, I mean first class, second and third class petty officers. I was still a seaman first class at that time, but we did have a few that were petty officers, and so they'd been around the horn a little bit.

Paul Stillwell: They were probably pushing up against the maximum age limit then for getting in.

Admiral Shelton: They were, and I was, too, because I was 21 when I got in. That was definitely on the older sides of the plebes. My roommate at the Naval Academy at one point was George Steele, Vice Admiral George Steele now.* He was only 17 when he entered the academy.

Paul Stillwell: I have interviewed him.

Admiral Shelton: Yes. He was one the youngest ones in the class. He was 17 when he came in. Here I was at 21. So that age difference played itself out over the years, and it was always there. The younger guys that were good and good performers always had an edge because of that two or three years' age difference. It didn't make any difference to me at the time. But I think later on I recognized that if I could have gotten in the academy out of high school, and if I'd been successful in staying in the academy and graduating then, I would have had a better shot at a lot of things.

Paul Stillwell: You would have been a classmate of Zumwalt, for example.†

Admiral Shelton: Wouldn't that have been great? [Laughter]

Paul Stillwell: Well, you have to play the hand that's dealt you, so you did.

Admiral Shelton: That's right, I did.

Paul Stillwell: George Steele never struck me as somebody who lacked in self-confidence at all. [Laughter]

---

* Vice Admiral George P. Steele II, USN (Ret.), has been interviewed as part of the Naval Institute's oral history program.
† Admiral Elmo R. Zumwalt, Jr., USN, served as Chief of Naval Operations from 1 July 1970 to 29 June 1974. He was in the Naval Academy class of 1943.

Admiral Shelton: Not at all. Not at all. His dad was a retired Navy captain. His dad had been the—I think I'm getting this right—he was a salvage officer at Pearl Harbor after the attack.

Paul Stillwell: Well, he may have been, but he moved to be a plans officer on Admiral Nimitz's staff.* Then he got command of the battleship Indiana and had a collision that pretty much ended his career opportunities.

Admiral Shelton: Maybe I'm wrong on that, but I thought that at least initially he had a big role in the salvage part of some of those ships.

Paul Stillwell: Well, he was the skipper of the Utah at the time of the attack.

Admiral Shelton: That's right. Incidentally, the St. Louis, the ship that I was on later in the war, did not get hit at Pearl Harbor. It was the first major combatant to get out of the harbor at that time.

Paul Stillwell: Well, back to prep school, did that really prepare for the exams that you were going to take?

Admiral Shelton: Oh, yes. I walked into those exams, and I thought it was a piece of cake. I think I made a 4.0 on all but one of them. I think the only one that I made a 3.6 on, and I can't even remember which one that was, but it was a pure momentary drop in focus or something, because I knew the answers and all that kind of stuff. Yes, I didn't have any trouble with the exams, and I felt quite confident. We all went on 30 days' leave as soon as we took the exams and came back to find out whether we'd passed or not.

---

* Admiral Chester W. Nimitz, USN, served as Commander in Chief Pacific Fleet and Pacific Ocean Areas, 1941-45. In December 1944 he was promoted to the five-star rank of fleet admiral.

Paul Stillwell: So that officer who was preparing you to succeed really did work.

Admiral Shelton: Yes, and I've seen him a number of times since then and I have told him. He's a rear admiral, retired Rear Admiral Fitzpatrick, and he became a communications specialist. Later on I was in the Pentagon at the same time that he was, and so I had a chance to tell him several times how good a job he'd done on me. [Laughter] And he had. He was a great guy. Both of them were. Norm Doudiet was killed in the Juneau, so I never had an opportunity to see him again.* But Admiral Fitzpatrick I've seen a number of times. Great guy.

Paul Stillwell: So now you were ready to become a midshipman.

Admiral Shelton: Yes.

Paul Stillwell: I'll bet your parents had a lot of pride when you showed up.

Admiral Shelton: Yes, they did. You know, I'm sure they had their doubts when I signed up to go in the Navy, but they never lost the bubble. They stayed with me.

Paul Stillwell: Well, in a way you were fulfilling what your mother had prepared you for.

Admiral Shelton: Oh, yes. Yes. If I'd have flunked that second exam, I think she would have had heart failure right on the spot, but there was no question about that.

So, anyway, when I got to the Naval Academy, as all the enlisted men did at that time, we went to the Reina Mercedes, which was still there.† That was a brig for bad midshipmen and the barracks ship for enlisted people. So that's where I berthed while I was getting ready to get sworn in.

---

* Lieutenant (junior grade) Norman W. Doudiet, USN, died 13 November 1942 when the light cruiser Juneau (CL-52) was torpedoed and sunk in the Solomons.
† USS Reina Mercedes (IX-25), an old cruiser captured during the Spanish-American War, served as a station ship at the Naval Academy from 1912 to 1957. Until 1940, midshipmen being punished for various disciplinary infractions slept and took meals on board the ship but continued to go to classes ashore.

As I recall, I was sworn in on July 2. At the physical I turned up with what the doctor said was a little heart murmur, and so we argued about that, and he said, "Well, I'm going to send you over to the hospital, and we'll see what they say." Well, there was an admiral at that time that was the head of the hospital. Very rare, I think, but anyway at that hospital.

So he came around to see me, and he took all the blood-pressure tests and all that kind of stuff, and he said, "I don't think there's anything wrong with you, but I'll tell you what we're going to do. We're going to keep you in here for a week, and I'm going to come around." He said, "You're scared of doctors. That's your problem."

I said, "Well, that may be."

But, anyway, he said, "I'm going to come around three or four times a day, and we're going to go through this routine every day, and at the end of the week you either go in the academy or you go out of the Navy." Well, I went in the academy, so that took care of that and I think I was sworn in on July 2.

Paul Stillwell: I interviewed one of your classmates, Andy Kerr, who had a go-around with the doctors too.[*]

Admiral Shelton: Andy Kerr and I were in the same company and for years, actually until just about eight months ago, we did not know that the New Mexico had played a key part in both of our careers. He's an Australian, and way back in the 1920s the New Mexico went to Australia.[†] There was a yeoman on the New Mexico that took an interest in Andy. Brought him out to the ship, showed him around, et cetera, et cetera, et cetera. That incident focused Andy on wanting to go to the Naval Academy. So that's what he did. He came back to Seattle, studied hard, and took a competitive exam. In those days the congressmen had a choice. They could either give you an appointment outright, or they could hold competitive exams to see who got their appointment, and that was the case with Andy. So he took the competitive exam and got in. But it wasn't until this last class reunion we had last June back at the academy that we both found out—and we were

---
[*] See the Naval Institute oral history of Captain Alex A. Kerr, USN (Ret.).
[†] In 1925 many of the battleships of the U.S. Fleet visited Australia and New Zealand.

in the same company at the academy the whole time—that we found out that the New Mexico had played a part in both of our lives.

Paul Stillwell: Please tell me about embarking on your career as a midshipman.

Admiral Shelton: Well, as a guy that had been in the Navy a couple of years by then, I probably had a different viewpoint of the whole thing than many did. The aspect of plebe year that seems to bother so many people, the hazing, didn't seem to bother me that much.* I don't know whether some of the upperclassmen thought because I'd been in the Navy that, well, maybe I wouldn't tolerate it too well or whatever. But anyway I wasn't bothered by it too much. I did all the stuff that all the rest of the plebes did.

Paul Stillwell: What was included in that?

Admiral Shelton: Oh, sitting out without a chair underneath you and all the things at the mess table: answering questions and shoving out and all that sort of thing. I just kind of took it as par for the course and didn't let it bother me too much. You always had a first classman that was supposed to kind of look after you and so forth, and that turned out to be James B. Osborn, if you know him.†

Paul Stillwell: I know of him.

Admiral Shelton: He's from Missouri, and he had dated my cousin, Laurabel Edmonston. He had dated her when they were both at Southwest Teachers College in Springfield. So he kind of looked me up really and said, "Well, let me know if you have any problems." That was the way Oz went about things.

---

* A midshipman in his or her first year is called a plebe; second year, youngster or third classman; third year, second classman; fourth year, first classman.
† Midshipman James B. Osborn, USN, graduated from the Naval Academy in the class of 1942. When the Navy's first ballistic missile submarine, the George Washington (SSBN-598), was commissioned on 30 December 1959, Commander Osborn was commanding officer of the ship's blue crew.

Paul Stillwell: So he spooned on you, to use the terminology.

Admiral Shelton: He spooned on me. And I never really had to use it very much. I used to go up to his room every once in a while, and he was a pretty smart guy. He always starred. That's the terminology for above 3.6 average. He always starred, and he had two roommates that both needed all of his help, so he spent most of his time at the academy helping them and helping me to some degree. But I didn't have too much trouble with the studies at the academy at that time, because I'd learned how to study from prep school. So I got through plebe year in reasonably good shape—and the rest of the years for that matter.

As I said, I didn't think the hazing was too heavy from my viewpoint, but some others thought it was. The only physical hurt that I ever got was at the completion of plebe year when the youngsters come back from their ball, they insist on standing on a cruisebox and whacking you with a broom and lift you as far as they can. I have to admit I didn't see the rationale for that, and it did hurt, and I did get lifted. The guy that lifted me was Jake Laboon.* [Laughter] So I had a little different view of Jake Laboon for a long time than maybe some others did.

Paul Stillwell: Any other memories of him specifically?

Admiral Shelton: No. He went to submarines, and I didn't. Actually, through the year he was just a good upperclassman basically. He had his share of eating me out every once in a while, just like everybody else did. Rosie Cowin's room was the room that I had the trouble with, Rosie Cowin and O'Brien and Schlichte.† Those three guys tended to make my life miserable, not for any good reason. They just decided they were going to have a little piece of me every now and then and they did.

---

* Midshipman John F. Laboon, Jr., USN, graduated from the Naval Academy in the class of 1944. He initially served as a line officer, later became a submariner and still later, a chaplain. He retired as a captain. The guided missile destroyer Laboon (DDG-58) is named in his honor.
† Midshipman Stanley J. Cowin, Jr., USN; Midshipman Clement E. O'Brien, USN; Midshipman George A. Schlichte, Jr., USN. All were in the class of 1943.

Paul Stillwell: Then Laboon became a priest, and he was pretty fierce in that role too.

Admiral Shelton: Even then, yes, that's right. So that sort of sums up my plebe year. I didn't have that much trouble. As I said, I'm a short guy, and so I was always at the rear end of the platoon.

I knew how to shine my shoes. I'd learned that. And I knew how to stay reasonably well dressed with my uniform, et cetera, et cetera, so I didn't get put on report too much. Biggest trouble I had was that I had a heavy beard even in those days, and I often had trouble convincing any of the OODs that I'd shaved that morning.[*] So most of the times I got put on report it was for improper shave, even if I'd shaved that morning. So that bothered me some, but it didn't bother me enough to worry about.

Paul Stillwell: Do you remember the news coming in about the attack on Pearl Harbor?[†]

Admiral Shelton: I remember it quite well. I remember that I was in the head sitting on the john when Oz the Poz, my first classman, came down the hallway looking for me, and he said, "Shelton, where are you?"

I said, "Here I am."

He said, "Goddamn it, I just heard that there's something about Pearl Harbor. Get off your ass and go find out what it is." And so I did.

Paul Stillwell: Literally. [Laughter]

Admiral Shelton: Literally. Literally. And so that's how I found out about Pearl Harbor also.

Paul Stillwell: Did that change the mood any in the academy?

---

[*] OOD—officer of the day.
[†] In late November 1941, the Imperial Japanese Navy dispatched from the Kurile Islands in the North Pacific a task force built around six aircraft carriers. A force of some 350 fighters, dive-bombers, and torpedo planes attacked U.S. military installations on the island of Oahu, Hawaii, on Sunday, 7 December 1941. The principal focus of attack was the collection of American warships at the naval base at Pearl Harbor. The U.S. Congress declared war on Japan the following day.

Admiral Shelton: Well, yes, I'd say so. Everybody that was there wanted to get out and go fight. The ones that were going to have to stay there for another couple of years, some of them began to debate whether they wanted to stay there for the rest of the tour or not. But Oz was a first classman, so he was about ready to graduate anyway, and so it didn't bother him too much. But the second, third and plebes, yes, I think there was a pretty uniform sentiment about wanting to get out there and see what was going on and do your part of it.

Paul Stillwell: Well, the first classmen got out there just a couple of weeks after that.[*]

Admiral Shelton: I know it was pretty close right after that. And of course then it wasn't too long after that, skipping ahead about another year, when they started bringing back some of the heroes from the war. I remember Butch O'Hare came back and some of those guys.[†]

Paul Stillwell: Any specific memories of him?

Admiral Shelton: No, other than he was Medal of Honor winner at that time and I thought, "Well, he's got to be good." And he was. I guess that just kind of helped jell my notions to get into the aviation part of things.

Paul Stillwell: Well, these were really role models that they were demonstrating.

Admiral Shelton: That's right, that they brought back, and I know there's some discussion these days on whether that was a good idea or not, but as far as I was concerned I thought it was a great idea. I thought it was one of the best things they could do. Of course, they were taking the guy, they were kind of giving him leave and letting him cool off a little bit and get his things back together. So that was kind of a lost time

---

[*] The Naval Academy class of 1942 graduated on 19 December 1941.
[†] On 20 February 1942, while a member of Fighting Squadron Three, Lieutenant (junior grade) Edward H. O'Hare, USN, shot down five of nine Japanese bombers approaching the aircraft carrier Lexington (CV-2), thereby saving the ship. He was awarded the Medal of Honor for his exploit.

there, but on the other hand I thought those guys all had a great effect on the midshipmen. At least they did me.

Paul Stillwell: Any others whom you remember specifically?

Admiral Shelton: No, I really don't. I remember him the most of any of them. If I heard the names I'd probably remember.

Paul Stillwell: I think John Bulkeley might have come back.[*]

Admiral Shelton: You know, if he did I don't remember him. But O'Hare, I remember him quite well, and I remember thinking, "Gee, that was really neat for them to bring him back here."

Paul Stillwell: I think he was uncomfortable in that role. He would have preferred being in a squadron.[†]

Admiral Shelton: Yes, I think so, too, as I've learned later. I didn't know it at the time, but as I've learned fairly recently I think you're probably right.

Paul Stillwell: What do you recall of the academics specifically and some of your instructors?

Admiral Shelton: The instructor I really remember the most was the one I had in mechanical engineering, and he was a lieutenant; he was a reserve. I liked mechanical engineering. I could really do that, the drawing part of it and precise and all that kind of stuff. I made good grades in there, and I got to know him a little bit. Even though he was an officer and I was a midshipman, I got to know him a little bit. I liked him and later on

---

[*] Lieutenant John D. Bulkeley, USN, received the Medal of Honor for his operations in command of a PT boat squadron around the Philippines in the early part of World War II.
[†] For details see Steve Ewing and John B. Lundstrom, Fateful Rendezvous: The Life of Butch O'Hare (Annapolis: Naval Institute Press, 1997).

during the Korean War when I was in a VC-3 night fighter detachment out there we were having trouble with the 20-millimeter guns. They would seize up and wouldn't fire. He was the one that was sent out from the Bureau of Ordnance to solve the whole problem. When he came aboard, he said, "Hey, Shelton, how are you doing?"

I said, "Well, doing great, but we need some solutions on these 20 millimeters." So he was there about four or five days, and the whole solution was that we had been greasing up the guns too much, and the thing you had to do was fire them dry. We went through a lot of barrels that way, but we also had guns that would fire when we pulled the trigger. So I ought to know his name, but it escapes me right now. He was a great guy.

Another one was Donald McClench, who had been head of the prep school. He came up there and was teaching navigation.[*] He was a good schoolmaster down at prep school, and he was an equally good head of the navigation department at the Naval Academy so I enjoyed taking navigation under him. Commander McClench took pains to keep track of his prep school grads.

We had a Spanish teacher named Vazquez.[†] I had not had any foreign languages. I'd had what they called English-Spanish and Spanish-English in junior high school but nothing beyond that. I enjoyed that. The math courses, I didn't enjoy any of those teachers too well. History? I don't remember any of the names. I liked history, and I liked English. I did pretty well in all those subjects. Didn't care anything about chemistry. That was probably my lousiest subject other than electricity.

I can remember that Pete Petersen, who is a classmate of mine, who has since deceased but who was an X-15 pilot and so forth and so on.[‡]

Paul Stillwell: Collier Trophy and CO of the Enterprise.

Admiral Shelton: All of those good things. He and I had electricity benches right next to each other, and I can remember that we both feared the time when one of us had to plug the thing in to see if it was going to work because more often than not it blew up.

---

[*] Lieutenant Commander Donald McClench, USN.
[†] Associate Professor Angel Cabrillo-Vazquez.
[‡] Midshipman Forrest S. Petersen, USN, who became a naval aviator and eventually retired as a vice admiral.

[Laughter] I think I'm lucky that I ever got through the electricity course there at the academy.

Paul Stillwell: What do you remember about the military subjects like navigation, seamanship, gunnery?

Admiral Shelton: They were all good. Of course, plebe summer you got turned over to a bunch of sailors, really to chiefs and first class, to take you out, learn to row a boat again. I emphasize again because I'd learned to row one before in boot camp. And they took you out on the YPs and taught you a little bit of that kind of navigation although most of that came later on.* But even plebe summer we got some of that. We got over on the rifle range quite a bit. As a matter of fact, I can still remember how hot it was over there in the month of August when we were over on the rifle range learning to shoot.

Paul Stillwell: Was that in that North Severn Naval Station across the river?

Admiral Shelton: Yes, across the river. And it was hot. And seamanship, we got a lot of that. We got a lot of knot tying, which I already knew. I spent a lot of my time on knots in the Naval Academy. I had learned when I was on the New Mexico how to weave belts with Belfast cord. So all the girls that I knew back in high school, I made them all a belt when I was at the Naval Academy and got one of the little dress belt buckles to put on it. Gave it to them while I was there, so I made three or four of those when I was at the academy and a couple of those were during plebe year. But, yes, we got our full dose of seamanship, nav, rifles and marching. We marched and marched and marched and marched. I guess I'm a little bit sad to say that I don't think they march enough back there anymore. You go back there and watch them march, and I come to the conclusion they need more practice.

Paul Stillwell: Well, when they went into the majors systems on the curriculum it wasn't practical.

---
* The YP was a yard patrol craft used for training of ship handling and seamanship.

Admiral Shelton: Yes, dropped all that out. And I guess there's a lot of argument about the majors system. I guess I shouldn't even have a vote in that, but I do still think that the academy has gotten a little further away from being a military school than it should have. I'd like to see them get back to it one way or another, majors or otherwise.

Paul Stillwell: How much do you remember about the competitive atmosphere among midshipmen?

Admiral Shelton: In athletics, yes. In academics the tops guys were pretty competitive, but they knew they were top, and they knew they were competitive. Most of us that were working for a living, so to speak, that had to study hard to make a 3.0, a 3.1, or occasionally a 3.4. Most of us were not too much worried about how anybody else did. We were worried about doing it ourselves. I had a lot of appreciation for the guys that starred all the time and wished that I could, but at the same time I knew that I had to spend more time than they did just making a 3.0. So I didn't worry about too much about that. Pete Peterson, for instance—hell, he was a star man. He did it with no problem at all. Engelmann, our number-one guy, I don't think he ever cracked a book when he went through the academy.*

I had a roommate named Jocko Reed, and he was pretty smart, but he didn't care to apply it, and so he would spend most of the study time reading Cosmopolitan or Redbook or whatever was a good thing to read in those days.† About the last five minutes of the study period, he'd say, "Hey, guys, what's it about today?" He'd go to class. He'd always make a 2.8 or a little better. Never failed. [Laughter] He was one of these guys you could say that could start, the logic was, "Well, it starts with A and ends with Z," and that's the way he applied everything in academics. He could take any of those subjects. Sometimes he really wouldn't know anything when he went to class about it, but he could figure it out while he was sitting there, and when he got his slip and had go to the board he could get a 2.8 or a 3.0 every damn time.

---

* Midshipman Richard H. Engelmann, USN, stood first among the 914 graduates in the class of 1945. He served two brief tours of active duty as a junior officer and resigned from the service.
† Midshipman John Hull Reed, USN.

One of my other roommates was Gene Spangler who also was enlisted and was on the <u>Augusta</u>.* He was about like me. He had to study like hell to make sure that he was passing all the time. He actually didn't do quite as well as I did but not because he didn't put the effort into it.

Our other roommate was a guy named Warren Hille, and Warren was a great gymnast.† Gene Spangler was pretty good, too, in many things, but Warren was a good all-around gymnast. He spent his time doing that or thinking about his girlfriend, Shirley, back in Milwaukee. The result of that was he bilged out at the end of plebe year like a lot of them did, and it really didn't bother him a bit. He went back and married Shirley. The next time I saw him he was one of those coast artillery officers at Pearl Harbor, sitting there with a machine gun. [Laughter] Warren was a good guy, but he was more concerned about marrying Shirley than he was graduating from the Naval Academy. There were a lot of them in the same boat.

Paul Stillwell: Well, you've got to look where your focus is and work toward that.

Admiral Shelton: That's right, and that's where his focus was. God, he went home at Christmas leave, and I thought he'd never come back. I thought he'd just stay there. [Laughter] But he flunked plebe year.

Paul Stillwell: What were the motivators that got you to work that hard?

Admiral Shelton: I'd have to say it was my mother. She was not mean about it at all, but she didn't tolerate lack of effort or lack of success.

Paul Stillwell: You were separated geographically, but you had internalized it by then.

Admiral Shelton: Oh, yes. Well, you know, even in those days I talked to her on the telephone every now and then, and I wrote a lot and she wrote a lot. She was a big

---

* Midshipman Eugene H. Spangler, USN.
† Midshipman Warren R. Hille, USN.

influence on that, and I knew I'd worked hard to get there. I didn't know what else I would be qualified to do if I didn't graduate, other than go back to the fleet or something like that. I didn't want to do that. As I said, I enlisted for six years when I came in, so that was a pretty big incentive to do well and get to the academy. Of course, I wasn't subject to that after I got there. But if I had flunked getting in, then I would have been back for the remainder of the six years. But after I got there it was mostly major effort to do as well as I could on everything but knowing that I probably was never going to star.

Paul Stillwell: How much involvement did you have in sports or other extracurricular activities?

Admiral Shelton: I had a little bit. Being a coxswain for the shell kind of intrigued me, so I spent plebe summer doing that. I was probably number-two coxswain for the plebe crew. There was another classmate from New Jersey I think that was better than I was, and his name was Flynn.*

I guess I got a little bit at crossroads with Bucky Walsh, who was the crew coach in those days, because the training was to learn how many beats, strokes per minute, you know, and all that kind of stuff. My music background gave me a very solid understanding of how many beats per minute and all this kind of stuff. My understanding was better than his. I think that's where we got at the crossroads, because I opened my mouth one day when I should have kept it closed about the stroke. He didn't exactly fire me, but he let me know that I wasn't number one on his list. And there wasn't enough athleticism to that for me to get any exercise out of it.

Warren Hille was a gymnast, Gene Spangler was a gymnast, my other two roommates, so they said, "What the hell. Come on over and start around the gym." So I did. But, you know, gymnastics is something you've got to start when you're a kid, or you're never limber enough to be a good one. So I never was that good, but I managed to get on the battalion gym team, which was not saying a whole lot. But that's essentially what I did. I didn't care for boxing, didn't care for wrestling. My dad was a hell of a good golfer, and how I missed out on getting some of his enthusiasm for that I don't

---

* Midshipman William J. Flynn, USN.

know. But in retrospect I probably should have taken up golf and worked at that as hard as I worked at some other things. I might have been pretty good. At least I've learned since then, and I'm not a bad golfer these days. I'm a 10 to 12 handicap. So that would have been pretty good. Sailing team? I probably should have gone out for that, because I knew a lot about it. But I don't know. I wasn't bent in that direction.

It seemed to me like some of those activities took more time than I could afford from the studies. So I kept protecting the study angle all the time. I wasn't on the radiator squad while I was there.* I avoided that. I was not a good swimmer, and I wasn't good as some at those things. Some of the things I could have been good at, I just thought it was going to take too much time from studying, and I had to study a lot while I was there. So that took care of that.

Paul Stillwell: Do you remember the excitement and pageantry of going to some of the Army-Navy football games?

Admiral Shelton: Oh, yes. Of course, the transportation was a big problem in those days. We rode the ferry up to the Army-Navy game my plebe year, and we almost didn't get there in time because there was so much fog up the Chesapeake Bay and that area and into the Delaware Bay there that we almost didn't get to Philadelphia in time. But we did. I always enjoyed that. I always thought the midshipmen parades, for instance, at the parade ground there on Worden Field were great.† I always enjoyed those. And I enjoyed, any time we had to go somewhere and parade. I enjoyed that, including the Army-Navy games.

I liked part of it because there were always a certain number of politically high people at those games. You know, the President would come or somebody almost as high, so I enjoyed all that. I enjoyed marching. Not many guys, I guess, would really own up to that, but I did. I always thought there was a certain amount of pleasure to a parade where it all got carried off really good. Our company my plebe year was the color company, so that was enjoyable. You know, you get a little pleasure out of that. But I

---

* "Radiator squad" was a nickname for midshipmen who didn't participate in athletics while at the academy; presumably they were sitting near a radiator instead.
† Grass-covered Worden Field is still the site of dress parades at the Naval Academy.

enjoyed the marching. I always did. I'm glad to say that I didn't have to spend too much of it as a result of being put on report.

Another classmate of mine was named E. P. Wilson.* We all called him Black Eep, synonym for Black Sheep, and he was always in trouble. I think he had the record for the most walking time for having been on report. I probably shouldn't admit this, being a retired naval officer, but the subject that I really had the most trouble with at the academy including electricity and chemistry was gunnery. I was not a very good gunnery student, and I had trouble with all of the terminology that they used. I studied hard, but I didn't do very well. If I was going to flunk out of there, it would have probably been on gunnery. I just didn't get it very well.

Paul Stillwell: The Naval Institute published that textbook, and it was about three inches thick.†

Admiral Shelton: I remember that. I remember having to pick it up all the time. [Laughter] It was the heaviest book I had, of course. But I don't remember who the gunnery instructors were. I think Commander Keith may have been one of them. I knew him fairly well. We got to know him pretty well after I graduated better than I did there. But I was not very good. The terminology, even though I'd been on the battleship and so forth and so on and had the seen the guns, had done my share of ammunition carrying and all that kind of stuff, I just did not understand any of the terminology very well. I'm lucky that I didn't fail the tests. I didn't do very well in them.

Paul Stillwell: What do you remember about summer cruises?

Admiral Shelton: Well, of course, our summer cruises were pretty much limited to YP cruises up and down the bay. With the war on, the ships weren't available for the old-time cruises like everybody had had before us. So we did our share of cruising, going over to the Eastern Shore in and out of Cambridge and a few other places, and I enjoyed

---

* Midshipman Edward P. Wilson, Jr., USN.
† Naval Ordnance: a Textbook Prepared for the Use of the Midshipmen of the United States Naval academy, by Officers of the United States Navy (Annapolis: U. S. Naval Institute, 1939).

that. You know, there was a little bit of practical application to navigation that you'd been trying to learn, and also you could drop anchor and pull up anchor and all that kind of good stuff. And they were pretty dependable little boats. They weren't all that big, but they were pretty dependable, so there wasn't too much trouble there. Other than that, there wasn't much to our summer cruises. We studied. We were a three-year class, and we made up the fourth year during the remainder of the summer.* So I've forgotten whether it was two months out of the summer or maybe just a month and a half, but at least half of the summer was academics, where it would not have been if the war hadn't been on because we were going to finish in three years.

Paul Stillwell: Did you still get leaves during the summer?

Admiral Shelton: Yes, we got our leaves, 30 days every summer. The trains were still running, so I could get back to Iowa, where my folks were living by then. And the YP cruises really weren't that long. They kind of condensed those down and fitted them in where they could, and we were still taking academics as I recall during the YP cruises. Not when we were out on the bay, of course, but otherwise the big effort during the summertime was to make up for the fourth year that you weren't going to have.

Paul Stillwell: Well, and the essence of what had been in those traditional summer cruises you had gotten as an enlisted man.

Admiral Shelton: That's true. I don't think I missed anything that way.

Paul Stillwell: Well, you'd had it in another form.

Admiral Shelton: Right.

Paul Stillwell: How much do you recall about a social life as a midshipman?

---

* During World War II the Naval Academy curriculum was shortened to three years. To return to the four-year format after the war, the class of 1948 was divided into A and B sections. A graduated in 1947 and B the following year.

Admiral Shelton: I didn't have any. A little bit.

Paul Stillwell: Well, they had the hops probably.

Admiral Shelton: Plebe year I didn't have any and junior and senior year Gene Spangler, who was my roommate, was from Germantown, Philadelphia, and his folks came down quite a bit. He had a girlfriend named Audrey that came down quite a bit, so I spent some time with them. When they came down we'd go out and have lunch, dinner, whatever. I did date a little gal over in Eastport. Her name was Barbara Windsor, and her brother was class of '44.[*] He had been in my company, and that's how I got to know her in the first place.

Paul Stillwell: Is that Duke Windsor?

Admiral Shelton: No. Duke is class of '41, I believe, and a different Windsor altogether.[†] I know Duke quite well, too. But, anyway, I dated Barbara Windsor some. And there was a girl that another guy in the company had introduced me to that came over from Washington. Her name was Libby O'Neil. She was the first southern girl that I'd ever really known, and I mean she was true southern all the way with the language and everything. She was a good gal, but we never did have anything serious going. So I didn't date very much, and I spent my time doing whatever we wanted to do otherwise.

Paul Stillwell: What other forms of recreation were there?

Admiral Shelton: Well, there was sailing, and I did a little bit of that. Not a whole lot. Softball, baseball, played some of that. Not too much else.

Paul Stillwell: Was there schooling in the social graces as in how to present your cards when you made a call on the captain?

---

[*] Midshipman James M. Windsor, USN.
[†] Midshipman Robert W. Windsor, Jr., USN.

Admiral Shelton: Yes, they had a course in that. I think when you were first class you had to go down and do a dining thing where you did all the etiquette with learning how to go from right to left and left to right with all the utensils and all that sort of thing. And you had to give a little five-minute talk of some kind. And there was a small class in etiquette, not too much, mostly the etiquette of calling on your seniors and what to expect in return. But that didn't seem to occupy very much of my learning experience.

Paul Stillwell: What do you remember about the Bancroft Hall organization, the company officers and so forth?[*]

Admiral Shelton: Oh, I thought it was good. Our company officer was a lieutenant commander named Mike Luosey.[†] Now, he had just come back from the war, or he did about the middle of plebe year, I guess. He'd been out there. I thought he was great. He expected you not to get into trouble, but if you did get into trouble he was the first one to want to know about it and the first one to want to help you as far as taking you up the chain or whatever was going to happen. I never got into that kind of serious trouble, but some of the guys that had class A's, he looked out for them.[‡] You know, he wasn't going to keep them out of trouble if they deserved it, but he was there to walk them through the line and make sure they didn't blasted out arbitrarily.

In those days there was the company officer, then the battalion officer, and then the commandant of midshipmen. That was it. The only time we ever saw the superintendent was at the Army-Navy game or if you were a first classman and the superintendent invited some of the first class over on occasion to see what it was like to be a superintendent. I did that once or twice. But basically it was the company officer, the battalion officer, and the commandant of midshipmen. In those days I thought they did it just exactly right. If you got put on report, the company officer got the report chit, looked at it, called you in, and said, "What's all this?" basically, and you went on from

---

[*] Bancroft Hall is the large multi-wing dormitory that houses Naval Academy midshipmen. It also contains the offices of members of the executive department, including the commandant, executive officer, and battalion and company officers.
[†] Lieutenant Commander Michael J. Luosey, USN.
[‡] Class A offenses were the most serious and carried the largest number of demerits.

there. But you did not end up with somebody else calling all the shots. And I appreciated that. I thought it was the right way to go about things. He kept us on the straight and narrow.

Paul Stillwell: Did the duty officers play this fox-and-hounds game where they try to catch you in discrepancies?

Admiral Shelton: Our biggest fox-and-hound game was with Uncle Beany.

Paul Stillwell: Beany Jarrett.

Admiral Shelton: Beany Jarrett.[*] We made him an honorary class member of the class of '45. I guess several other classes did, too, but I think we were the first one. He was a great guy. He made no bones about it being a cat-and-mouse game, but he was not unjust about it. You know, if you could talk him out of it, why, he'd be talked out of it. If you couldn't talk him out of it, why, you were on report. But he was good.

Some of the duty officers I thought were a little bit—I wouldn't say it got around to being hazing or harassment, but it got pretty close at times. Some of them kind of felt like it was their beholden duty to go out and put people on report, and I didn't think that was the right attitude. But, all in all, the duty officers did their job, and, of course, once in a while you were made the duty officer's orderly, so you got to go around with him and keep the pencil and the pad and all that kind of stuff, take names so to speak. So you got that experience, and it was good experience to get that side of the argument too.

Paul Stillwell: There was no formal honor code. What was the sense of personal honor in the academy?

Admiral Shelton: You know, you bring up a really good point, because I thought that the honor back there was handled the way it should be, which was company officer, battalion

---

[*] Lieutenant Commander Harry Bean Jarrett, USN, was in the Naval Academy's executive department in the late 1930s and early 1940s. The frigate Jarrett (FFG-33) was named in his honor.

officer, and commandant of midshipmen. At the same time West Point, as I recall, did have an honor system at that time, and I think the sentiment among most of the midshipmen was that they didn't think that it worked very well at West Point. I certainly didn't think it worked very well. I don't think that they need one at the academy. Even today I don't think they need one. If they've got the right system of discipline and the old chain of command, I don't think they need an honor system. We knew exactly what a class A was. We knew that if we managed to go out and screw up and get a class A that we were in trouble. And if there were circumstances where they didn't want to throw you out, why, they didn't throw you out. But you also knew that if you were bound and determined to get into trouble, they were there to throw you out if that's what became necessary.

Paul Stillwell: And there are some people who try to beat the system.

Admiral Shelton: And they did. [Laughter] There were a lot of them that beat the system, and there were a lot of them that tried and didn't. [Laughter] I didn't ever think that we needed the kind of thing that says that, "Oh, he just got a slip to the next class or something. I'm going to tell on him."* I didn't appreciate the fact that some guy was getting the answers for slips that we were going to get in math class or something like that, and a lot of them beat the system that way academically. But at the same time I didn't think it was my job to go spill the beans on them, and I still don't think so. I think that that's the wrong way to go about it. Everything has a way of evening up, and the guys that beat the system that way didn't beat it later on. That's the way I see it. So I didn't think we needed a codified honor system at all, and I don't think they need one back there now. I think I am right when I say that the only codified honor system in the fleet is your oath and obedience to the UCMJ, and, of course, the chain of command, so why a codified honor code just for the academy?†

---

* A frequent practice in Naval Academy classes of the period was for the instructor to hand out slips of paper containing questions, and the midshipmen would then go to blackboards to write their answers.
† Following the unification of the U.S. armed forces in 1947, a new Uniform Code of Military Justice (UCMJ) was enacted for all the services and put into effect on 31 May 1951.

Paul Stillwell: Well, and also there was a sense of people seeing what they could get away with, for example, frenching out.*

Admiral Shelton: Oh, we had two or three guys in my company that were extremely good at that. I never tried it. I just have to say that it wasn't that I didn't think I could succeed because I really thought I could. But I didn't want to take the chance of getting a class A and a chance of getting thrown out. I wasn't there to get thrown out. I was there to graduate and do my thing. So we had some guys in my company that were very good at going over the wall. Most of the ones that succeeded in that were also guys that could star pretty easily most of the time because they were that smart. But I didn't go for that—not because I had any regrets about the fact that they succeeded, but my view of why I was there was different.

Paul Stillwell: Different set of values.

Admiral Shelton: Different set of values, I guess. The whole time I was there I don't think I ever had an inclination to go over the wall. First place, most people out in town were not very sympathetic toward the whole thing. [Laughter] They could tell who you were, and they weren't going to help you. And just to beat the system I didn't think it was worthwhile. Also, I didn't really know anyone out in town. I don't think the sponsor system was in effect at that time, where a family out in town sort of adopts you and provides a place where you can visit and sort of relax and let your hair down.

Paul Stillwell: How much could you keep track of the progress of the war while you were there?

Admiral Shelton: That was pretty good. They kept the news coming in pretty well, as I recall. We knew about all the major things that were happening. I'm not sure we got all the single instances, but all the big happenings we were pretty well brought into.

---

* "French out" is midshipman slang for leaving the Naval Academy without authorization.

Paul Stillwell: There were some grim days, I would suspect, during that first year.

Admiral Shelton: That's right. We heard about a lot of losses and not so many victories part of the time there.

Paul Stillwell: You said that you were attracted to aviation. How much was there in the curriculum about aviation at that point?

Admiral Shelton: Very little. That was part of the summer thing that went out the window, too. They used to have the old yellow N3Ns there on floats at the academy, and those all went down the drain when the summer curriculum was changed so we could graduate in three years.* So we didn't get much. The only aviation indoctrination we really got was when we graduated and we all went down to Jacksonville and/or other places for 30 days for indoctrination. And we didn't all go right from the academy. Some of us went on leave first and then went back down to Jacksonville or someplace, but that's when we got our aviation indoctrination. We got very little of it at the academy. I do remember, however, that they did have PBYs over across the river there.† Not a squadron or anything like that. Just a couple or three that were there for experimental duty. I do remember that that's where they developed JATO takeoffs.‡ I remember that one of them caught on fire from the JATO, but he got it back in the water and didn't lose the airplane, so that was pretty exciting.

Paul Stillwell: Pretty dramatic to watch.

---

* "Yellow Peril" was the nickname for the yellow-painted N3N trainer, a biplane equipped with a centerline pontoon. It was 26 feet long, had a wingspan of 34 feet, gross weight of 2,792 pounds, and a top speed of 126 miles per hour.
† The PBY Catalina was a twin-engine flying boat that performed extensive service before and during World War II. Across the Severn River from the Naval Academy was an experimental station for Navy equipment.
‡ JATO—jet-assisted takeoff. In propeller-driven seaplanes, rockets were used to give the aircraft additional boost when taking off from the water.

Admiral Shelton: Pretty dramatic to watch, that's right, because it was all right there. They just taxied out from the ramp over there, and that's where they did their thing. But we really didn't get very much in the way of aviation indoctrination.

Paul Stillwell: In retrospect how would you assess the quality of the education you got from the Naval Academy?

Admiral Shelton: I'm possibly the wrong one to ask, because I thought it was great. You know, there are a lot of arguments about it because a lot of the guys had other college experience. For instance Oz the Poz, my first classman—I think he'd already graduated from the University of Missouri when he went there. And there were several guys in my company, Jack Riley and Pete Petersen and several others, that had had at least one or two years of college.[*] So plebe year and to a certain extent a lot of the youngster year was pure nothing for them, and I sort of resented that.

On the other hand, I think there was something to be gained in those days by requiring everybody to take the same course, go through and you graduate. That benefited some guys because they'd already had it, and they could star easier than others. I guess that's basically the reason they finally got around to the majors system, and perhaps that's okay. But I think there's some other things that went down the drain with the majors system that we had, and marching to class was one of them. Sounds crazy, but I thought that was a pretty good idea. I still think so.

Paul Stillwell: Not everybody shares your enthusiasm for marching.

Admiral Shelton: That's right. Not everybody does. And there's a lot of them. But Peggy can tell you, my wife. She can tell you when we've been back there to visit, and you drive around the yard there, and I go over and I find places there where midshipmen are sitting on the benches with their arm around a girl, or they're sitting there smoking a cigarette. They didn't do that when I was there. They did not do that when I was there, and I thought for good reason. I still think for good reason.

---

[*] Midshipman John R. Riley, USN.

Paul Stillwell: Anything else to mention about your years at Annapolis?

Admiral Shelton: Well, I was going to say in connection with that that I guess you could say that it's probably a good thing that I didn't ever go back there as commandant of midshipmen, company officer, or anything like that, because I would have had a totally different outlook on things than what I perceive back there these days. So it's just as well that I was there when I was, got out when I did, and did not go back there under the present circumstances.

Let's see, I think we got 750 bucks a year or 785 dollars a year back there then, and we had a passbook that we kept all the tally in. I remember that it always came out pretty close every year. When I graduated I wasn't in debt, but I didn't have enough money to buy my uniforms. My dad coughed up the money to buy my raincoat and the things that I needed to buy for uniform to be outfitted, cap and all that kind of stuff.

I sang in the choir back there. Bob Baldwin is a classmate of mine, and we sat next to each other in the choir, and we were both first bass in those days.* And I've always thought very highly of the church or the chapel. It's the most beautiful building in the world.

Paul Stillwell: And you had mandatory attendance in those years.

Admiral Shelton: That's right. You had your choice of going there or going out in town. I didn't feel seriously enough about going out in town to any of the churches, so I was glad to go right there. No, I didn't mind it. I thought it was a good idea then. I think it'd be a good idea now. Those that haven't really availed themselves of that acquaintanceship with that chapel don't know what they're missing.

Paul Stillwell: That's where the civil libertarians muddied the waters.

Admiral Shelton: They really did, and I think it's a big mistake.†

---

* Midshipman Robert B. Baldwin, USN, who eventually became a vice admiral and served as Chief of Naval Personnel.
† As a result of legal challenges, mandatory church attendance for midshipmen ended in the early 1970s.

Paul Stillwell: What do you recall of the graduation itself?

Admiral Shelton: It was in Dahlgren Hall in those days, and I remember that the guys with honors got to go up there and get theirs first. All the rest of us went alphabetically. The anchorman in the class was in my company also.* That was Benny the Penny.† I mentioned Black Eep, but he and Benny the Penny were running against each other all the time to see who could get in the most trouble. Benny became a Marine and wasn't too successful at being a Marine. Later on he straightened out and became vice president of Convair, something like that. So he wasn't all bad. And Black Eep, he's back there still in Maryland and he's been a youth athletic coach back there for some years, a successful coach. So I don't have anything bad to say about them. They were good guys that just didn't care whether they got in trouble or not. They kind of went out of their way to get in trouble, and it didn't seem to bother them.

Paul Stillwell: Did you go directly from there to the aviation indoctrination?

Admiral Shelton: I did. I went from there down to Jacksonville and then on leave and then from leave on out to San Francisco. I spent, as I recall, about two weeks in San Francisco. At that time they had a nice little system there at Com 12 for all the new ensigns that came out there that were waiting for transportation.‡ When they put them on a ship to go somewhere, they put them in charge of a draft of men. I remember that occasion quite well. They put me in charge of a draft on an Army transport. It had an Army captain, but it had Navy armed guard on it.

The draft of men that I had was a whole ship full of stewards that were going to Hawaii. Never been to sea before. As it can often be, it was rough out there off of San Francisco and almost all the way to Pearl. They got so sick that you couldn't believe it. They had these big 50-gallon cans down there that they were all supposed to heave into

---

* "Anchor man" is a term for the midshipman with the lowest class standing in a given year.
† Midshipman Walker Gardner Bennett II, USN.
‡ Com 12—Commandant of the 12th Naval District, which had headquarters on Treasure Island in San Francisco Bay.

when they got sick. Eventually they got so sick that they didn't care whether they heaved into the can or whether they didn't, so it got to be a pretty big mess. I'd been up to see the captain a couple of times to see if he couldn't let some of them come up to get some fresh air, but he wouldn't let anybody topside. He was scared of the submarine threat if there was one. I never did know whether there was one or not, but that's what he was afraid of, so it wasn't until we were about a day out of Pearl that any of those guys ever got topside for a breath of fresh air.

Paul Stillwell: And fresh air is what you really need.

Admiral Shelton: And that's what they needed. Even five or ten at a time would have been great. No soap. No soap.

Paul Stillwell: I don't see how that's a problem with a possible submarine menace. You're better able to abandon ship if you're topside.

Admiral Shelton: Yes, that's right. You know, I say that's the reason. I think that's the rationale that he used. At the same time, there wasn't very much to eat, and as I recall we subsisted on crackers and cheese the whole trip. That wasn't too unusual, I found out later, because when I finally got to St. Louis, and we got out there and we were at general quarters a lot of the time, why, crackers and cheese was what we got to eat. But at least that draft of men going there I never will forget. There was only one steward out of that whole bunch that didn't get sick, and his name was Mitchell. I will never forget, he came and he said, "Mr. Shelton, what can I do to help in this situation?"

I said, "I don't know. Unless we can get these guys up for some fresh air, there's not much you can do except try to keep it as clean as you can." And so that's what he did, but it was a poor situation.

Paul Stillwell: Were they all black?

Admiral Shelton: Yes, every one of them. Boy. So we got to Hawaii, and I was going to gunnery school there, the 40-millimeter and 20-millimeter gunnery school out around past Barbers Point.* So I spent two weeks there. I think I reported on board the St. Louis in Pearl Harbor.† I was sent to Hawaii because the St. Louis was due there in a couple of weeks, and I used those two or three weeks going to gunnery school. Then we went out to Eniwetok or Ulithi, someplace there.

Paul Stillwell: What month did you report aboard?

Admiral Shelton: Oh, I got there in late July or the first of August. I know one of the first ports, if you want to call it that, that we got into was Ulithi, and that was my first view of what that Pacific Fleet looked like.‡ I know there's a lot of pictures. You see a lot of pictures of the fleet at Ulithi and, man, there were ships there that you couldn't count. More ships, I guess, than we probably have in the Navy today almost.

Paul Stillwell: Probably.

Admiral Shelton: It was something else again. There was that little old island there called Mog Mog that was the recreation island. The only recreation really was softball and drinking beer.

Paul Stillwell: Was the beer cold?

Admiral Shelton: Yes, it was cold. I didn't drink beer, but I don't think it was very much of a beer for beer drinkers. It was either Ajax or Shaefers as I remember, and I don't recall those being very good beers. But we carried that beer around down there in GSK,

---

* Barbers Point is at the southwest "corner" of the island of Oahu, Hawaii.
† USS St. Louis (CL-49), name ship of her class of light cruisers, was commissioned 19 May 1939. She had a standard displacement of 10,000 tons, was 608 feet long, and 62 feet in the beam. Her top speed was 33 knots. She was armed with fifteen 6-inch main battery guns and eight 5-inch dual-purpose guns.
‡ Ulithi is an atoll in the Western Caroline Islands. It had a large lagoon that provided a sheltered anchorage for the ships of the U.S. Third Fleet.

down underneath the hangar back aft in general stores.* It got all bombed out later on, as we'll get to, I guess. But Ulithi was the first place I can remember, and from there on, we went on out, and by the time we got to Leyte Gulf, it was November.

It was November 27 that we got hit.† We were just covering a landing there like all the rest of them were, the Denver and the Maryland and the Columbia and all the cruisers. We were all there in Leyte Gulf, and to refuel we would do a Lufbery circle around two tankers, and then one ship at a time would peel out of the Lufbery circle and go in and get alongside and take on fuel and go back out and get in the Lufbery again till everybody had gotten fuel.‡

The Lufbery, of course, was for protection, because theoretically the Lufbery circle that got its name from World War I. It's an aviation term where the fighters could get in a circle and protect outboard of the circle for any danger and that's what we did with the ships. Theoretically they could all shoot outboard as they went around the circle. But we got banged. That was the beginning of the kamikaze attacks, as I recall, and we might not have been the first, but that's when all the kamikazes started.§ We had a 13-plane attack, and six of them managed to hit us. The others we shot down. The two that did the most damage, one of them hit us in the port side right in a little space that was the ship's armory, which was right between the boiler operating spaces. One other one went right down the hangar deck right all the way down into the GSK where the beer was and where all the aviation fuel was also. Another hit in the superstructure without a lot of damage.

You'd have thought that the one who hit near the aviation fuel would have been a horrendous explosion, but the lucky thing—if there was any luck—was that the kamikaze that went down there broke all the foam lines at the same time. So he started the fires but started the fire system automatically, so he put all the fires out basically. The guy that

---

* GSK was the designation for a storage area.
† On the morning of 27 November 1944 the St. Louis was hit by a Val dive-bomber on a kamikaze suicide mission. The plane's bomb exploded on the port quarter, in the vicinity of the aircraft hangar, and started fires. Soon afterward another suicide plane crashed near the port side and tore numerous holes in the ship's hull. All told, the ship lost 15 killed, 1 missing, and had more than 40 men wounded.
‡ The Lufbery circle is a defensive maneuver in which airplanes fly in a ring, each one protecting the tail of the plane ahead. It was named for Major Raoul Lufbery, a fighter pilot in World War I.
§ The first deliberate kamikaze suicide plane attack of the war came against the escort aircraft carrier Santee (CVE-29) on the morning of 25 October 1944, during the Battle of Leyte Gulf.

did us the most damage was the guy that hit us in the port side, in the ship's armory, because it was right between the boiler operating spaces. The bulkheads were weaving in and out. We were dead in the water. We lost all power. Couldn't even shoot a gun. That was late in the morning, and we drifted with the current outside the Lufbery circle until about 2:00 o'clock or 2:30 that afternoon when the kamikazes came back. For reasons I've never understood to this day, they obviously could see that we were dead in the water, but not a one of them made a pass at us. They went back and hit the Colorado and some more of the ships up in the Lufbery circle, maybe because they were bigger. I don't know.

Paul Stillwell: Where were you when all this was happening?

Admiral Shelton: We went to our air-defense stations. I was not in the 5-inch guns or anything like that. My job was down in the wardroom to help the medics find the wounded and try to get them down there, which is what I did. To this day I can't believe it, but there was a guy in one of the 40-millimeter mounts that had had just the top of his head pretty much shaved but not very deep. He wasn't conscious, but he wasn't dead. He was a big guy, probably weighed 180 or 190 pounds, and I weighed a 125 or 130. But I managed to carry him over my shoulder all the way down to the wardroom, and to the best of my knowledge he lived, which I was always glad about. But I didn't have much to do other than that.

Paul Stillwell: How many were wounded?

Admiral Shelton: We lost 16 killed and I don't know how many wounded. You know, if they'd have passed the word, "We need somebody to man this gun or that gun or something else," I was prepared to do that because I had gone through gunnery school and thought I could do it. But you were in the way if you were trying to do that otherwise.

Paul Stillwell: Do you remember a sense of fear in that environment?

Admiral Shelton: Not really. I remember thinking, "What the hell is going on?" because when that guy hit us in the port side I was not too far from that. I was just in the passageway outside the wardroom, and that was kind of above in the center of the ship just a little lower and to the port side where he hit. I can remember that it knocked me flat on the deck. And I can remember that the whole ship just reacted like a giant rubber sheet, where somebody had flipped one end of it and watched the wave travel from one end to the other. I thought, "My God, that really is something." I didn't know what the hell had happened, really.

Paul Stillwell: Your classmate, Andy Kerr, was in the Honolulu that got torpedoed, and he said he barely escaped being killed in that ship.

Admiral Shelton: Yes. Well, we had a lot of them that barely escaped a lot of things in those days. But it was exciting. I would say that. I guess I wasn't smart enough to be scared, not that scared anyway, panicked or anything.

Paul Stillwell: Well, but also you wouldn't see them coming directly in either.

Admiral Shelton: That's right. I didn't, no. I was topside for part of that but not when the guy hit us in the port side. Well, anyway, they shored up the two bulkheads the best they could, and we finally managed to get under way that night, making four knots all the way down to Manus for preliminary repairs and then came back to Long Beach to get everything fixed up.[*] The thing I remember was that we didn't have any air cover that day, which was why we got pranged, I guess. The squadron that was supposed to provide cover for us from Leyte or from Tacloban was Major Bong's outfit, P-38s.[†] So we got some kind of a communication from them later on in the day saying words to the effect

---

[*] Manus in the Admiralty Islands was the site of a forward logistic-support base that had extensive ship-repair facilities.
[†] Major Richard I. Bong, USAAF, was the leading U.S. fighter ace in World War II. He shot down 40 Japanese planes while flying P-38s in the Pacific theater and was awarded the Medal of Honor. He was killed in an accident in August 1945 while testing a new plane at Muroc, California.

that they were sorry they hadn't done any better, but they couldn't get out of the mud over in Tacloban. So I guess the truth is we really didn't have many fighters airborne that day for good reason.

Paul Stillwell: What was your job in the ship when you reported?

Admiral Shelton: I was a turret officer for number-three turret, which was right in front of the bridge. Under the air-defense setup, they didn't man those turrets. I never did quite understand why they didn't, but they didn't.

Paul Stillwell: What were the duties involved being in a turret?

Admiral Shelton: Well, you were responsible to know all the safety precautions, and theoretically you were responsible for all the actions in there. As a matter of fact, you had to rely on the petty officers to a great degree, because you weren't where a lot of action was going on, and it was the petty officers that were. So you were up there, and your job if you were going to shoot at a ship of course, you helped make sure the pointers were matched and all that kind of thing. Take a look through the periscope and make sure you were shooting at the right thing. We never did shoot at a ship while I was on there, so that never happened. But we did shoot a lot at practice targets and fired shore bombardment. So I spent a lot of time in the turret. That was later on. We didn't do any bombarding at Leyte Gulf, but later on when we got to Okinawa we did a hell of a lot of bombarding, so I spent a lot of time. Ten or 12 hours in GQ was nothing unusual at all in that circumstance.*

Paul Stillwell: Those 6-inch guns had a high-speed capability.

Admiral Shelton: Yes, they did. I'm not sure whether the St. Louis and the Brooklyn were the only ones that had those 6-inch guns, the Helena.

---

* GQ—general quarters, in which the ship's crew is at battle stations.

Paul Stillwell: I think the whole Brooklyn class.

Admiral Shelton: I guess the whole Brooklyn class had those, but I'm not sure that any of the other cruisers did at that time. I don't think they did. I think it was a new gun.

Paul Stillwell: It was that class.

Admiral Shelton: Yes. And we bombarded a lot. Well, that's getting ahead of the story, but anyway we got to Manus. We went into one of those floating dry docks down there and got some emergency repairs. My sister's husband was an Army medical corpsman at Manus, so while I was there I got to go over and see him for about a half an hour. But other than that we were there not very long. Four days, five days, maybe a week if that long and then came back to Long Beach for major repairs on what had been damaged. We were back in Long Beach. We got back here probably around Christmas time, a little before.

Paul Stillwell: Well, in many ships the crew members were delighted when the ship was damaged enough to get them back to the States.

Admiral Shelton: I've got to say that was not the case on the St. Louis. If I've ever seen a gung-ho bunch of guys that wanted to get back out there, it was all the guys I knew on the St. Louis. We had a quite active JO bunkroom on there, and any time when we weren't at GQ we were shooting craps or sleeping because the watches then were mostly one in two, not one in three.* And we had a good JO bunkroom. They were a terrific bunch of guys. All the officers on that ship I really enjoyed knowing.

[Interruption]

Paul Stillwell: Well, as I remember before we broke for that delicious lunch, we were just getting your ship back to Long Beach for repairs.

---

* JO—junior officer.

Admiral Shelton: Oh, yes. Well, we weren't there too long. Everybody was eager. You asked me what the mood was on there, whether they were glad to be get back or whatever, and yes, everybody was glad to get back for good liberty and all that sort of thing. But basically they were all eager to get back out there and do their bit. So they fixed the ship up. We went out, and, of course, after you've done something like that you always have to go out, and you have to go through a series of tests to make sure everything is put together right and that everything still works right.

I think I mentioned to you the other day one of the occasions where we went out, and we were going to test the guns and the turrets and all that kind of stuff. I came as close to closing out my naval career as I ever did right then. We were checking out the turrets, firing them, and we were checking the safety sectors and all that sort of thing. Well, the idea was that some of the firing circuits weren't working maybe as right as they should have been. That's why we were checking them. So we were out off San Clemente and shooting at targets out there or whatever. And a lot of times we were just firing out in the ocean because the exercise was just to fire the guns and not at anything in particular. So we were training the turret back and forth and firing in different sectors.

We got a little bit out of the safety sector, and the procedure was that if you pulled the trigger and it didn't fire, then you assumed a firing circuit failure. You checked through your periscope and checked the range, and if the range was clear, you went ahead and kicked them out, as they say, by percussion. So we had that done several times already, and we trained over in an area, and it's probably safe to say that we didn't realize that we'd trained back as far as we had. But anyway we had trained just very slightly—thankfully, just very slightly—into the safety sector on the port side. So pulled the trigger and nothing happened, which means that the cutout for the safety sector probably had worked correctly, and it wasn't a firing circuit failure as we had had in several other places.

So we did what we had done before, which is that we checked down range through the periscope and everything and kicked them out. We fired very slightly into the safety sector close to the bridge, that being the turret that was closest to the bridge. And we fired right over a 40-millimeter mount and close to the bridge. So probably if we'd have trained another five or eight degrees further to port and done the same thing, hopefully we would have seen the corner of the bridge. But if we hadn't, we would have cleaned out that part of the bridge, and I wouldn't be talking about it now I don't guess. They didn't tolerate that kind of thing very well, and you can't blame them for that.

Paul Stillwell: Who was your gunnery officer that you worked for?

Admiral Shelton: Well, that was Ben Sarver, and he knew his gunnery.* He was a first-class member of the Gun Club.† He knew all about it, and he knew what to do and what not to do, et cetera. He was not the easiest man to be around if you were a junior officer on the bridge or anything of that sort, because he didn't pay too much attention to you except when you did something wrong, and then he let you have a full blast of what you'd done wrong.

Paul Stillwell: Do you remember any specifics in that regard?

Admiral Shelton: Yes, I do. It was a rainy night. St. Louis had an open bridge, and Lieutenant Bunch, who was my division officer, was there. He had the OOD, and I had the JOOD, and Commander Sarver had the command duty.‡ Well, he was sitting in the command duty chair there on the open bridge, on the starboard side of the bridge.

Paul Stillwell: He was sort of the captain's watchdog.

Admiral Shelton: He was the captain's watchdog. And Mr. Bunch and I were dutifully looking ahead into the rain, and I made the mistake of turning around for about a minute to get out of the rain. In the meanwhile, a steward from the wardroom had brought up a hot pot of tea to Commander Sarver. I think I happened to mention something about, "A

---
* Lieutenant Commander Ben W. Sarver, USN.
† "Gun Club" was the unofficial name for surface officers who served in battleships, cruisers, and destroyers. Its members often had specialized ordnance training. The term had a somewhat derisive meaning in that the officers were considered slow to recognize the ascendancy of the aircraft carrier's capability as a strike force.
‡ OOD—officer of the deck; JOOD—junior officer of the deck.

hot cup of tea sure would be good at this point." And he let me know that a hot cup of tea was not my privilege at that point. My privilege was to stand there and look ahead as a lookout. He never said anything more about it, and I don't think he held any grudge on it or anything like that. But I did notice that after that he never had the tea out on the bridge. He always took it in the charthouse, so to speak, and drank his tea in there. And I couldn't blame him. A good hot cup of tea in those days about 3:00 o'clock in the morning wasn't a bad thing to have.

Paul Stillwell: It's interesting they had those open bridges, because that's not conducive to good visibility or the health of the watch standers.

Admiral Shelton: Not at all. The helm was actually inside protected, but the bridge itself, where all the watches were stood, was outside, right out in the weather. I know that the CO of the ship was a captain named Roberts.[*] He was even shorter than I am, and they called him Shorty Roberts. For him to see over the edge of the bridge coaming there they had to literally build him a little platform inside of that open bridge so that when he was on the bridge he could stand on that little platform and be able to see out over the ship. So I never understood really why they didn't have an enclosed bridge, but they didn't.

Paul Stillwell: What other experiences do you remember from standing bridge watches?

Admiral Shelton: Well, I got qualified, of course, and that was good.[†] I stood most of my watches with Mr. Bunch, and he was not an Academy graduate. He was from Seattle, Washington, as I recall. I thought he was really a good man. He was not tolerant of mistakes or anything like that, but when you were on watch with him, he had an interest in educating you. Part of his job, he felt, as the OOD was to make sure that you understood certain things about standing a watch and why you did it this way and why

---
[*] Captain Ralph H. Roberts, USN, served as commanding officer of the St. Louis from 12 October 1943 to 3 January 1945.
[†] This refers to qualifying as officer of the deck.

you didn't do it some other way and what to look for and what not to look for and how to look for it.

Paul Stillwell: It was just what you needed.

Admiral Shelton: Yes. Such simple things as how to make the best use of your binoculars and a lot of things. So I always appreciated him, and I never had a problem with standing a watch with him. Really, I stood the watch very seldom with anybody but him. I don't know why it was that way, but that's the way it was. And occasionally we even got to go in and take a peek at the radar, which we had by then. But it was inside, too, so the command duty officer who made a lot of decisions or the OOD if they were going to do anything that involved checking the radar, they had to go inside the bridge shack, as we called it, and check the radar there because there wasn't any out on the open bridge.

Paul Stillwell: How much formation steaming did the St. Louis get involved in?

Admiral Shelton: Not a whole lot, to tell you the truth. I can remember it wasn't until, oh, after Leyte Gulf. We got in a little bit going up to Okinawa.* But the most of it was after Okinawa when we went on up in preparation for the invasion of Japan. If you remember then the old task force, they had about five big circles that went right down the row there. So there was a certain amount of steaming in formation there. You learned how to look at the ship ahead of you and keep station by how much the ship filled of your binoculars. And you could get quite good at it, as a matter of fact. You could get good enough to stay within, oh, easily within 25 yards of where you were supposed to be.

Paul Stillwell: Of course, the radar could be very helpful in that regard too.

---

* U.S. forces invaded the island of Okinawa, only 340 miles from the closest point in the Japanese home islands, on 1 April 1945.

Admiral Shelton: Except that it was inside the shack. So we learned to keep station with binoculars. I guess that's really kind of one of the fundamentals of all station keeping is to be able to do that with looking through binoculars. But we didn't do a whole lot of steaming in company as it were until that time when we got up there off Japan, and we did quite a bit then.

Paul Stillwell: Were you involved in the battle of Leyte Gulf per se there in late October?

Admiral Shelton: No. As I recall, we got there about the time that that finished.

Paul Stillwell: Did you get to Iwo Jima?

Admiral Shelton: No. We never did get to Iwo Jima. We steamed close by, but we never went there. We spent a lot of time at Okinawa.

Paul Stillwell: Well, please tell me about that.

Admiral Shelton: We were on both sides of Okinawa basically, the west side and the east side. The west side was where most of the early bombarding all took place, and that's where again where all the kamikazes starting showing up. We never got hit there. We were right in close to the beach. We were a couple of thousand yards off the beach doing the bombarding, sometimes closer than that.

I do remember that one Sunday we had to replenish ammunition, and so we backed off of the beach about another, I don't know, 4,000 or 5,000 yards, maybe more. It was Sunday, and so here was this merchant ship that had all the ammunition, and they would not man the hatches. They wouldn't man any of the winches, wouldn't do anything. It was Sunday and that wasn't in their contract. They were very nervous about being there anyway, and I couldn't blame them for that, because all it took was one big mistake, and they would have been a big mistake. But, anyway, we had to send over our personnel from the St. Louis to man the hatches, the winches, handle ammunition, the whole bit in order to get that ammunition back over to the St. Louis.

We saw a lot of action there. We saw a lot of kamikazes. A couple of times we went down to Kerama Retto for one reason or another, which is a little set of islands to the south there of Okinawa. I guess all of the destroyers that were able to when they had been hit by kamikazes went down there and went in the north entrance there, and there was a shallow beach inside Kerama Retto there. They were able to go in and turn in to the beach and just drive the destroyer right up on the beach. I've forgotten how many destroyers you could see in there at any one time, but I don't think 35 or 40 was a low number. Maybe more than that. I know there are pictures that show them, and it was just amazing.

Paul Stillwell: How would they get back off the beach? Just with propellers?

Admiral Shelton: A lot of them didn't. They were hurt too bad. But if they were able to make repairs, why, they could otherwise be towed off it. It was so shallow that they didn't get embedded very much. It was well protected, but if they could get emergency repairs they could do that, and so you'd get towed off or back off, one of the two. But some of them were there permanently.

At one end of the Kerama Retto harbor, I think it was the south end, was where the PBMs, the seaplanes were flying from in those days. My brother was in VP-21, one of the PBM squadrons there at the time.[*] He was a jaygee. The mother ship for him was the Chandeleur.[†] I had put in for flight training but had not had an opportunity to get a flight training physical, which you had to have to send your application in. So there was about five of us from the St. Louis that they gave us a boat, and we went trundling over to the Chandeleur from the St. Louis while we were in Kerama Retto there. Lieutenant Ted Wolfe, the flight surgeon in my brother's squadron, gave us all a flight physical, and I spent a little time with my brother. Then we got in the boat and drove back to the St. Louis.

---

[*] Lieutenant (junior grade) Robert F. Shelton, Jr., USNR.
[†] USS Chandeleur (AV-10) was a seaplane tender that had been commissioned in 1942.

Paul Stillwell: Did you have any sense of encouragement or discouragement from the people in the St. Louis about looking into aviation?

Admiral Shelton: Not too good really. There were several on the St. Louis. They were good guys. I don't mean to say otherwise. But for one reason or another they hadn't gotten into aviation. Either they had flunked the physical or they didn't want to, one or the other. But anyway they didn't, and they didn't particularly encourage anybody getting into it.

The executive officer that we had by that time was Andrew Jackson Smith, and he had come to the St. Louis from Missouri.[*] He'd been the damage control officer on the Missouri, as I recall. He had gone to flight training, but he had flunked out. Any mention of going to flight training around him was like waving a red flag. He thought he had been had when he got bilged out of flight training, and he didn't particularly care whether anybody got to flight training or not.

I'm getting ahead of the story a little bit, but a little later on, when we were down in Subic after the bomb was dropped, my orders came through to go to flight training.[†] That was in early August '45. So I waited around there expecting that maybe somebody would let me know when I could leave the ship to carry out my orders. I finally went down and asked to see the exec, and he wanted to know what the hell I wanted. I said, "Well, I'd like to know when I can count on being detached to go to flight training."

He said, knowing full well that I had a set of orders, said, "Do you have any orders?"

I said, "Yes, sir."

He said, "What do they say?"

I said, "They say 'When detached in August.' "

He said, "You come back and see me at 2330 the last day of August." [Laughter] Then he told me all about going to flight training and bilging out of flight training and

---
[*] Smith was a commander.
[†] In the first combat use of atomic bombs, U.S. B-29 bombers hit Hiroshima, on the island of Honshu, on 6 August 1945 and Nagasaki, on Kyushu, on 9 August. Subic Bay is a protected anchorage on the island of Luzon in the Philippines. It borders the Bataan province and is about 35 miles north of the entrance to Manila Bay

how much he didn't give a shit about naval aviation, to be exact. [Laughter] So I went back up, and I had this kind of figured out, living in the JO bunkroom.

This is getting ahead of the story, but from Okinawa finally we went back down to Subic, and that's where we were on the 25th of August. Then the ship got orders to go to take the surrender of Formosa. So at 3:00 o'clock in the morning on the 25th he sent his messenger up to the JO bunkroom with the message that there would be an LCS alongside in 30 minutes.* If I was on it, I was going. If I wasn't on it, I wasn't going.

Well, I'd sort of had something like this figured out in the back of my mind at least, so I had my seabag packed. So when that word came, man, it couldn't have been more than five minutes later I was standing on the quarterdeck with another one of my classmates named Gene Mahan, who had the deck.† It was raining like it can only rain in the Philippines, straight down in large drops. The quarterdeck was about six inches deep in water, and Gene Mahan was in no mood to be very happy. But, sure enough, that LCS came alongside about 3:00 or 3:30 in the morning. I went over and I laid down on the cover they had over the cabin they had there, and it was just a plain old canvas cover. I threw my seabag down where it wouldn't get too wet, and I climbed up on the top of that thing. I waved good-bye to the USS St. Louis. [Laughter] Rode to Manila on that LCS. And I can get into that a little bit later on.

But, going back to Okinawa, it was exciting. We had a rapid, real-time account all the time of the destroyers that were up on the point getting hit by the kamikazes. Then they would try to limp from there down to Kerama Retto and make repairs or whatever. But every one of those destroyers that had the point duty eventually was bagged one way or the other. So those were pretty exciting times. Later on we were around on the other side of Okinawa, on the Buckner Bay side. They had a net across that harbor, and we had gotten inside the net. I don't know, we were there a week or ten days I guess. And every night the little LSMRs fired rockets.‡ Every night was a real Fourth of July, believe me. Man, I'm telling you. I guess they'd had 50 or 60 of those little ships in there and, man, they all put out their rockets every night, you know, and everything like that. And it was real show.

---

* LCS—landing craft (support).
† Ensign Eugene Mahan, USN.
‡ LSMR—landing ship medium (rocket-equipped).

Paul Stillwell: I saw them fire in Vietnam 20 years later.

Admiral Shelton: Oh, spectacular.

Paul Stillwell: One of the crew members told me that for them R&R meant reload rockets. [Laughter]

Admiral Shelton: I guess that's right because, man, they really did put them out. But there we were, anchored in the bay, not maneuvering or anything like that. There were a lot of ships in there, and so you couldn't be under way very much, and that was still kamikaze time. By that time they'd gotten down to the old biplane float airplanes with just a big bomb essentially tied to the float or whatever. But they would come down there. They didn't come down in the daytime, because it was too easy to shoot them down; they were so slow and cumbersome to do anything like that. But they would come down every night.

Our defense against that basically was to put out smoke. We had a smoke generator on the fantail, and all the rest of the ships had them too. We would generate smoke. And we would generate smoke, and we would generate smoke. That whole bay was covered with smoke. The only thing sticking up out of that smoke would be the top of your mast. Whichever one had the highest masts, those masts would be sticking up out of the smoke. Well, I had the watch several times up there in the crow's nest, and it was pretty interesting, because here would come these kamikazes every night, and there would be maybe three or four of them at a time and maybe only one sometimes.

They would fly around and fly around and fly around and looking for ships. Couldn't see the ships, but they finally got wise enough so they'd get low enough and try to match off the masts against any discoloration so that they could see the masts. Didn't happen very much, but they did manage to hit a couple of ships. But by that method they would get down low enough to where they could finally see the mast against the hills or the horizon or whatever. Then they would dive on that mast. So it was kind of exciting, but for the most part they were pretty ineffective because of the smoke that we just kept on generating, and they couldn't see the ships.

Paul Stillwell: Did you have any trouble breathing in all that smoke, or did you stay inside?

Admiral Shelton: Yes, a lot of trouble breathing because that stuff is pretty heavy stuff. People complain about jet fuel these days. This was pretty heavy stuff. But it worked.

Paul Stillwell: What do you remember from being inside the turret during those bombardments?

Admiral Shelton: Ten to 12 hours' GQ at a time and having to go to the head and no head to go to. And cheese and crackers for breakfast, lunch, and dinner.

Paul Stillwell: The ammunition-handling procedures were all well rehearsed and so forth?

Admiral Shelton: Yes, that was just not a problem. Everybody was well versed in that, and we shot a lot. But that kind of bombardment usually, unless there's some call for a specific kind or whatever, it turns out to be a kind of rotating sort of thing. Turret number one fires, and a little bit later turret two or turret three and so forth. So it was very seldom that we fired more than one turret at a time under those circumstances. But we fired constantly, pretty much. When we were at GQ like that for 10 or 12 hours, we fired for 10 or 12 hours.

Paul Stillwell: Did you have spotted fire from airplanes?

Admiral Shelton: Yes, we had some of that. Not as much as you might think but quite a bit of it. And we had a lot of whatever you want to call the ground guys over there that were calling for fire. We had a lot of that. Well, anyway, there we were anchored in Buckner Bay over there and call-fire, we did do a lot of it at that point because they were still trying to get them out of the cave and all that sort of thing. So they needed a lot of ammunition put on a certain point, and that was call-fire so we got a lot of that.

But the interesting thing that happened there was, I've forgotten how long we'd been in there, three or four days I guess, and we got the word somehow that a Japanese mini-sub had gotten inside the gate, so to speak. Nobody saw it or anything like that. I was up in the 5-inch sky watch, sky aft, and all of a sudden we saw this torpedo coming. I think I was the first one to see it. I'm not sure. I just said, "Torpedo coming, port side." There wasn't any time to do anything. There we were, anchored. We didn't even have time to go to GQ or anything like that, although watertight integrity was always set. But that torpedo went right by the bow, or the stern, I've forgotten which, bow I think, and hit the old Pennsylvania that was sitting next to us on the other side.[*] Now, Buckner Bay was pretty shallow. It hit the Pennsylvania, and the Pennsylvania just kind of, as I recall just kind of sank until it was sitting on the bottom.

Paul Stillwell: She went down by the stern. I've seen pictures of that.

Admiral Shelton: Yes. So there we were. We just watched it. There it was. But they never fired another one. They only fired that one torpedo, as far as I know. I don't know whether they turned and ran or whether a destroyer got on him and sunk him. I don't remember that part of it at all, strangely enough, but I don't think we ever got it. I think he went back out the net and was glad to go.

Paul Stillwell: Your classmate, Ed Snyder, was in the Pennsylvania.[†]

Admiral Shelton: Yeah? I'll be damned. Later the New Jersey.[‡]

---

[*] On 12 August 1945, a Japanese aircraft torpedoed the battleship Pennsylvania (BB-38) while she was anchored in Buckner Bay, Okinawa. The battleship, which was hit well aft, suffered extensive damage. Twenty men were killed and ten injured. After preliminary salvage work, she left Buckner Bay under tow on 18 August and arrived in Apra Harbor, Guam on 6 September for dry-docking.
[†] Ensign J. Edward Snyder, Jr., USN.
[‡] As a captain, Snyder commanded the battleship New Jersey (BB-62) in 1968-69, during her only deployment of the Vietnam War.

Paul Stillwell: Well, that's where I knew him. He was my skipper.

Admiral Shelton: Yes, he was a good man.

Paul Stillwell: Yes, indeed. You've talked about the cheese and crackers on your long GQs. Did you have normal meals? I mean, how good was the logistic supply of food for replenishment?

Admiral Shelton: Pretty good, as a matter of fact. I don't think we ever wanted for too much really. The biggest thing we ever wanted for was a good old Coca-Cola.

Paul Stillwell: Interesting.

Admiral Shelton: We never had many of those, and I can still remember one time when a destroyer came alongside; he wanted to get some ammo, I guess it was. I've forgotten what it was he wanted. But, anyway, it was Ed Dexter, who had been the assistant commandant of midshipmen when we were there. Our class as a class had gotten to know Commander Dexter quite well. And I'd gotten to know him from one of the classes that I had. He was CO of this destroyer when it came alongside, and I was up there on the port bow and helping to handle lines, that kind of stuff.* He looked over, and he picked up the megaphone, and he said, "Hey, Shelton, how are you doing?"

I said, "I'm doing great."

He said, "Would you like a cold Coke?"

I said, "I'd die for one." [Laughter] And so he sent me over a cold Coke by highline. Great.

Paul Stillwell: That's a wonderful memory.

---

* Commander Edwin B. Dexter, USN, was commanding officer of the destroyer Barton (DD-722).

Admiral Shelton: He never sent over a case or anything, but he did send over one. [Laughter] But Ed Dexter, he was a great guy.

Paul Stillwell: Usually it was the bigger ships that supplied smaller ships with goodies like that.

Admiral Shelton: That's true, but if I can remember correctly, and I do think I remember pretty correctly, I don't ever remember that we ever had any adequate supply of Cokes. Everything else, food, yes, we had plenty of that. But when you're at GQ there was no way of getting to that, so we had crackers and cheese.

Paul Stillwell: Did you get any ship-handling experience, taking her alongside an oiler or something like that?

Admiral Shelton: Not at that point I didn't. It was all underway steaming, out in the open sea, keeping station. No, I never did get to. Later on, on carriers, I got to go alongside and that kind of stuff. But not at that point I didn't, no. As a matter of fact, except for the time alongside that ammunition ship I can't ever remember that we were alongside. Well, in Leyte Gulf we had to go alongside the oilers, but that was not a time to train somebody. That was a time to get in there and get your oil and get out. So I'm sure they didn't have any time to waste on trying to get a JO educated on how you get alongside a tanker.

Paul Stillwell: Did you normally fuel in Kerama Retto then?

Admiral Shelton: Yes. I guess really that's probably why we were over there from time to time and just to relax a little bit. But all the re-ammo was basically done right there off of Okinawa, just a little further out. But I didn't think it was very far out.

Paul Stillwell: Not far enough.

Admiral Shelton: Not far enough. There were still ships all around us, you know, so we weren't very far away from the beach. And we certainly weren't far enough away as far as kamikazes were concerned.

Paul Stillwell: You said you went to Chandeleur for that aviation physical. Was that more demanding than a regular physical?

Admiral Shelton: Only from the standpoint of blood pressure and eyes, I think. I've thought about it a lot of times, and I remember the name of the flight surgeon was a fellow named Ted Wolf. I've often thought maybe he was as tired as we were and said, "Let's get this over with." [Laughter]

Paul Stillwell: Well, what had really inspired your interest in naval aviation?

Admiral Shelton: Well, as I had indicated, you know, when I was a kid I saw Lindbergh, and I got a ride with Roscoe Turner in his Condor. And I had watched some of the aviation PBY business there at the Academy, and Butch O'Hare had come back. My time both on the battleship as an enlisted man and on the St. Louis as a JO, I hate to say it this way, but I always thought the naval aviators had the best of it. I liked it. I liked that idea. I thought, "Well, when you're flying your own airplane, to some extent you're the master of your own destiny. You're either going to make it, or you're going to get shot down or whatever's going to happen to you, but at least you have a certain amount of control over whether you're going to survive certain situations or whether you're not." My brother was already a PBM driver in the war, and he loved it. So I thought, "Well, that sounds good to me." So I had put in for it as soon as I could.

Paul Stillwell: So it was really a combination of things.

Admiral Shelton: Yes, a combination of things. But, anyway, I had put in for it, and it wasn't too long really after they sent those all in. I thought that was pretty miraculous, really, because that couldn't have been any later than about June or July, something like that, when I put in my application. I'd have to look back. No later than that.

Paul Stillwell: At that point BuPers didn't know the war was going to end so soon, and it needed to keep that pipeline going.*

Admiral Shelton: That's right. They needed to keep the pipeline going, and I've thought about that a lot, too, because probably, oh, six months later they shut that pipeline down. I wouldn't have gotten out of there maybe at all or at least for another year or whatever. So I was glad to get off there and get back.

Paul Stillwell: Well, what happened between Okinawa and then during that summer till you were detached?

Admiral Shelton: Went down to Subic Bay, and we stayed there for a month maybe. I don't remember how long. About a month. Then, as I said, I got detached at 3:00 o'clock in the morning on the 25th of August.

Paul Stillwell: What do you remember about first the news of the atomic bombs and then the news of the end of the war?

Admiral Shelton: You know, my recollection is that that bomb was dropped before we left Buckner Bay. I think we got the news while we were still in Buckner Bay that they had dropped the bomb. I didn't know what the damned thing was, and I guess there might have been somebody on the ship that did know. But basically we just got the news that we had dropped one hell of a big bomb and that the figuring was that the Japanese were going to capitulate.

Paul Stillwell: Was there a sense of relief when they did?

---

* BuPers—Bureau of Naval Personnel.

Admiral Shelton: Hard to say. Yes, let's see. I know that we had been up north, and we'd been in the task forces up there and then came back down to Buckner Bay, or maybe it was while we were still up there off of Japan that we got that news. I'm not really sure. I'd have to go back and check the St. Louis book that I have. But one of the interesting things that did happen while we were up there off the coast of Japan is that one of the things I had in the turret, of course, was a very strong periscope. I could really see a lot of things. We were just one circle removed from the Franklin when she was hit, so I had a first seat observation of that whole thing.*

Paul Stillwell: That was in March. That was before the invasion of Okinawa.

Admiral Shelton: Okay. March. Okay. Well, then we'd been up there before we went back down to Okinawa. I couldn't remember that schedule. But that was really something to see that ship get hit.

Paul Stillwell: What is in your mental picture of that experience?

Admiral Shelton: One big cloud of black smoke—I mean, huge—and the ship starting to list a little bit. Other than that, you weren't close enough to see very much of the actual action on the deck or anything like that, so it was really that. It had only been a couple of nights before that I think that there had been a wave of 60 Bettys, as I recall, coming down the pike.† The two task forces up ahead of us, again my recollection is that they shot down every one of those 60 before they got to the task forces. So there was a lot of action going on. From the turret you didn't see all that much of it, but I happened to be able to see the Franklin thing head on. That was pretty interesting. Anyway, the news of the bomb was pretty much along those lines. It wasn't any big headline kind of broadcast

---

* The carrier Franklin (CV-13) was hit by bombs near Japan in March 1945, resulting in great damage and loss of life. After her fires were extinguished, she was able to return to the United States under her own power, though she never did go back into active service.
† The G4M (known by the Allied code name Betty) was a Mitsubishi Type 1 two-engine, land-based torpedo bomber.

or anything like that. On the other hand, it seemed pretty firm that the Japanese would capitulate. Well, anyway, I think that was before we went and got down to Subic.

Paul Stillwell: That first one was on the sixth of August.

Admiral Shelton: The sixth of August, yes. Okay, well, we were either on our way down there or we were there at Subic. So from the sixth of August then until the 25th of August, we were sitting alongside the pier at Subic just waiting to go somewhere.

As I said, they sent the ship to take the surrender of Formosa, and that's when I got off the ship. Went to Manila on that LCS. Checked in to the old Wilson Bank Building up there, which was the headquarters for everything. They had a first class yeoman taking care of getting everybody out of there, the transportation officer. He was on about the third floor, and the Red Cross girls were all up on the fifth floor, and we were on the first floor or something. But, anyway, the Wilson Bank Building was right downtown. It was the only building that still had elevators running, so that was why they had everything in that building.

Paul Stillwell: Was there kind of a happy-go-lucky atmosphere at that point?

Admiral Shelton: Yes, very much so. Everybody was trying to go home. I told you about Gibson's Dairy. One of the Gibson daughters, Anne Gibson, who was not in my class—she was a couple of classes after me—was in the Red Cross in Manila.

Paul Stillwell: This was a Springfield girl.

Admiral Shelton: Yes, so I had an opportunity to go find her, and we had dinner someplace. I've forgotten where. I think it was in the Army O-club or something like that.* So, anyway, I stuck around there for a couple of days, just trying to find out how long it was going to take me to get out of there. I had a bottle of Old Overholt with me. You know what Old Overholt is. It's rye, and there's not very many people that would

---

* O-club—officers' club.

call it good drinking whiskey or sipping whiskey. I certainly didn't, but anyway I had it with me. I walked up to this first class petty officer, and I said, "When do you think I can get out of here?"

He said, "Oh, I don't know." Same routine as you get many times.

I said, "Well, I've got a bottle of Old Overholt here." I said, "I don't want it. You can have it if it'll help get me out of here."

About a half an hour later he said, "Mr. Shelton," he said, "You're going out of Manila this afternoon [laughter] on Admiral Nimitz's airplane. He won't be on board, but it is his airplane." It was a B-25 that Admiral Nimitz had configured, as I recall. So I rode from Manila to Guam on Admiral Nimitz's airplane and was there in Guam for, I don't know, maybe four days, five days or a week. They were pretty efficient by that time at setting up the Magic Carpet.* They put me on the USS Cabot, which was a CVL of some renown.† I don't know whether this was the first load on the Magic Carpet or not. It probably was.

Paul Stillwell: Probably so, yes.

Admiral Shelton: Yes. But, anyway, we got on there and everybody on there was going home for one reason or another. So we sailed directly from there to San Francisco. Did not stop in Honolulu, Hawaii. The biggest thing I remember about that trip was that, again, it was almost all cheese and crackers. [Laughter] There were so many people on there they couldn't hope to serve any kind of a meal to speak of.

Paul Stillwell: Did they have people berthed in the hangar deck?

Admiral Shelton: They had people berthed every place there was to berth anybody. It was full. The biggest thing that I remember about that trip back was that there were four warrant officers and a lieutenant that had a huge poker game going. Without getting too

---

* Magic Carpet was the nickname for the use of Navy ships, including combatants, to bring servicemen home to the United States from overseas once World War II ended.
† USS Cabot (CVL-28) was an Independence-class light carrier.

close, I kind of tried to observe the whole thing, because it was just kind of interesting. This lieutenant was cleaning them out.

Warrant officers, being the renowned poker players that they are, normally didn't cotton too well to this lieutenant cleaning them out. Just before we got into San Francisco, a night or two out, I remember that the four warrants all had really good hands. One had a straight flush, and the other one had a full house or something like that. Big hands anyway. And this lieutenant was sitting there with a pair of deuces. And this was pot limit stuff. I think that pot was up around 2,500 bucks, which was a lot of money back in those days. Of course, they had a lot of money. Everybody was betting, though, the four warrants and the lieutenant. The lieutenant didn't have a damn thing to show except this pair of deuces. He drew the other pair of deuces, and he cleaned them out again. [Laughter] That broke up the poker game. The warrant officers were so POed [laughter] that they didn't ever want to see that lieutenant again. I don't know. He must have cleaned up $10,000-12,000 during that trip.

Paul Stillwell: You seldom hear of somebody winning a hand with four deuces

Admiral Shelton: Yeah, that's right, but he did. I'll never forget that.

Paul Stillwell: Where did you sleep during this voyage?

Admiral Shelton: I don't even remember. I really don't. I've thought about that from time to time, too, but I do remember that there was a whole bunch of kind of staterooms like there would be on a carrier, staterooms and everything associated around the wardroom and a lot of cots on the hangar deck. So I either was sleeping in the wardroom or I was sleeping in one of those staterooms with a couple of other guys. I don't know, but that's about as much as I really remember about sleeping on it.

Paul Stillwell: Your homecoming to the West Coast was probably not as dramatic as it was for some people because you'd been there relatively recently.

Admiral Shelton: Yes. I was mostly anxious to get through San Francisco back to Missouri and see my parents and get on down to Dallas to start flight training. That's what I did.

Paul Stillwell: Well, please tell the story about flight training.

Admiral Shelton: Before that I went back to Philadelphia to see a beautiful young lady that I'd gotten to know slightly my last year at the Naval Academy. I spent a couple of days in Philadelphia taking her out and found out that wasn't going to do any good. So I got back on a train and rode back to Springfield and then a couple of days later went on back down to Dallas.

Reported in to Dallas in October '45 and started flight training right away. Didn't have too much trouble. I seemed to pick up on it pretty good, and my primary flight instructor was a young jaygee that I liked pretty well. His name was H. R. Way, and he asked me several times, "What kind of this naval aviation do you want?"

I said, "Well, I think from what I've seen I want to get back to the carriers," never having been on one.

He was a reserve, and he said, "Well, I'm going to get out pretty soon. I've already got a job working for the airline." So, as far as I know, he had a very successful career flying for the airlines.

A long-time Springfield buddy of mine was an instructor down there at the time, a guy named Gene Newman, who later became a GS-17 in the OSHA organization, the national director of compliance and federal safety.[*] He lives back in Middletown, Virginia, at this point. By the way, he also had a hand in setting up that Ozarks History Museum in the old Bentley House in Springfield. But, anyway, he had a couple of rides with me, and he said, "Well, you look like you're doing all right. I guess I can't do too much harm to you," so he didn't give me a down or anything like that.[†]

Paul Stillwell: What were you flying?

---

[*] OSHA—Occupational Health & Safety Administration, U.S. Department of Labor. Lieutenant Gene Newman, USNR.
[†] A "down" was an unsatisfactory grade given by an instructor pilot during a check flight.

Admiral Shelton: N2Ss at that point.* And I marvel at that, too, because we flew from a couple of round asphalt mats out there in the middle of the field, between Hensley Field and the old Chance-Vought plant.† The system was that the airplanes would taxi out there, and they would all be out there at the same time on this octagonally shaped mat. They would all turn into the wind, and they would all pick their little piece of wind and go that way. Then they did the same thing landing when they came back. I've always thought, "I don't know how in the hell you could get through primary without somebody driving into somebody else, either on takeoff or after landing, and lose control or something." But to my knowledge that never did happen.

Paul Stillwell: Well, there's some aptitude involved in flying. Did you seem to have that?

Admiral Shelton: Oh, yes. I seemed to have that. As a matter fact, one of the things you had to demonstrate in primary was what they called spot landings. This was simply you picked a spot in a field, and you made a turn so that at the end you could sideslip down and then roll out and plant it right in the middle of that spot that you'd picked. When we first started doing this, H. R. Way said, "Well, let me show you what we're going to be doing here." So he showed me, and he said, "Okay, now you try it." So I did several of what I thought were pretty goddamned good, and when we got all through he said, "I don't need to teach you that. You're doing it better than I can." [Laughter] So I began to feel pretty comfortable.

Paul Stillwell: Sure. That's a great confidence builder.

Admiral Shelton: The only part of it that was coming up that I wondered about was the aerobatics, and I thought, "Well, you know, that's kind of the true test." I guess it was in

---

* The Stearman N2S Kaydet was the Navy version of a biplane trainer first ordered by the Army as the PT-13. It was 25 feet long, had a wingspan of 32 feet, gross weight of 2,717 pounds, and a top speed of 124 miles per hour. Deliveries of the plane to the Navy began in 1935.
† Hensley Field at Naval Air Station, Dallas, Texas, was named for Colonel William N. Hensley, Jr., who was prominent in the reserve program during the 1920s.

a way, but I never had a tendency to get sick or anything like that, and I understood the aerodynamics of it. So, again, H. R. Way was a good instructor, and Gene Newman was too. So the times that I had in aerobatics I didn't have a problem and enjoyed it. Finished up there in December.

Paul Stillwell: Did you solo before you left there?

Admiral Shelton: Yes, you had to solo before you left there, and that was not a problem. While I was at Dallas I saw one of the most extraordinary things I've ever seen in my life, and that was an officer getting drummed out of the Navy. If you've never seen one of those, you talk about pageantry or whatever you want to call it, that's something you don't really want to have to see.

Paul Stillwell: Well, I never have, so could you describe it please?

Admiral Shelton: Yes. This guy was a lieutenant, and he was one of the instructors there. And he was dating a good-looking blond WAVE, and he wasn't supposed to be dating her, because she was enlisted and he was a lieutenant.* She decided to go AWOL for whatever reason.† And she decided that staying with him while she was AWOL was a good idea. A big mistake on his part, because that got him a general court-martial and got him drummed out of the Navy. That was the sentence. And the CO of the base presided. All the cadets—they called us cadets there in flight training—everybody on the base was out there at the front gate in parade formation. They marched that lieutenant out there. They walked up. They clipped his buttons off. They took the braid off his arms, took the insignia off his cap, marched him out of the gate and said, "See you later." And that's pretty amazing.

---

* WAVES—Women Accepted for Voluntary Emergency Service. Until the 1970s, when women ceased to have a separate organization within the Navy, the term WAVE was used to refer to a Navy woman.
† AWOL—absent without leave. The Navy equivalent for this term is UA—unauthorized absence.

Paul Stillwell: Well, your wife was telling a story here when we had our lunch break about some people getting fined $30,000 apiece for injuring Torrey pine trees. An example like that goes a long way toward teaching other people.

Admiral Shelton: I've got to tell you there wasn't anybody on that base that didn't understand. [Laughter] Ooh.

Paul Stillwell: There would be no more fraternization.

Admiral Shelton: There'd be no more fraternization. Not on that base anyway. It was really, it was impressive. I mean, it was impressive.

Paul Stillwell: As it was intended to be.

Admiral Shelton: As it was intended to be. But, you know, you really wonder if anybody has the guts to carry through on a thing like that. It takes quite a bit of something to do it. But they did—and no ifs, ands, buts, or fors about it. Marched him out the gate, and all he had on was a uniform that didn't have any insignia on it.

Paul Stillwell: Did you have ground school as a component of your flight training?

Admiral Shelton: Oh, yes.

Paul Stillwell: What did you cover?

Admiral Shelton: Oh, primarily navigation and aerodynamics, and you learned all about the engine in an airplane and what the carburetor does and what it doesn't do and what the magnetos do and what they don't do and all that sort of thing. Anything that has to do with running the airplane. And all the aerodynamics of throttle and stick and elevators and rudders, et cetera, et cetera, et cetera. But it was primarily navigation and aerodynamics.

Paul Stillwell: Was the N2S a pretty forgiving plane for a novice?

Admiral Shelton: Yes. It was a great airplane, but as many people have said you can kill yourself in that airplane just like you can any other. One of my classmates and St. Louis shipmates did just that, Hank Oates.* But, yes, it was great. As I said, it was always amazing to me to see so many N2Ss in one place at the same time and never hit each other because there were a bunch of them. You know, there would be 25 or so of them in the air all at one time, and basically most of them coming and going at the same time because there was a schedule.

I can remember back in those days the Chance-Vought factory there almost next to, well, part of Hensley Field. But they had produced P-51s for the last part of the war.† I can remember that they were trundling brand-new, spanking new P-51s and taking them out there and putting them on flatcars to go get demolished. I thought, "Oh." Of course, today you wouldn't think of doing that, and nobody thought about in those days what kind of an image the P-51 would be in later years. But, yes, countless of them. They just took them out and put them on the flatcar and trundled them away.

Paul Stillwell: The threat had evaporated overnight.

Admiral Shelton: Overnight. We've seen that happen several times too.

Paul Stillwell: Right.

Admiral Shelton: I went from there down to Cuddihy Field at Corpus Christi.‡ And a distant cousin of mine, third or fourth cousin, I guess, was the CO of Cuddihy, so I enjoyed being able to see him. His name was Babe Edmondston, and he had been a pretty good fighter pilot in the war.§ Eventually he ended up up in Seattle, and I think he

---

* Ensign Henry N. Oates, USN, died in a plane crash at Dallas, Texas, on 24 November 1945.
† The P-51 Mustang was a fighter plane widely used by the Army Air Forces in World War II.
‡ Cuddihy Field at Corpus Christi, Texas, commissioned on 3 September 1941, was named in honor of Lieutenant George T. Cuddihy, USN, a test pilot who was killed in a plane crash in 1929.
§ Commander Lilburn A. Edmonston, USNR.

finally crashed an F6F someplace up there in Puget Sound and drowned. I'm not sure of that, but something like that. But, anyway I was able to see him while I was down there, and he kind of kept me on the right track.

I didn't stay there. That was SNJ time.* I went from there over to Pensacola. And at that time going through the syllabus at Pensacola, why, you went through both single engine and multiengine planes—multiengine being both Beechcrafts and PBYs, the single engine being SNJs.† So I did all that. Got 27 hours or so in the PBY and the same amount in the SNBs and more than that in the SNJs. It came time to get your wings and where you were going to go for what kind of airplane you were going to fly. And at that time there was a big problem with what kind of airplane you were going to go fly, because they didn't have a system of recommending you for fighters or attack or anything like that. They pretty much told you what kind of vacancies there were, and you drew straws for what was available.

Paul Stillwell: So your whole career could depend on what straw you drew.

Admiral Shelton: That's right. If you didn't like what you were going to go do, you had a problem. I was lucky enough that I drew fighters, as did my roommate from the Naval Academy, Gene Spangler. He went to F4Us at Cecil Field, and I went to F6Fs at the old NAS, Banana River, which is now Patrick Air Force Base down at the launch pads.‡ So I got my wings February 6 1947 and went on over to Banana River. Spent the spring over there until July and got out of there and got assigned to VF-1 on the West Coast, which

---

* The SNJ Texan was a training aircraft manufactured by North American Aviation. The Navy first ordered a version of the airplane in late 1936; the Army designation was AT-6. Versions of the Texan continued in use for Navy training well into the 1950s.
† The SNB Kansan was a training aircraft manufactured by Beech Aircraft Company. The Navy first ordered a version of the airplane in 1941; the Army designation of the equivalent plane was AT-11. When DoD introduced its unified designation system in 1962, SNBs still in use became either TC-45Js or RC-45Js.
‡ Grumman F6F Hellcat fighters first entered fleet squadrons in early 1943. The most commonly employed version of the airplane was the F6F-5, which was 34 feet long, wingspan of 43 feet, gross weight of 15,413 pounds, and top speed of 380 miles per hour. Patrick Air Force Base is near Cape Canaveral, Florida.

elated me because they had just gotten F8F Bearcats, which was one great airplane, as I learned later.[*]

Paul Stillwell: What do you mean you learned later?

Admiral Shelton: Well, when I got to San Diego and checked in, they had a little pipeline, so to eliminate the pipeline they sent everybody down to Ream Field to go through an electronics course.[†] While I was at Ream Field, my orders were changed to VF-1E. I thought, "Man, my luck is getting even better," because at that point VF-1E had the FR-1, the old Ryan Fireball, more commonly know as the Fart Cart.[‡] [Laughter] But anyway the FR-1 Fireball. And I thought, "Oh, boy, this is great."

Well, of course, I was the junior guy in the squadron, so they weren't going to check me out just right away. But in a period of about three weeks or so I had done my handbook, and I'd done everything that was required. If you can believe this, I was sitting in the airplane to taxi out for my first flight. They got a dispatch grounding all the FR-1s, and they never flew again.

Paul Stillwell: Why not?

Admiral Shelton: It didn't work out. It had a prop forward and a jet aft, and they had a lot of problems with the airplane. Reliability was its biggest problem. They couldn't count on the jet engine when they needed it. There was nothing wrong with the recip engine because it was a good one. It wasn't fast enough. It was a lot of things. It was a good experiment at the time, but it was not going to be a good airplane in the fleet.

---

[*] VF-1—Fighter Squadron One. Grumman F8F Bearcat fighters first entered fleet squadrons in 1945. The F8F-1 version was 28 feet long, wingspan of 35 feet, gross weight of 12,947 pounds, and top speed of 421 miles per hour. It was one of the best piston-engine planes ever to serve the U.S. Navy but had a short operational life because of the advent of jet fighters.
[†] Ream Field at Naval Air Station Imperial Beach, California, was named in honor of Major William R. Ream, USA, a medical officer on North Island, Coronado, California, in the World War I period.
[‡] The Ryan-built FR Fireball was a composite fighter plane that had a propeller forward and a jet engine in the rear fuselage. The FR-1 first entered an operational squadron in March 1945 in VF-66. The FR-1 was 32 feet, 4 inches long; wingspan of 40 feet; gross weight of 11,652 pounds, and top speed of 404 miles per hour. The plane was withdrawn from naval service following carrier-based exercises in 1946 and 1947.

Doniphan B. Shelton, Interview #1 (2/10/00) – Page 95

Paul Stillwell: So you almost got to fly it.

Admiral Shelton: I almost got to fly the FR-1 but not quite. And instead of that they rolled in some F6F-5Ns. That's when I got introduced to night fighters, and essentially that's where I stayed from then on out.

Paul Stillwell: So in a sense it was luck of the draw that determined what you did from then on.

Admiral Shelton: Absolutely. Yes, very much. Basically I think always I've been pretty lucky. A classmate of mine was Bill Hoover, whose dad was ComFairWestCoast at the time.[*] Bill and I were living in the BOQ at North Island.[†] Well, he did go to VF-1, and he was in F8Fs, so we had a lot to talk about. But basically at that time I was getting more flight time than he was, and I was getting more carrier landings than he was. So I thought that was pretty good. He was getting his on the big carriers like the Tarawa, Valley Forge and so forth. I was getting mine on the Bairoko and Badoeng Strait, which were CVEs.[‡] Didn't bother me very much. I guess I didn't know any better at the time. It was a carrier, and that was all I needed. But it was a small boat on a big ocean, and they rolled a lot and couldn't develop very much wind over the deck if they needed to, so there were some problems with operating.

Paul Stillwell: How far along was night fighter doctrine in development at that point?

Admiral Shelton: Not very far along. It was right after the war and the early part of the war there were some guys, one of whom kind of a personal hero of mine, Chick Harmer,

---

[*] Ensign William H. Hoover, USN. His father was Vice Admiral John H. Hoover, USN, who served as Commander Fleet Air West Coast during the latter half of 1945.
[†] BOQ—bachelor officers' quarters. North Island Naval Air Station is on the end of the Coronado peninsula, across the harbor from San Diego.
[‡] CVE designated an escort carrier, which was considerably smaller and slower than the attack carriers.

R. E. Harmer.* Another was W. I. Martin.†

Paul Stillwell: They'd both been in Enterprise.

Admiral Shelton: They'd both been in Enterprise, and they were two of a kind of carrying the torch for night fighters and night attack. Pete Aurand and Bob Holden were in that group.‡ A guy named Cecil Kullberg was in that group.§ Kullberg was a former enlisted pilot and was Chick Harmer's exec when VF(N)-101 was first formed. When Chick took the squadron to the Enterprise from Hawaii, Kullberg took half of the aircraft and pilots as a detachment to the Intrepid. When the Intrepid was torpedoed and headed for Pearl Harbor for repairs, Kullberg's detachment was essentially knocked out of the war.

There were a number of them, and basically, in numbers, you could probably boil all those guys down to about 10 or 15. Not a big group, but they were all avid about it. And as time has come on, they led the way—none of which I knew at the time when I was trying to get my F6F-5N on and off the Bairoko or Badoeng Strait.

I don't know, I've often thought maybe it was for lack of anything else to do, but we were essentially what they called a hunter-killer group. VF-1E had F6F-5Ns. VA-1E had the old TBM.** The idea was that the F6F-5Ns were supposed to patrol and so would a VA-1E TBM, but we were supposed to report if we saw a periscope or something like that, and a VA was supposed to come along and tag him. Well, I spent a lot of time at 100 feet over the water, day and night, looking for periscopes. [Laughter] I don't remember that I ever saw one, but they were out there. I mean, they were there for

---

* During World War II Lieutenant Commander Richard E. Harmer, USN, was commanding officer of VF(N)-101, the first carrier-based night fighter squadron, flying F4U Corsairs.
† In the last year of World War II, Commander William I. Martin, USN, commanded Night Air Group 90 on board the USS Enterprise (CV-6). It was the Navy's first carrier air group specialized for night operations.
‡ Lieutenant Commander Evan P. Aurand, USN. Lieutenant (junior grade) Robert A. Holden, Jr., USN.
§ Lieutenant Cecil L. Kullberg, USN.
** The Grumman-built TBF Avenger was the U.S. Navy's standard carrier-based torpedo plane from mid-1942 through the remainder of World War II. The TBF-1 model had a wingspan of 54 feet, length of 40 feet, gross weight of 15,905 pounds, and top speed of 271 miles per hour. It was armed with one .30-caliber machine gun (two .50 caliber in the TBF-1C). The first TBF-1s reached the fleet in the spring of 1942. The General Motors-built version of the Avenger was designated TBM.

exercises. They were there, and we were supposed to be finding them, but I don't really recall that we ever found one.

Paul Stillwell: That's not really a fighter role.

Admiral Shelton: No, it wasn't, and I didn't think it was either. But we did get to go up here around Ramona and shoot rockets and some aerial gunnery and that sort of thing, so it was good.

Paul Stillwell: Butch O'Hare had gotten killed on a true night fighter mission.[*]

Admiral Shelton: Yes, that's right.

Between VF-1E and VA-1E there was an SNJ, maybe two of them, that were assigned for instrument training. That was kind of the early days of any instrument training in the squadrons. There had been some in the war but not a whole not, not very much.

Paul Stillwell: Please tell me about how far along it was at that stage, how sophisticated.

Admiral Shelton: Well, it was needle-ball and airspeed and an altimeter and gyro horizon. You went up, and you practiced the old Charlie pattern and the Bravo pattern. And you had a hood on in the back seat, and the instructor was in the front seat, and you'd go out for an hour and a half and practice nothing but instruments. I'm not sure whether we even had GCA in those days or not, but we didn't make any anyway that I can recall.[†] So it was all airborne instruments. There wasn't much practicing to make instrument approaches as such to land, although I guess we could have. But, anyway, you spent a lot of time doing that.

---

[*] Lieutenant Commander Edward H. O'Hare, USN, was killed the night of 27 November 1943. He was the pilot of an F6F Hellcat while it flying with a radar-equipped TBF. See Eugene Burns, "Butch O'Hare's Last Flight," The Saturday Evening Post, 11 March 1944, page 19, and Steve Ewing and John B. Lundstrom, Fateful Rendezvous: The Life of Butch O'Hare (Annapolis: Naval Institute Press, 1997).
[†] GCA—ground-controlled approach, in which a radar-equipped controller on the ground sends signals to a pilot in low-visibility situations to facilitate getting the plane down safely.

I'd been in the squadron, oh, just about a year I guess when in May 1948, they were going to break up. Johnny Magda and Tom Sedaker and a couple other guys went over to VF-51A when they got the FJ-1 Fury.[*] I was not one of those that got the lucky call on that, so there I was still in F6F-5Ns. But about that time Air Group One was signed on to go around the world on the Tarawa, and that was Bush Bringle's air group.[†]

Paul Stillwell: Tell me, how did the N version differ from the regular day version of the F6F? You had that pod on the wing, didn't you?

Admiral Shelton: You had the APS-6 radar out on the right wing, and you had a little scope right in front of you. Basically, when you were intercepting, it had an altitude differential type of thing where two dots showed on a screen, and if the target dot was above you, that meant he was above you, and it gave you range also. It was good, and if you worked hard enough at it, you could do a lot of things. There was always a guy up there that you were supposed to intercept, and then he was supposed to do maneuvers of various kinds to try to throw you off. So if you got good enough, you could follow him through a good many maneuvers. I didn't get good enough that early in the game. Later on, when I was out at Barbers Point, I got that good. But I just qualified in the basic intercept at that time.

Paul Stillwell: Did you do a fair amount of night work with this?

Admiral Shelton: Yes, quite a bit. Practically day and night as far as converting over from day ops to night ops. Flew more nighttime than I did daytime.

Paul Stillwell: How about night carrier landings?

---

[*] The FJ-1 Fury, built by North American Aviation, was the first jet fighter to go to sea operationally. The only squadron to get the FJ-1 model was VF-5A, later VF-51. The first carrier landings were on 10 March 1948. The FJ-1 was 34 feet long; wingspan of 38 feet; gross weight of 15,600 pounds; and top speed of 547 miles per hour. It was armed with six .50-caliber machine guns. Lieutenant Commander John Magda, USN; Lieutenant Thomas S. Sedaker, USN.

[†] Commander William F. Bringle, USN, Commander Carrier Air Group One. Bringle eventually retired in 1973 as a four-star admiral.

Admiral Shelton: Yes, I got night qualified on both the Bairoko and Badoeng Strait.

Paul Stillwell: Were they set up with some kind of light system to facilitate that?

Admiral Shelton: It was pretty primitive. They had some dustpan lights back in those days. They called them dustpan lights that kind of shined from the port and starboard catwalks onto the deck but not very much lighting like they have today.

Paul Stillwell: The dustpan being so that a ship outboard couldn't see the light?

Admiral Shelton: Right. They just reflected, oh, probably a maximum of eight or ten feet onto the deck. So the centerline of the deck really was still pretty dim, even though they did have a little string of centerline lights. In those days they did not have the thing down the stern of the ship to show you the centerline or any of that. They had just had the dustpan lights and the LSO had a fluorescent suit and fluorescent paddles to work you, and they still used the same old carrier pass in those days.[*] In other words, downwind at 150 feet and turn and make your approach to the carrier just like the standard carrier approach.

I'd become very good friends with a jaygee in the squadron named Dave Williams, and he and I were very competitive as far as flying was concerned.[†] And so, much to his wife's chagrin, they wanted some volunteers for the night fighter detachment on the Tarawa for the round-the-world cruise. So I badgered Dave until he and I both volunteered to go in that. So the night fighter training outfit out in Barbers Point had sent a team back to North Island to train us, so to speak. Clancy Rich was the head of this training unit, so we got a lot of nighttime.[‡] Another guy named Fish Trout, Rock Trout, and myself and Dave, we spent a lot of time there getting ready, and so then we went

---

[*] LSO—landing signal officer, a naval aviator, who stands on a platform on the port side of the carrier at the aft end of the flight deck. He signals to incoming aircraft in order to coach them onto the deck for recovery.
[†] Lieutenant (junior grade) David T. Williams, USN.
[‡] Lieutenant Clarence E. Rich, USN.

around the world on the Tarawa.* This was still in the time when night fighters had a tendency to interfere with the operations of the ship, because everybody wanted to fly during the daytime, and they didn't want to have to put up with losing their movies at night to let the night fighters fly. So if it hadn't have been for Commander Bush Bringle, I don't know how much night time we would have gotten. That was on the Tarawa.

Paul Stillwell: So there was some resentment of your presence?

Admiral Shelton: Yes, I would say that. Maybe not so much resentment as just the fact that, "You guys are screwing it up for us here. We like to fly during the daytime, and you guys are interrupting our movies at night. Why don't you go somewhere else and do it?"

Paul Stillwell: I've heard a great deal of admiration for Bringle. What are your impressions of him?

Admiral Shelton: He was certainly in the top two or three officers I've ever known.

Paul Stillwell: What qualities would you cite?

Admiral Shelton: Oh, integrity, loyalty down, knowledgeable, understanding, didn't get upset about a lot of things. He was just a hell of a leader.

Paul Stillwell: Any specific incidents you recall that would illustrate his qualities?

Admiral Shelton: Yes. There was one night up in Ready I, and that was where CAG

---

* USS Tarawa (CV-40) was an Essex-class aircraft carrier, commissioned 8 December 1945. She had a standard displacement of 27,100 tons, was 888 feet long, 93 feet in the beam, and had an extreme width of 148 feet. Her top speed was 33 knots. She had 12 5-inch guns and could accommodate approximately 90 aircraft. Lieutenant Commander R. L. Trout, USN, was officer in charge of the ship's night fighter detachment.

was, and that was VF-1, and that's where they put the night fighter team.* We were getting ready to don our night fighter gear, and, of course, in those days we had the night-vision goggles that we put on in the ready room to night-adapt our eyes. One of the guys in VF-1 was starting to make noises about, "Here you guys are again. We can't have our movie," and all that kind of talk.

I didn't know it, but Bush Bringle was there at the time. But anyway I'd about had my fill of this kind of stuff. So I turned around and I had my Mae West in my hand. I threw it at this guy, and I hit him.† [Laughter] Pretty good really. I wasn't still holding onto it, but I hit him. I used words that I won't care to use here right now. But anyway I let him know that I didn't appreciate the fact that he didn't appreciate that maybe we had something to offer too. About that time, Bush Bringle stepped in, and he said, "All you guys in VF-1, go down somewhere else and get lost and leave these guys alone. They're going to fly tonight." He did it in such a way that no big problem, and he never lectured me. [Laughter]

Paul Stillwell: And he commanded enough respect that that would be the end of the incident.

Admiral Shelton: That was the end of that.

Paul Stillwell: They would do as he said.

Admiral Shelton: That's right. That was the end of it forever, the rest of the cruise. There was no big problem after that.

---

* CAG—commander carrier air group. A carrier air group comprised all the planes assigned to the ship. The air group commander was the senior pilot in a flying billet, as opposed to being part of ship's company. In 1962 the Navy began using the term CVW, carrier air wing, in place of carrier air group, but the abbreviation CAG is still often used to denote the air wing commander.
† "Mae West" was the nickname for an inflatable life jacket that fit over a man's head and chest. When not in use it was rolled up into a pouch that he carried on his belt. The life jacket was named for a buxom movie actress of the period.

Doniphan B. Shelton, Interview #1 (2/10/00) – Page 102

Paul Stillwell: Well, last night I was at a reception with Vice Admiral David Richardson, who was the CAG in Princeton at the same time that Bringle was in the Tarawa.* He said there was kind of a rivalry between the two ships.

Admiral Shelton: Oh, yes. Well, I know Admiral Richardson, too, and I know his son, who is the VF-14 CO, just relieved in early December, I think, on the Theodore Roosevelt. Know them both. Yes. But there's none better than Bush Bringle.

Paul Stillwell: He said the ships were going to WestPac and kind of leapfrogging each other.†

Admiral Shelton: Yes, that's right. But the round-the-world cruise, it was sort of so and sort of not, but there were some interesting parts of it. We went in to Tsingtao, China. That's when the Marine squadrons were being thrown out by the Communists, so we covered their evacuation. In the meantime, we went back up to Yokosuka a couple of times for liberty and so forth, but we came back to Tsingtao.

There were a lot of things interesting about Tsingtao. The most interesting, of course, was that it was known then, I guess it still is, as the garlic capital of the world. When you were steaming in there, there was no doubt in your mind, because you could smell it from 15 miles at sea. And after a while when you're in there, of course, you got numb and didn't smell it anymore.

The other thing is there were two O-clubs there. There was one downtown and one out at, I think it was the old—I think the name of it was the Edgewater Beach Hotel, and that's where Admiral Cooke and Rear Admiral Freddie Boone were.‡ They and their staffs were aboard the command ship Estes. And at either place you could go and you could get filet mignon for 75 cents for dinner. [Laughter] And the drinks were equally cheap. And that's where my friend Dave Williams was going to prove that he could do

---
* Commander David C. Richardson, USN, was Commander Carrier Air Group 13. His oral history is in the Naval Institute collection.
† WestPac—Western Pacific.
‡ Vice Admiral Charles M. Cooke, Jr., USN, served as Commander Seventh Fleet, 1946-48. Rear Admiral Walter F. Boone, USN.

what the guys did in the Western movies. I forget the guy in the Western movies, but he had a thing where he could take a cigarette out and grind it out in his hands, you know. Well, old Dave, we were sitting around there having a couple of drinks, and Dave decided he was going to prove he could do that too. Meanwhile he'd been holding some ice in his hand, and he thought that was sufficient. So comes the true time of reckoning, and he took the cigarette and ground it out, and, sure enough, there was a big blister all over the palm of his hand. So we never let him forget that.

But we left there. We went on around and went to Singapore and Ceylon and went on around, went into Jidda. And before that we went into Aden.

Paul Stillwell: Please tell me about some of those Middle Eastern ports.

Admiral Shelton: Well, Aden at that time was still British. They had a British squadron there. And they had a lieutenant in that British squadron that anytime he was sufficiently provoked would prove that he could eat a glass. So he presumed to literally take a water glass and chew it up and swallow it. Couldn't believe it, but he did. We had a good time with the Brits. They were at Singapore, too, and they did an air show for us around the carrier and all that kind of stuff. But Aden was good, and we were only there a couple of days.

Went on around and went into Jidda. And so for whatever the reason, I'm not sure I know, but they wanted some planes to come to the beach, so I guess it was Bush Bringle who decided, "Well, we'll send the night fighters over there." So there we went, six of us. We went over there, and we landed at the airport there. The guy that was the head of our team, R. D. "Ace" King out of '42, landed off the runway in the sand, which was fairly easy to do.[*] That wasn't too good, but at least he didn't do any damage to the airplane.

The colonel that came out there to host us and everything—he wanted us to come into the operations building there and have what amounted to coffee and whatever. If you've ever been in that part of the world and they offer you coffee, whatever it is, it's brewed in a brass pot. It takes on the taste of the brass. And I'm telling you, it is

---

[*] Lieutenant Commander Richard D. King, USN.

something else again. We all managed to get through one small demitasse cup of that. And you have to know all the hand signals, or you're going to get another cup. We all got another cup, because none of us knew the hand signals. [Laughter] And, you know, by the time we got out of there I'm telling you we could hardly see straight from the effects of whatever it was.

Paul Stillwell: You took the carrier inside the Persian Gulf?

Admiral Shelton: Oh, yes. Yes, we were right there in Jidda Harbor. And we catapulted at anchor from there. I think we could have landed at anchor too. There was enough wind there that no problem. There were 40 or 45 knots of wind across the deck anytime you wanted it there. We stayed downtown Jidda that night. We stayed in an old hotel there, and it wasn't all that great, but it was clean. Dave and I both got up early the next morning and went up to the parapets or whatever you want to call them and listened to the natives yodel to the East. I thought that was all pretty interesting.

Paul Stillwell: I got awakened when I was in Bahrain once by that, and it was about 5:00 in the morning. [Laughter]

Admiral Shelton: Yes. Well, they will wake you up. [Laughter]

Paul Stillwell: Yes, it did. [Laughter]

Admiral Shelton: But it was interesting. At that time of the morning there in Jidda it was one of those times when it was just perfectly calm, beautiful. Sun coming up and all that sort of thing. It was really quite a sight. And there was not a lot of noise around. The town wasn't under way yet, and in those days Jidda wasn't very big anyway. So we had a good time.

Paul Stillwell: What was the purpose of going into a place like Jidda?

Admiral Shelton: I presume it was because the British were still trying to hold onto various places there like Aden, etc. And Jidda was giving them a bad time at that time, as I remember. So I think it was just a minor show-of-force type of thing.

Paul Stillwell: Solidarity?

Admiral Shelton: Solidarity, yes. There was no liberty, so there certainly wasn't anything of that embellishment.

Paul Stillwell: Well, it had to be for a political reason rather than military.

Admiral Shelton: Had to be for a political reason, and, of course, at my level I never saw the message that said anything about it. But we enjoyed it. So that afternoon, why, we got in gear again and flew out, landed again. Went on through the Suez. And that was pretty interesting. I'm not sure I'm going to get this right, but you can't have too many ships in there at the same time.

Paul Stillwell: Well, the canal has holding areas where you can congregate.

Admiral Shelton: They have holding areas where you have to do one or the other, because as you're going through one part of it, the water actually rises quite high because of the displacement of the ship. Then you get into the central holding area and then you can go on into the other one and that sort of thing. But, anyway, we went on through. We did not stop at Port Said, which we thought we were going to, but we didn't.

We went on up to Istanbul, and in those days Istanbul was a little bit rustic. There were people there that put on several really nice dances and parties for the whole ship, enlisted, officers and everything. So everybody had a good time there. We were there about three days, and, of course, everybody went over and went through the underground bazaar and all the temples or whatever.

Paul Stillwell: How receptive were the Turks to that visit?

Admiral Shelton: Not too. The ones we talked to were quite receptive, but as a whole you felt that they would just as soon we hadn't come in. But it was interesting being right there. We anchored right there almost in the Bosporus. And, of course, that's pretty heavy current right in there.

Paul Stillwell: Yes, indeed.

Admiral Shelton: So we saw some interesting ships coming through and all that, and when they come through there they come through. So it was interesting. It's a busy little intersection of the world and it was interesting to see all the ships and how they navigated, etc.

Paul Stillwell: Were there any receptions ashore for you?

Admiral Shelton: Yes. They had receptions, and, as I said, they had dances and parties for everybody, the enlisted men and the officers. I found out right away that the Americans are not the only smart people in the world, because every girl that I talked to at one of those dances spoke seven languages. I figured out right away that I was not in that league. They were all well educated. It was really nice. There was nothing bad about it. We went on to Athens. Athens was great. Went on to Gibraltar. Gibraltar was great. Enjoyed that. Then we were supposed to go to Portsmouth, England, and have side trips to Paris and other places in Europe. Got a dispatch saying, "The money has run out." So the Tarawa sailed from Gibraltar to Norfolk direct, and they off-loaded the air group. Then I don't think it was even a month later that the Tarawa went on up to New York and got decommissioned.[*]

Paul Stillwell: Was Captain Ruble the skipper of that ship?[†]

---

[*] The ship arrived at Norfolk, Virginia, on 21 February 1949. Following an inactivation overhaul she was decommissioned on 30 June 1949 and became part of the Atlantic Reserve Fleet.
[†] Captain Richard W. Ruble, USN.

Admiral Shelton: Yes.

Paul Stillwell: What do you remember about him?

Admiral Shelton: Good man. I liked him. You know, there I was, a lieutenant (j.g.), and there he was captain, and so I didn't see that much of him but what I did see I liked.

Paul Stillwell: You had been before in a CVE. Please draw the contrast when you got into a full-sized CV.

Admiral Shelton: Oh, well, yes. Felt like it was landing on a big airport.

Paul Stillwell: Well, and bigger all throughout the ship.

Admiral Shelton: All throughout the ship.

Paul Stillwell: Accommodations and so forth.

Admiral Shelton: Oh, yes.

Paul Stillwell: A huge wardroom.

Admiral Shelton: Huge wardroom, and it was a wardroom in every sense of the word of a good wardroom. I'd like to say that I wish they still had that today, but they don't.

Paul Stillwell: One thing in ships of that vintage that surprised me, they'd have the bulkheads in the staterooms would not go all the way to the overhead. There'd be an opening. I've never figured out what the reason was for that.

Admiral Shelton: I never did either. I just wonder if today with women aboard if they tolerate that same airspace up there. I doubt it. [Laughter]

Paul Stillwell: I doubt it.

Admiral Shelton: So I had orders. At that point both Dave and I had orders to proceed. Since we were in VFN we were a detachment of VCN-1 at that point, which shortly thereafter became FAWTUPAC.*

Paul Stillwell: Well, could you talk about the flying during that long cruise?

Admiral Shelton: Well, we got our share of it, and, as I say, after that incident in Ready I we never had a problem with the day boys. And we got a pretty good share of time. I've forgotten how many landings we got or how much time we got, but we got a pretty good share of it.

Paul Stillwell: Did you run a fair number of night intercepts?

Admiral Shelton: Oh, yes. Anytime we were airborne at night we were running intercepts.

Paul Stillwell: Was there any doctrinal development during that period?

Admiral Shelton: No, not that I recall. As far as I can remember the doctrine, if there were going to be any development, it would have been pretty severely hampered by the fact that the equipment was still the same. The shipboard radar was essentially the same. I think we had reasonably good altitude determination gear on the Tarawa, but before that there really wasn't much in the way of altitude determination. They could put you within a ballpark altitude of the bogey, but then when you got him on your scope you could determine whether he was above you or below you and act accordingly.† But any doctrine was pretty much hampered by the equipment that you had, and that was

---

* FAWTUPAC—Fleet All-Weather Training Unit Pacific.
† "Bogey" is a term used to designate an unidentified air contact.

essentially the tail end of the World War II equipment, APS-6 radar on the airplane and the same type of intercept radar on the ship.

Paul Stillwell: How capable were the air controllers?

Admiral Shelton: Pretty good. They had a good training course for controllers by that time, which was quite a level of improvement over what was available when Chick Harmer was on the Enterprise, for instance. They really had to work to get somebody to be a good controller in those days. See, Chick Harmer was on there in the early part of '44, and this was '48, three years. By that time VCN-1, and later FAWTUPAC, came into existence out at Barbers Point.

VCN-1 had a good stable of different types of aircraft: F6F-5N, TBM, F7F-3N, F8F-1N (an experimental and never successful night fighter version of the F8F-1), and SNB-3N. These were all for night fighter and night attack training. The initial instruction was in the SNB-3N, which provided one-on-one instructor/trainee familiarization with the APS-6 radar. After a few flights, training progressed to the F6F-5N for fighters and TBM for attack trainees.

The initial flights in the F6F-5N were in the daytime, primarily for safety purposes, then regularly on into night flights. The APS-6 had a 6-mile range for initial contact, in most cases, then a one-mile intercept/shoot range for close in. The APS-6 presentation had two dots on the scope, one at your own altitude and one for the target. It displayed the range and the altitude differential above and below you. The idea was to close the range and match altitudes until you were in gun range. Although it was possible to shoot solely by radar, the best tactic was to close slightly below and behind the target for a visual and then shoot. In fact, some or most rules of engagement required that you obtain a visual and identify the target before shooting.

With practice you could detect a target's movement quite well, that is, whether the target slowed down, sped up, dived, turned hard, etc. With even more practice, you could follow a target in various evasive maneuvers such as a split-S, Immelmann, loop, etc. Naturally, the hope always was that the target did not know you were there. GCAs ended almost every night flight.

During my training at VCN-1/FAWTUPAC, Captain Paul H. Ramsey was the CO, and Commander W. I. Martin was exec.

So they set up the training out there, and they had trained quite a few intercept people, like Clancy Rich, the guy that came back to San Diego; he lives out in El Cajon here I think. But he came back to San Diego to qualify Dave and myself principally, because the other four guys already were graduates of the FAWTUPAC or VCN-1. Clancy was just as good as they come, and as good as they've ever been. He was good. He did not go around the world with us, and I've forgotten who the night controllers were on there. They were ship controllers, but they had gone through the school. They belonged to the ship. They did not belong to our team, as I recall.

Paul Stillwell: Was there anything so formal as a textbook then on how you should do night fighter work?

Admiral Shelton: No, not that I remember.

Paul Stillwell: So it was passed on by word of mouth, from Chick Harmer onward.

Admiral Shelton: Word of mouth and here's how you do it, with the hands, you know.

Paul Stillwell: Was Harmer kind of the founding father or he and Martin in that area?

Admiral Shelton: Yes, they were. Chick Harmer had been on the Saratoga flying F4Fs, and he got shot up a little bit. Had to come back to Pearl Harbor, and when he finished that tour his name was pretty much drawn out of a hat, and he was sent back to Quonset Point, Rhode Island, for project Affirm. He and Pete Aurand and this fellow Kullberg, Gus Widhelm, Bob Holden, and some others where there, and when they finished there there was kind of a scramble to see who was going to get back out there first.[*]

Gus Widhelm couldn't wait. He was senior, so he grabbed what he wanted basically. He grabbed what he wanted of the people that were training there and left

---

[*] Lieutenant Commander Evan P. Aurand, USN; Commander William J. Widhelm, USN.

Chick Harmer with the rest. Gus shoved off and went to Pearl and set up his squadron and they ended up shore based, I believe, at either Guadalcanal or Majuro with F6F-5Ns. Chick Harmer—about that time they brought in 30 or 31 F4U-1s, which they converted to F4U-2s, the only difference was putting the early AIA radar out on the wing and the scope in the cockpit. Then Pete Aurand left and he also got F6F-5Ns. He ended up on the Intrepid a little later, I believe. Incidentally, Chick was checked out in the F4U by Charles Lindbergh.

So then Chick got his group together, and that was VFN-75 at the time. They went to Barbers Point. About December the first of '45 his squadron was split in two, and his half became VFN-101. They had the F4U-2s. The other half became VFN-76, I believe, and they had F6F-5Ns, shore based and then on some other ship. So Chick and his little outfit, VF-101, were on Enterprise, and at that time W. I. Martin was on there with VT-10. Between the two of them, they managed to make a few inroads into breaking down the day-only flight schedule type thing.

It wasn't easy. Chick Harmer had to go rescue some forlorn cruiser and battleship airplanes that got lost and couldn't find their way back to the battleships before he could make a name for the night people, and that's how he did it. But in the time that they were on there, I think Chick was credited with three and a half night kills and Bob Holden was—I forget how many but in that squadron I think they were credited for the time they were on there with five or six night kills, which doesn't sound like a whole lot, but that was five or six more than they didn't have before that.

Paul Stillwell: Well, Enterprise became a night carrier, didn't she?

Admiral Shelton: Yes, later on, and so did the Independence, I believe. But that was still a little later on. It took a lot of time in those days for things to catch on and still does in some respects, I guess. But, anyway, between Chick Harmer, W. I. Martin, Pete Aurand, and this Kullberg, who all stayed in the Navy—some of the others later got out pretty soon—but between them they managed to kind of keep the fire going on the night business.

Then, of course, W. I. Martin ended up back at Barbers Point a little later on as exec of FAWTUPAC when Captain Paul H. Ramsey was CO. That pretty much kind of set into pretty solid gear the night training business. It was still slow, but it did get going, and it certainly wasn't all weather for a long time after that, but that was a good beginning. I knew Chick Harmer because when I went from Norfolk out to Barbers Point, I stayed there about a year, then I came back to VC-3 at Moffett Field when it was first commissioned.* Lew Hardy was the officer-in-charge initially, and then Chick Harmer came there as CO.† I believe he had just finished Stanford for a business degree and came and took VC-3. He was very active. He went out to the carriers all the time. He was a great CO, and he made me want to do the night bit without really standing on the stool and soapboxing the whole thing.

Paul Stillwell: How did he accomplish that?

Admiral Shelton: Well, he put it to you as a challenge. For instance, when he was there, I did not know his background on the Enterprise, but I knew he knew something about night fighters; I could tell that. He said, "You know, one of these days this is going to be the thing. You're in the forefront here, and you need to really pay attention to what you're doing and learn all you can about instrument flying and learn what you don't want to do while you're doing it," and all that kind of stuff. And he did it by example. He went up and did it too.

Paul Stillwell: So he was an inspirational leader.

Admiral Shelton: He was inspirational. And he was good. So I was there—let's see, that was '51. I was there about a year and a half. I had been out on the Boxer and came back, and about the time the Korean War got going I wanted to go back out there, and I did. I went out on the Princeton and the Philippine Sea.

---

* VC-3—Fleet Composite Squadron Three. Moffett Field Naval Air Station, Sunnyvale, California, was located ten miles north of San Jose, at the southern tip of San Francisco Bay. It was named in honor of Rear Admiral William A. Moffett, USN, first Chief of the Bureau of Aeronautics.
† Lieutenant Commander Lewis R. Hardy, Jr., USN.

Paul Stillwell: We're kind of jumping ahead. I just want to get a little background on night fighters. What happened after Tarawa?

Admiral Shelton: Oh. Went back to Barbers Point, and one of the things to this day that I'm really POed about was what happened to my gear. They gave me a set of orders, and when I left Norfolk, I was a bachelor. You know the old saying, "Take it with you when you go, because nobody's going to send it to you." Well, I still had all my gear when I got to Norfolk. I put it in a big chest and shipped it to Barbers Point. I'd been to Barbers Point about a month, and the supply officer called me down and said, "You owe me $400.00 for shipping your stuff from Norfolk to Barbers Point."

I said, "What do you mean? I got a set of orders. How am I supposed to get my stuff here."

"I don't know, but you owe the system 400 bucks." I had to pay them 400 bucks, and I never ever got it back.

Paul Stillwell: That was a lot of money!

Admiral Shelton: Well, it was a lot of money and not only that, I thought it was out-and-out robbery. But I never did get it back.

Well, anyway, Barbers Point was kind of nice in a way. There wasn't any carrier deck there, and we didn't get any carrier deck time, which I resented because I thought we should because they were going to deploy teams from there. They were always waiting for the team to go to whatever ship it was going to go to before they would get any carrier deck time. I thought they should have gotten the carrier deck time right there at Barbers Point as a part of the syllabus.

Well, we didn't, but anyway they did have F8F-1Ns there on an experimental basis, which I didn't get to fly, and they weren't there very long because the big radar bulb out on the end of that little F8F just slowed it down and made it a non-fighter. Ruined the stability on the airplane and everything. But they had F7Fs there, and they

had several other airplanes, so we got our share of flying some pretty nice airplanes.*
And there again the syllabus was that for your checkouts in an airplane you hadn't flown,
it could be daytime. Otherwise it was all night time. And we could. And that was about
a year of it.

Paul Stillwell: And Hawaii was probably a pleasant place to live at that stage.

Admiral Shelton: Yes. You know, Barbers Point in those days was pretty far out there, but it wasn't too far. I had a '47 Ford convertible that managed to make it into Honolulu every now and then. I do remember that one morning after I got back from downtown on a weekend, I got a call to come up to see the exec, W. I. Martin. I thought, "Oh, hell, what have I done now?" He didn't even know me at that point, but he called me in and said, "Mr. Shelton, I just want to thank you for changing my wife's tire on the way back to Barbers Point the other morning." [Laughter]

About halfway out to Barbers Point there was this car over here. I didn't know who it was from the man in the moon. Never recognized her. But she was obviously a woman that needed some help, because she was standing there with a flat tire. So I stopped, and I changed her tire for her and never even knew who she was. So after that, as those things happen, W. I. Martin always knew my name after that. He always spoke to me, all that kind of good stuff, and I met him a number of times in later years and happen to think a great deal of him.

Paul Stillwell: Well, please tell me more about him.

Admiral Shelton: Well, he was a pioneer, more on the night attack side than the night fighter-intercept type thing. He had tried to do a night bombing thing down around Majuro someplace there. I forget. I'd have to look up the proper place. But, as it turns out, I think he fell and broke an arm or an ankle or something, and he himself did not get

---
* Grumman F7F Tigercat fighters first entered Marine Corps squadrons in early 1943. The F7F was the U.S. Navy's first twin-engine fighter to be produced in quantity. The F7F-3 version of the airplane was 45 feet, 4 inches long; wingspan of 51 feet, 6 inches; gross weight of 25,720 pounds; and top speed of 435 miles per hour. Grumman built 60 of the F7F-3N night-fighter model, which had a radome in the nose.

to make that flight.* But his exec did, and that was kind of the forerunner, and it was quite successful.† They found a bunch of Jap ships there in the harbor and pretty much blew them up, ships, and that was really about the first night attack thing that anybody had pulled off. And later on, I think he did the same thing at—what's the harbor at the south end of Taiwan? Anyway he did the same thing there. So he was big on going in at night, getting on the attack side, getting them in the harbors, etc., etc., or hitting whatever installations you wanted to hit.

Paul Stillwell: When people wouldn't expect airplanes to come.

Admiral Shelton: When people would not expect airplanes to be there. And it's kind of strange, because that was in the Pacific largely. In Europe they'd been experiencing that kind of thing for, seven or eight years. But then on the other side Chick Harmer was the VFN, the night fighter type thing. So they complemented each other, and they both had a lot to do with getting the show on the road. And both of them outstanding guys. Chick Harmer was in that top three.

Paul Stillwell: Well, what else about Barbers Point and your time there?

Admiral Shelton: I spent a lot of time on the beach trying to learn to body surf. I never did try to learn to surf otherwise. The BOQs weren't very good, and you woke up with scorpions in your shoes most of the time [laughter] and all that kind of thing. It was pretty serious stuff. We flew most every night and a lot of days. Weekends off to go into town and whatever you wanted to do. In those days, you could go into the old Moana Hotel, and at that time across the street from the Moana they had the old Moana huts, which were on stilts. For six bucks a night you and six or seven other guys could rent the

---

* On 31 January 1944 Lieutenant William I. Martin, USN, commanding officer of Torpedo Squadron 10, slipped and fell while exercising on the forecastle of the Enterprise (CV-6). He broke his elbow on the steel deck.
† The Navy's first night bombing attack by carrier planes came during the predawn hours 17 February 1944, when 12 radar-equipped TBF-1C Avengers attacked shipping in Truk Atoll in the Caroline Islands. The low-level attack by the planes from Torpedo Squadron Ten of the USS Enterprise CV-6) resulted in several direct hits on Japanese ships. Lieutenant Van V. Eason, Jr., USNR, the squadron's executive officer, led the attack.

whole shebang, so we had some good times down there. And we had some good times out at Barbers Point, but Barbers Point was essentially flying. There wasn't much screwing around with anything else.

Paul Stillwell: I walked through the lobby of the Moana last year, and they had a menu posted up in kind of a museum setting from 1945, and I think you could get about a five- or six-course dinner for 50 cents or so.

Admiral Shelton: Oh, Geez, it was great. The whole idea was that there were a lot of young schoolteachers downtown in those days, and at that time there was some kind of a transportation strike. Nobody was coming into Honolulu, so we really had it all to ourselves. Like I said, you could go down there and rent this whole cottage, which had probably about six rooms, so you could rent the whole cottage for six bucks a night. It was pretty good. Then you could go across the street and sit under the banyan tree and have a couple of drinks.

Paul Stillwell: Pleasant living.

Admiral Shelton: Pleasant living. Very good.

Paul Stillwell: What came next?

Admiral Shelton: Well, let's see. Well, I went out to Korea. I guess it was while I was on the Princeton and Danny O'Neill was the O-in-C of that detachment, I believe, at the time.*

---
* Lieutenant Commander Hugh Daniel O'Neill, USN.

Doniphan B. Shelton, Interview #1 (2/10/00) – Page 117

Paul Stillwell: She got pulled out of mothballs at Bremerton.*

Admiral Shelton: Yes. I didn't have any part of that, but anyway went out there, and while I was there, why, Chick Harmer came out and wanted me to escort him on a mission, so I did. He wanted me to lead, so I did. We went over, and I was lucky enough to get a couple of trucks that night, and he was lucky enough to get shot at and not hit. So he didn't get any trucks or anything, but it was right at dusk when we took off and came back and made night landings, as I recall.

Paul Stillwell: Were you still flying Hellcats at that point?

Admiral Shelton: No, F4U-5Ns at that point, which was a big difference.† There are some people that say that the F6F was a better airplane than the F4U, and there's a lot of people that will argue about that. But at least in the night fighter business the F4U-5N had the APS-19 radar by then, and I don't think it was any better than the APS-6 on the Hellcat. But airplane-wise the F4U-5N was a better airplane than the F6F-5N. No question about it.

Paul Stillwell: In what ways?

Admiral Shelton: More power, better airplane. It even flew better.

Paul Stillwell: Did you have a problem seeing over that nose when you landed?

---

* USS Princeton (CV-37) was commissioned 18 November 1945. She had a standard displacement of 33,300 tons, was 888 feet long, 93 feet in the beam, an extreme width of 148 feet on the flight deck, and had a draft of 29 feet. She had a top speed of 33.5 knots and could accommodate approximately 90 aircraft. The ship was inactivated at Puget Sound Naval Shipyard and decommissioned on 20 June 1949. She was reactivated and recommissioned on 28 August 1950, shortly after the outbreak of the Korean War. The Princeton was reclassified CVA-37 on 1 October 1952.
† The Vought F4U Corsair was in production longer than any other U.S. fighter plane of World War II. It first entered fleet squadrons in 1942. The F4U-1 was 33 feet, 4 inches long; wingspan of 41 feet; gross weight of 14,000 pounds; and top speed of 417 miles per hour.

Admiral Shelton: Yes, you know they always say that, and they didn't it call it Hose Nose for nothing.*

Paul Stillwell: That's right.

Admiral Shelton: But you learned to accommodate to that. The night-fighter version was even a little more ticklish because up where the exhausts were they actually had a little cowl thing built up there to shade your eyes from the exhaust glow from the exhaust. So that was a little bit of an impediment also. But you got pretty used to that, and I loved that airplane. I thought it was absolutely great.

Paul Stillwell: Well, tell me about a night mission going in against Korea then.

Admiral Shelton: Basically there were two times that you would launch. You either launched about 3:00 o'clock in the morning, or you launched about dusk. When I was out there it was during the cold time. It was January and February, the early part of March. Colder than I've ever been anywhere in my life. Snow all over the deck most of the time. About zero temperature across the deck, and I believe I'm right in saying that that's when the terminology "wind-chill factor" came into being, because people began to recognize that with 40 knots across the deck it wasn't just zero degrees. The effect of it was a lot more than that. So a chill factor of 30 below was nothing at all out there in those days.

The 3:00 o'clock launches were by far the hardest, because you had to get up there about midnight and cold, bitter cold, and the engines wouldn't start even though they'd been turned up maybe an hour before that. I can remember time after time after time, it was not singular to anybody—every time you tried to start one of those birds you ended up with dripping fire out of the exhaust one way or another until you finally got it started. And then you had to keep it running. You didn't shut it down again until you were going to launch. One of the things about that was that the two buttons you used to start the airplane, the primer and the starter, weren't so that you pressed down on the

---

* The F4U had a long engine-and-cowling arrangement that extended forward of the cockpit.

buttons. They were located on the panel, so that you had to push forward on the buttons. By the time you got airborne, your two fingers were so sore you didn't even want to touch them. And you knew that it was going to repeat itself the next flight that you had, so you had two sore fingers the whole time you were there in that cold weather because it took that long. It would take 45 minutes to get started.

We had Bendix gasoline heaters in the F4U-5N, but you weren't supposed to use them until you got airborne, and then they were not bad. They didn't all work as well as they should, but when they worked at all it was better than nothing, so it was pretty good.

Your missions were basically about three, three and a half hours, sometimes four. So if you launched at 3:00 you recovered just about dawn, a little after dawn. If you launched at dusk, then you recovered about 10:30 or 11:00 at night. So you sort of shifted back and forth. You did one and then did the other. Sometimes you even got a daytime hop in, but most of the time they used us pretty regularly for what we were there for, which was night interdiction. We didn't get any shot at intercepting aircraft. Some of the shore-based guys did. Some of detachments that were shore based at Taegu or elsewhere actually got some intercepts in, and some of them even got some kills.

Paul Stillwell: So the North Koreans were flying at night too?

Admiral Shelton: Some of them were. They weren't flying much out over around Hungnam, up in that area where we were operating there. But over further inland they were flying at night. Further up toward Pyongyang, up in that area I guess it was. I'm not sure about that. So that's the way that went.

Paul Stillwell: How would the radar that was used for intercepts, how would that work on a ground target?

Admiral Shelton: Didn't work at all. It was mostly visual. The one good thing during that time of the year at least was that even though it was as cold as it was, with snow on the ground over there, it was usually pretty clear. You could see stuff on the ground, I would say, equally well as you could in the daytime, at least part of the time. So you could pick up trucks on the highway, and you pick up trains on the railroad tracks, all this kind of stuff. The one thing you couldn't pick up that was easy in the daytime would be any cables across the way or anything like that, so you kind of hoped.

Paul Stillwell: Did you just strafe, or did you carry any stores?

Admiral Shelton: Oh, no. We carried bombs and did strafing. We carried 250-pound bombs for the most part. During the daytime—the ADs did more of this than we did—but the few times that we were called on to do what they call tunnel busting, why, we did that in the daytime.* That was carrying either a 1,000- or 2,000-pound bomb down the railroad track and throwing it in the tunnel. [Laughter] Pretty interesting. It was a real technique there, because if you dropped too far out it was going to drop and hit the railroad tracks, and you were likely to see it bounce up in front of you. So you had to get close enough to throw it in the tunnel but not so close as to not be able to pull up and not hit the tunnel entrance. We didn't do very much of that. I think I had maybe two hops doing that. But basically we stuck to night interdiction.

Paul Stillwell: How close to the deck would you get for one of those tunnel drops?

Admiral Shelton: Oh, ten feet—right down the railroad tracks. Right down the railroad tracks. The only exception to that is if there happened to be any poles and there weren't usually, but if there were well then you couldn't do that. But, yes, you were right down there.

Paul Stillwell: What kind of thoughts went through your mind about the need to perhaps bail out in that kind of cold.

---

* Douglas AD Skyraider propeller-driven attack planes first entered fleet squadrons in late 1946. The AD-2 version was 38 feet long, wingspan of 50 feet, gross weight of 18,263 pounds, and top speed of 321 miles per hour. In September 1962 Skyraiders still in service were redesignated A-1s.

Admiral Shelton: A lot. I had a real experience along that line. One morning, 3:00 o'clock launch, I took off with a guy named Hotdog Mayfield, Harley Dean Mayfield.[*] You didn't fly together. You didn't try to fly together. You just kept in radio contact. "I'm going here, I'm going there." And what altitude, etc., etc. So we took off, and our trip was to go into Wonsan Harbor and then fly north up along the coast. So we got right over Wonsan, and there's a little island there named Yodo. Yodo was supposedly friendly, had friendly people on it. The rest of Wonsan Harbor was supposedly not friendly. I never tested the veracity of that, but that's what they told us.

When we got over Wonsan at 8,000 feet, Hotdog called and said, "My engine's quit."

So I said, "Well, tell me what you're going to do." I said, "You can bail out over Yodo there, or are you going to try to get down to Taegu, or are you going to try to get back to the carrier, or what are you going to try to do?"

He said, "Well, I'm probably going to have to bail out, because I can't get it started." Well, that's all I heard for about a minute or so. In the meanwhile, he had climbed out on the wing and was ready to jump. The engine started running. He climbed back in, got it running on the prime, and then got it running. Called me up and said, "I'm going to try to get back to the carrier," which he did.

Okay. So I said, "Fine." By that time I was ready to start my trek north, so I started my trek north up the coast to Hungnam and back. I got back over Yodo about, oh, two and half or three hours later. My engine quit. Same deal. I climbed out on the wing, one leg still in the cockpit. Started ticking over again. I climbed back in. Got it running on the prime. Here again, you're pressing forward on the two buttons, not down on them. I was a little over 8,000 feet at the time, about 8,500, and the carrier was somewhere between 50 and 75 miles. So I got it ticking over at about 1,100 RPM, maybe a little more at times. That is above idle but not much.

As long as I would keep feeding it, it would keep running. If I stopped feeding it, it stopped. And I did this experimenting while I was circling Yodo Island. And so I finally figured, "What the hell." By that time one of the AD Guppies had joined up on me, and he said, "Well, I'll escort you back." He couldn't see me, but he knew where I

---
[*] Lieutenant (junior grade) Harley D. Mayfield, USN.

was. He said, "I'll stay right with you here. You tell me when you're going to leave, and I'll stay as close as I can," and all that kind of stuff. "And then I'll be able to help you maybe."

So I called the carrier and told them what my situation was, and I got back. They gave me the option again of going to Taegu. I said, "No, I think I'll try it." So here I am, punching the primer button and beating my way out to the carrier. By the time I got back out to the carrier, I still had just about 3,000 feet left. The LSO was a guy named Bill Spell.[*] I don't know whether you've ever come across him or not.

Paul Stillwell: No.

Admiral Shelton: He was one of the best—one of the very best—and he had worked with me a lot. I had a lot of confidence in him, and I'd like to say that I think he had pretty good confidence in me. So I told him, "I'm running this thing on prime at 1,100 RPMs, and I can't take a waveoff. If I have to wave off, pick me up out of the water, please." [Laughter] And so you talk about when I was in primary flight training and H. R. Way and the spot landings? Did it again. So I started about 3,000 feet, kept turning in there as I saw fit. I got it on board and shut it down in the arresting gear. What had happened was that—up where I started at 8,000 feet it was just barely cracking dawn you know, starting to get a little light. Down where I was shooting the landing was still not dark, not pitch dark, but it was dark enough to need the flight-deck landing lights and the illuminated LSO.

What they found when they got into it with both Hotdog's and my airplane was that they had come out with a fuel filter which was supposed to be non-freezing. It was right in the belly of the airplane where all fuel filters are in that kind of airplane basically. So when they got in there, it was gasoline frappe. And there's no way that either one of those engines was going to run at full power except that his developed early, cleared out I guess enough so that the engine would run. He got back, and by the time mine had had a good solid freeze, it wasn't going to do that.

---

[*] Lieutenant Billie C. Spell, USN.

So you asked me about going in the water. I had thoughts about it, and I was dumb enough, and I really say probably stupid enough, that up to that point I had considered the poopy suits as an unnecessary piece of gear.[*] Cumbersome, hard to get into, took a long time to get into them, hot, sweaty when you got in there, all that kind of good stuff. So I did not have a poopy suit on. And I can guarantee you that every flight after that I had a poopy suit on. [Laughter]

Paul Stillwell: Who was your CAG and squadron commander in that operation?

Admiral Shelton: Let's see. The CAG on the Princeton was—not really sure. The CAG when I went over to the Philippine Sea was Ralph Weymouth.[†]

The only reason I shifted to the Phil Sea was because in the middle time of all this, when I was back at Moffett, I had put in for Test Pilot School. I had gone back to Patuxent to find out if I could get in a certain class which was going to be class number four. The director of the Test Pilot School, Commander Tom Connolly, said, "Class is full."[‡] He said, "But you can go up to BuPers. If you can talk Honest John Sweeney [the detailer] into letting you come in, why, I'll take you. Otherwise can't do it."

So I went up to see Honest John Sweeney in BuPers, and he said, "Well, it's just really full. You got aced out by a classmate of yours whose father had a little more influence than you do." [Laughter] And so I didn't go. So I went back to Moffett. Well, it wasn't time to go again yet so what Honest John Sweeney had told me was, "You go on back out there, and I'll guarantee you that next time around, if you still want to go, why, you'll get orders." So I was sitting out there on the Princeton, and it wasn't time to go back there yet, and I wanted to stay out there anyway. So I asked for permission to stay out there.

I sent a note back to Commander Harmer, and I asked him to let me stay out there and shift me over to the Philippine Sea because the Princeton team was going somewhere

---
[*] The "poopy suit" for aviators was designed to provide insulation protection in the event they had to land in cold water.
[†] Commander Ralph Weymouth, USN, Commander Carrier Air Group 11.
[‡] Commander Thomas F. Connolly, USN. The oral history of Connolly, who retired as a vice admiral, is in the Naval Institute collection.

or something, I don't know. But, anyway, I needed to shift over if I was going to stay out there. Ralph Weymouth was CAG of the Philippine Sea, and I had to get his permission to stay out there. He looked at me like I had rocks in my head [Laughter] and said, "If you're dumb enough to want to stay out here, I'm dumb enough to let you stay." [Laughter] So I stayed. So then not too long after that, I got back to Moffett. But before I forget—that the hop that I flew with Chick Harmer out there, I didn't know it at the time, and I didn't know it for quite a while afterwards, a number of years afterwards, because that was his last carrier-based flight.

Paul Stillwell: Now, when did that take place?

Admiral Shelton: That was when we were on the Princeton out there, and I think that was in March of '51.

Paul Stillwell: Were Ray Hawkins and John Magda on the Princeton when you were there?[*]

Admiral Shelton: Yes, they were. I watched them fly.

Paul Stillwell: Magda got killed, didn't he?

Admiral Shelton: Yes, sure did. He got hit. Got bagged.

Paul Stillwell: They had taken the nucleus of the Blue Angels and made a fighter squadron of them.[†]

---

[*] Lieutenant Commander John J. Magda, USN, was commanding officer of Fighter Squadron 191 at the time he was killed in March 1951. Lieutenant Arthur R. Hawkins, USN, was a member of the same squadron. The oral history of Hawkins, who retired as a captain, is in the Naval Institute collection.
[†] Blue Angels is the name of the Navy's flight demonstration team, which has done close formation flying for air shows and other events since 1946.

Admiral Shelton: Yes, that was it. I used to know all the guys that were in that initial outfit out there, but I've long since forgotten some of them. But I knew Johnny Magda quite well because he was the exec of VF-1E, my first squadron and I liked him. Thought he was a good guy. Handsome guy. Ladies' man all the way. But a good fighter pilot.

Paul Stillwell: When did you come back to Moffett?

Admiral Shelton: I came back to Moffett probably about in the first part of, May, April or something like that, and then I left there that summer to go to Test Pilot School. And, true to his word, Honest John Sweeney sent me a set of orders. I didn't have to reapply. I didn't have to go find out if I was going to get to go or anything else. He sent me a set of orders.

Paul Stillwell: What do you remember about your time in Philippine Sea?

Admiral Shelton: Not much. Not much. Princeton was my primary thing and primarily because that's when Chick Harmer came out there. Danny O'Neil and I liked him, and he was O-in-C of detachment. He had a certain amount of fame to him. He'd been down there around Majuro, Guadalcanal, and he'd been shore based. He's the one that they tell the account about at least—and I think it's true—that on one of O'Neil's night hops he was test firing his guns and he shot down a Betty. [Laughter] Now, how true that is I'm not 100% sure, but that's the story they tell. But he was good, and I liked Danny and still do. So I knew more people on the Princeton than I did on the Phil Sea.

Paul Stillwell: Well, Alan Shepard, one of your classmates, was a test pilot also.[*]

Admiral Shelton: Yes. Al was one or two classes ahead of me, I think, in Test Pilot School. I like to tell people that I graduated from the academy one number senior to Al

---

[*] A decade later, on 5 May 1961 Commander Alan B. Shepard, USN, became the first American astronaut to fly into space. He completed a 15-minute sub-orbital flight in a Mercury spacecraft. After splashdown he was recovered by a helicopter and landed on the deck of the aircraft carrier Lake Champlain (CVS-39).

Shepard, and I always have been. [Laughter] Doesn't make much difference sometimes, but I like to tell it. Now, Al was a superb pilot.

Paul Stillwell: Well, Admiral Ramage spoke well of him in his oral history.[*]

Admiral Shelton: Oh, yes. He should. Al Shepard saved his ass.

Paul Stillwell: That's right. [Laughter] Well, what motivated you to want to go to Test Pilot School? Was it sort of like what motivated you to get into aviation in the first place?

Admiral Shelton: Yes, that was one of the things that the good guys were trying to do, and I thought I ought to try to be a good guy. I did not have a real yearning to go to the Blue Angels, and as a matter of fact I probably couldn't have gone anyway because back in those days the Blue Angels were all NavCad wingers.[†] No academy guys went in there. They've since changed that, and there are academy people going in there now, but in those days it was all NavCads. I really hadn't given it much thought to try to get into the Blues, and I don't think I would have anyway. That wasn't really my bag. As much as I appreciated it, that wasn't my bag.

But I did want to go to Test Pilot School. I thought that was a great thing, and I did not want to go to some shore duty, namely Washington or some other place at that time. So I was really lucky that I got to go there. I was in class seven. Joe Moorer was in that class.[‡] A number of Marines, including Jack Hanes.[§] A couple of civilians in there, Billy Sunday from Chance-Vought and David North from McDonnell. We started in August of '51 and finished in January, I think, '52—six months basically. And, as in the Naval Academy, I didn't exactly star, but I managed to be somewhere respectable.

---

[*] See the Naval Institute's oral history of Rear Admiral James D. Ramage, USN (Ret.).
[†] NavCads—pilots who had been trained in the naval aviation cadet program before being commissioned.
[‡] Lieutenant Joseph P. Moorer, USN, younger brother of Admiral Thomas H. Moorer, USN, who served as CNO from 1967 to 1970.
[§] Captain John V. Hanes, USMC

Paul Stillwell: Was that a competitive atmosphere?

Admiral Shelton: Not too much, but, there again, it was competitive if you were good enough to think you were going to stand number one. Other than that, I don't think it meant a whole lot. The guy that stood number one in our class, Tom Kilgariff, got out of the Navy very shortly thereafter.* He went to work for Douglas, test pilot, and got pranged in an A3D up at Edwards Air Force Base.† So you know those things have a way of evening out over the long term.

Paul Stillwell: And luck plays a big factor too.

Admiral Shelton: Yes. I've mentioned Dave Williams that was in VF-1E when we went around the world. We were always in contact, and he got in this same class. He got in there by being back at Patuxent River and being on the staff at Test Pilot School, because he did not have the—and this is nothing against Dave, but at the time he did not have the basic education that they were requiring, engineering degree or any of that kind of stuff. But he deserved to get in, and he got in, but he had a hard time with the academics, a really hard time. So there were several of us, myself included, that spent part of our time helping Dave. He got through okay, and he did great. He got caught in that dilemma that BuPers caused for going back to chief, going back to jaygee, going back to chief, going back to lieutenant. He finally retired as a commander and deserved every bit of it.

Paul Stillwell: Had he been an enlisted pilot?

Admiral Shelton: Yes, he had. He was gung ho, and he deserved every good thing that he got.

Paul Stillwell: Joe Moorer was another classmate.‡ What do you recall of him?

---

* Lieutenant (junior grade) Thomas G. Kilgariff, USN.
† The Douglas A3D Skywarrior first entered fleet squadrons in 1956 as a carrier-based heavy bomber. Edwards Air Force Base in California is the site of a good deal of flight testing.
‡ Moorer was also in the Naval Academy class of 1945 with Shelton.

Admiral Shelton: [Laughter] Handsome Joe. A good guy, great pilot. We've always had good times together. We played golf a lot together. I never will forget I shot a 75 one day there at Patuxent and got beat three down by him and he didn't shoot a 75. [Laughter] He shot something like an 81 or something, and I owed him five bucks or something. I couldn't forget it for a long time. [Laughter]

Paul Stillwell: What was the curriculum that was so demanding when you were in the school?

Admiral Shelton: Well, there was a lot of studying, and you had to write a lot of flight reports. Every time you flew an airplane you had to go write a flight report. That was practice for what you were going to do when you got to one of the test divisions. And there were a lot of exams. I don't recall exactly how many, but we'll say one a week in everything, and some of it was pretty stiff stuff. The theory of jet propulsion at that time was pretty new. There were a lot of theories that hadn't been tested at that time, how to get the best performance out of a fighter plane, all this kind of stuff. So there was quite a bit of theory involved, a lot of engine work involved as far as understanding both jets and recips.[*]

And we did a lot of flying. We flew seven or eight different types of airplanes. We had the F8F there. We had a PBY. We had an F2H, and that class I was in did a number of time-to-climb types of things.[†] That isn't what it really was but performance climbs for Bob Fuhrman, who was one of the instructors there at the time. He wrote his master's thesis, I believe, on how to get the most out of your performance climb so that you still have the most fuel and the best fighting speed when you got there.[‡] He later on became president of Lockheed, so he didn't do too badly.

---

[*] Recips—reciprocating engines, that is, the ones with propellers on them.
[†] McDonnell's F2H Banshee was a jet-powered fighter-bomber that first entered the fleet with squadron VF-171 in March 1949.
[‡] Robert A. Fuhrman, a civilian, was a project engineer at the Naval Air Test Center from 1946 to 1953. He later worked as an executive for Ryan Aerospace and the Lockheed Corporation. He received his master of science degree from the University of Maryland in 1952.

Paul Stillwell: Was the F2H the first jet that you flew?

Admiral Shelton: No, the F3D, believe it or not, was the first jet that I flew and that was back at Moffett Field when I was still in VC-3.* A fellow named Brown, who at that time was chief test pilot for Douglas, had been a TWA pilot before that, and he brought the F3D in its infancy up to Moffett Field to see what we thought of it. I can remember thinking, "They'll never get this truck aboard a carrier." [Laughter] I didn't know it at the time, but I think Commander Chick Harmer was even more pointed in his remarks. There actually was a detachment from the East Coast, VC-4 maybe, that did take their airplane aboard, but they put them ashore over in Korea, so I'm not sure it did a whole lot of good. Marines used them pretty successfully from shore bases in Korea. But it never was a carrier airplane. Just was not destined to be.

Paul Stillwell: How much adjustment did it take for you personally to go from a prop to a jet engine?

Admiral Shelton: Zero practically. I thought it was a piece of cake. I wondered what all the fuss was about, really.

Paul Stillwell: Didn't have to fight the torque anymore.

Admiral Shelton: No, didn't have to fight the torque. There was a lot of things you didn't have to fight. There was a little adjustment getting used to it. With a prop, when you pull the throttle back, you slow down real fast. In a jet that's not necessarily so unless you put out the speed brakes. And there were things like that, and taking off is a little different. Not a whole lot but a little. And coming aboard, everything is a little faster. You know, you're flying at a little faster speed, basically about 94 knots compared to about 130 or 134 knots, in that ballpark. But I didn't think it was too much.

---

* The Douglas F3D Skyknight was an all-weather jet fighter used by the Marines as a night fighter and for electronic countermeasures. It was first delivered to VC-3 in 1951. The plane's two-man crew of pilot and radar operator sat side by side. The F3D-2 version was 46 feet long, wingspan of 50 feet, gross weight of 26,850 pounds, and top speed of 600 miles per hour. It had four fixed forward-firing 20-millimeter guns.

Paul Stillwell: And you'd been used to flying on straight-deck carriers because you didn't know any alternative.

Admiral Shelton: Didn't know the difference. I had to admire all those guys that did, but I don't think I ever took a jet aboard a straight deck. I think all mine were on the slanted deck, on the canted deck, angled deck.* But there were guys that did that. It wasn't a very long period of time there before the straight deck was dead. They got around that pretty fast. Remarkably so for the Navy and the way of what they have done at times about other things. But, you know, they recognized that right away, that that just wasn't going to sell. I think there was one occasion where a Banshee took a high cut and floated right on across the barriers and landed in the pack up on the bow and that, if nothing convinced them: "This is not going to sell."

Paul Stillwell: Well, you measure the cost of wiping out a lot of airplanes. That adds up.

Admiral Shelton: Absolutely. You bet.

Paul Stillwell: Well, did getting into Test Pilot School live up to your expectations?

Admiral Shelton: Every bit of it. I enjoyed it, and I worked hard. It wasn't easy getting through there. There'd been a gap of time since I had last introduced myself to mathematics and some of those things, so it was largely the mathematics. There wasn't much history or English or anything like that. [Laughter]

Paul Stillwell: That's right.

Admiral Shelton: And no electricity to speak of, so it was basically math and performance and parameters of performance and all that kind of stuff. Enjoyed it. Got

---

* The U.S. Navy began adding angled decks to its aircraft carriers in the 1950s to prevent landing aircraft that missed arresting wires from crashing into planes farther forward on the deck.

out, went over to service test. Joe Moorer and I both went to service test. There again, we had a lot of projects there. We had the F2H series, all of them. We had the F9F series, all of them.*

We had some interesting projects. Back in those days they did not have any systematic air-start system. If your engine shut down for some reason, you did not have any bona fide procedure for getting it started again, and so that was one of the interesting projects we had. The first good starters we had were kind of borrowed from the English, again from the Canberra, which was a shotgun starter. So we spent a lot of time first chasing the Pratt and Whitney guys in an F9F doing a shotgun start. And then, after they got through proving it, then we went up and did some ourselves.

There were a lot of other interesting projects. We had an F7F there that had a back seat configured, which we didn't know at the time, as kind of a lay-down couch. That was the forerunner of trying to figure out what kind of couches would be best in the Mercury capsule.† The flight psychologist there was a flight surgeon, and he was also an aviator and he ran that project. So all of us took our turn at getting in the back seat of that F7F and flying it lying down and looking at the instruments and telling them what we thought and everything. Of course, we were all different sizes so that's why they wanted it. Then the F7U came along about that time.‡ I had the project there at service test, and the first airplane was the old banana-nose F7U. It had a longer nose. Had J-71 engines in them. It was not the production version. So we flew that for a little while and then got the production version, which was the F7U-3 with the J-46 with afterburner.

---

* The Grumman F9F-2 Panther was first delivered to an operational unit, Fighter Squadron 51, in May 1949. On 3 July 1950 the Panther became the first U.S. Navy jet ever used in combat. The F9F-5 model was 39 feet long; wingspan of 38 feet; gross weight of 18,721 pounds; and top speed of 579 miles per hour. It was armed with four 20-millimeter guns. It had wings that were perpendicular to the fuselage. The swept-wing Grumman F9F-6 Cougar was first delivered to operational units in November 1952. The F9F-5 model was 42 feet long; wingspan of 36 feet; gross weight of 20,000 pounds; and top speed of 690 miles per hour. It was armed with four 20-millimeter guns.
† The one-man Mercury capsule was used in the earliest U.S. manned space flights.
‡ The Vought F7U Cutlass was a swept-wing jet fighter of an experimental design. It had two vertical stabilizers but no tail per se. It first entered the fleet in 1952. The F7U-3 version was 44 feet long; wingspan of 39 feet, gross weight of 31,642 pounds, and top speed of 680 miles per hour. It had four fixed forward-firing 20-millimeter guns and provision for four Sparrow missiles. For more on the faults of this airplane, see the oral history of Rear Admiral James D. Ramage, USN (Ret.).

Paul Stillwell: What was it like to fly an airplane that sort of had a tail and sort of didn't? [Laughter]

Admiral Shelton: Well, that airplane comes in for a lot of criticism, and justifiably so, but one of the things it did do pretty well when it was in the air was fly well. If you stalled it out and got into the post-stall gyration, you wouldn't think that, and you got a hell of a ride out of it, and maybe you got an ejection out of it, as several did. But basically if you didn't run into trouble of some kind, one way or another, it was a pretty good flying machine. Didn't have the power it needed, particularly around the carrier. If you got a little low and slow in the groove, it didn't respond fast enough with enough power to really be safe in that respect, you know.

It had a lot of kind of advanced features in the airplane. It was the first Navy airplane at least, and I think maybe the first airplane, to have 3,000-PSI hydraulic system, and it not only had one but it had two. It had a tandem system. The power boosts on it were all tandem, and it had the best speed brakes that I've come across yet. You know, one of the old tests for speed brakes you get up there, and you simply pick out a point as a target, and you put out the speed brakes at different speeds to see what effect it'd have. That thing stays right on the pipper. So it had good speed brakes.

It did not have good engines. The J-46 was one of the first if not the first that had a modulated afterburner. But it also had a hell of a tendency to stall out the engines under certain circumstances, and when it did, the results were not very good most of the time. Fortunately, you usually only stalled out one engine, hardly ever two. I don't know of a case where they stalled out two at the same time. But when it did it was fortunate one way. It just corn-cobbed all the blades on the turbine but didn't blow up. When you got back down and looked in the tail cone, there was about five feet of molten metal right down in the bottom of the tail cone. So there were a lot of things. And the engine casings on the engine were magnesium, which was obviously a fire hazard.

I tell the story quite frequently about Bud Sickel and I taxiing out to take off behind a guy that had come down to Moffett to pick up an airplane that had been on loan to NASA, Ames, and he started his takeoff roll, F7U-3.* Started his takeoff roll, went into burner, and the left engine exploded. So he trickled on down the runway, which was an asbestos runway up there, the 32 Left was asbestos, 32 Right was cement. So where he stopped it was right in front of the fire department. He got out of the airplane. The airplane burnt to a crisp right on the runway, and burned about a foot and a half pattern of an F7U-3 right into the runway.

Paul Stillwell: When did that happen?

Admiral Shelton: Oh, that was probably 1954.

Paul Stillwell: How was the F7U as a dogfighter?

Admiral Shelton: Not much. They later converted it mostly to an attack role really, and the only way it would have ever been successful as a fighter, not a dogfighter certainly but as a fighter, would be for you know AIM-9s or something like that, Sidewinders, whatever.† But basically as a fighter it wasn't that good. First of all, the guys were very leery to get very tight with the airplane, because that was one of the ways that you got into this post-stall gyration. You pulled too many G's too tight and got too slow and stalled it out. Then you were more than likely in the post-stall gyration right away. So there would be a common tendency not to get to the limits that you should be able to get to. Up at VC-3 there at Moffett we had investigated and asked Chance-Vought about the possibility of using the wing slats in that situation where you get wrapped up tight and don't want to stall out. Could you extend the slats and get away with it? Well, they never said, "Yes" but they said, "No, mostly." They didn't know whether the slats would withstand it, and they didn't want to try to find out.

Paul Stillwell: That's right. [Laughter]

---

* Lieutenant Commander Horatio G. Sickel, USN. See Admiral Ramage's oral history for more on Sickel's involvement with the F7U.
† Sidewinder is an air-to-air infrared-homing missile with a speed of approximately Mach 2.5. It has been operational, in various forms, since 1956.

Admiral Shelton: So we never really used the slats in a combat dogfight situation.

Paul Stillwell: Now, was it the delta-winged version of the F9F that you were flying?

Admiral Shelton: Yes, yes. We had the F9F-2s, 3s, 4s, 5s, and 6s and 8s, all the way up. Of course, the 2s, 3s, 4s, and 5s were straight-wing, and the 6s and 8s were swept-wing. I was always a little surprised that they had trouble with the F9F-6 when they brought it into the fleet because I didn't think it was that difficult. Maybe I was wrong. But, anyway, the primary difficulty that they had with the airplane getting into the fleet was that most of the pilots that had not flown jets before. They set up a transitional training unit at VC-3 but the F9F-6, later the F9F-8, the F7U-3, the FJ-4, F2H-3.

Paul Stillwell: How did the swept wings improve performance?

Admiral Shelton: Well, you could go supersonic if you really tried. Didn't have enough power, really, but it was just a better airplane all the way around. Faster. Could maneuver better. Mostly it just had more capability all the way.

Paul Stillwell: How would you describe its characteristics similar to the way you described the F7U?

Admiral Shelton: Oh, easier and not as susceptible to as many tricks, either engine-wise or aerodynamic-wise.

Paul Stillwell: So more reliable.

Admiral Shelton: Yes. I believe the number of major accidents in an F7U-3 was 90 in about four years. Now, that's a lot of major accidents.

Paul Stillwell: Yes.

Admiral Shelton: And that doesn't count blown tires, all this kind of stuff, but major accidents. You cannot imagine in today's world buying an airplane that's going to have 90 major accidents in four years. That's just not going to happen.

Paul Stillwell: Can't afford it.

Admiral Shelton: Can't afford it. That's right. At the price per airplane that we pay these days, that's not going to be. But there was a fair amount of that back in those days—both Navy and Air Force.

Paul Stillwell: Do you have any memories of Tom Connolly as the skipper at that school?

Admiral Shelton: Oh, yes.

Paul Stillwell: Do tell. [Laughter]

Admiral Shelton: Tom was not bashful about almost anything, and he particularly was not bashful about letting you know that he was director of the Test Pilot School and what a great school it was. And that he and Syd Sherby had set it up and this kind of thing, and he and Dan Dommasch had written the book for it, which they did.* And so I would say he was kind of the right guy at the right time. Joe Smith took over from him, and so most of the time that I was there—and maybe all the time I was there—Joe Smith was the director. But I knew Tom Connolly by then fairly well. I later had OP-506, which was naval aviation military requirements in OpNav. I was director of that branch, head of that branch when he was OP-05.

Paul Stillwell: He had that job for a long time.†

---

* Commander Sydney S. Sherby, USN. Dommasch worked in the program as a civilian.
† Vice Admiral Thomas F. Connolly, USN, served as Deputy Chief of Naval Operations (Air) from 1 November 1966 to 31 August 1971. Admiral Connolly's oral history is in the Naval Institute collection.

Admiral Shelton: Yes, he did. He had it quite a while because in one way he wanted to get that F-14 born and in the air, and if he left there he had no certainty that that would happen.* And he's probably right.

Paul Stillwell: Well, he also didn't probably have too much certainty that he could get another job after that either.

Admiral Shelton: Yes, he had a problem with that. [Laughter] There were a number of guys in his bailiwick that didn't get along too well with the head shed.

Paul Stillwell: Any other planes that you spent quite a bit of time with when you were in service test?

Admiral Shelton: Well, I flew all of those. The F7U came along about halfway through my tour there, so I spent most of my time in the F9F and F2H series. Flew some helicopters at the same time, that sort of thing, but that was about it.

Paul Stillwell: What can you say about the F2H?

Admiral Shelton: Oh, a real nice airplane to fly. I mean, there was nothing about that airplane. I always felt, "Man, anybody that gets in trouble in this is airplane is really sick; he's a non-aviator," because that airplane was a joy. I never did take the F2H aboard ship. I did take the F7U aboard. I never did take the F9F-6 aboard a carrier, but all the guys that I ever talked to that flew any part of the F2H series loved it.

Paul Stillwell: And McDonnell was still relatively a young company at that point.

---

* Grumman F-14 Tomcat fighters first entered training squadrons in late 1972. The F-14A version was 64 feet long, wingspan of 38 feet, normal takeoff weight of 55,000 pounds, and top speed of Mach 2.34. It was equipped with a 20-millimeter cannon and was designed to carry a variety of types of missiles—Sparrow, Sidewinder, and Phoenix—and later equipped to deliver bombs as well.

Admiral Shelton: Oh, yes. Absolutely. Of course, they later on got into the F3H series, and I was ops and then exec of the first West Coast Demon squadron F3Hs.* I left TTU at Moffett, and Wally Schirra and I both came down to VF-124 at Miramar.† I was ops and then exec of that squadron, the first West Coast Demon squadron. Still in the night business. All my life.

Paul Stillwell: Any more about that tour of duty that you want to put on the record?

Admiral Shelton: Oh, not a whole lot. The CO of that squadron when I got there was Shannon McCrary, who had been out at Barbers Point when I was there.‡ He was the CO, and he was killed on a GCA one night so they moved Paul Payne over from VF-121.§ I moved up from ops because the exec, a fellow named Shorty Ewing, experienced one of the engine failures that at that time was sort of common to the J-71 in the landing pattern of all places.** He would have made it, except that he forgot to drop the outside hydraulic-ram air turbine, RAT. He ended up sliding down the runway, and he ended up having to retire from the Navy due to physical disability from the accident. So I moved up to XO of that squadron. CAG was Bob Elder.†† Tom Sedaker was the CO of VF-121.‡‡

Paul Stillwell: Now, what squadron are we talking about here?

Admiral Shelton: 124 I'm talking about, the Demons.

---

* McDonnell's F3H Demon was a jet-powered fighter-bomber that first entered the fleet in the 1950s but was relatively unsuccessful in fleet service. The F3H-2 version was 59 feet long, wingspan of 35 feet, gross weight of 33,900 pounds, and top speed of 647 miles per hour. It had four fixed forward-firing 20-millimeter guns and provision to carry bombs or rockets under the wings.
† TTU was the transitional training unit to facilitate propeller pilots making the transition to jets. Lieutenant Walter M. Schirra, Jr., USN, later became one of the nation's initial seven astronauts. Miramar Naval Air Station was near San Diego, California. It has since been turned over to the Marine Corps.
‡ Lieutenant Commander Shannon W. McCrary, USN.
§ Lieutenant Commander Paul E. Payne, USN.
** Lieutenant Commander James W. Ewing, USN.
†† Commander Robert M. Elder, USN, commanded Air Group 12 from March 1956 to November 1957. For a detailed article on his career, see Barrett Tillman, "Where Are They Now? Bob Elder," The Hook, Fall 1989, pages 12-17.
‡‡ Lieutenant Commander Thomas S. Sedaker, USN.

Paul Stillwell: Okay, you went there from—

Admiral Shelton: Moffett.

Paul Stillwell: Well, where did you go from Patuxent?

Admiral Shelton: Oh. From Patuxent I went to FASRON-7 at Miramar, where they set up a thing called Project Cutlass.* Myself and a fellow named Floyd Nugent, who had been in flight test on the F7U-3, and several others including Burt Shepherd, Wally Schirra were collected here in Project Cutlass to make fleet introduction for the F7U-3.† That happened almost simultaneously with the time that then Commander Ramage was getting TTU set up up at Moffett Field. So before long myself, Wally, Burt Shepherd, and all went up to Moffett Field. I headed up the F7U team and had myself, Wally, Burt Shepherd and Jake Ward, J D Ward.‡ That was the F7U team.

We spent our time there putting pilots and maintenance personnel through the F7U syllabus that we had there. I came out to Project Cutlass in about January of '53. Went up to Moffett in about a year later and stayed there about a year and a half and then got involved in the fleet introduction program for the F3H. Went back to Patuxent for a short while for that. Came back to VC-3 (TTU) and then detached. Came down to Miramar to be ops and then XO of VF-124. So that's the sequence there.

Paul Stillwell: Okay. What more can you say about the F7U introduction team?

Admiral Shelton: Good team. Four good guys, knew how to fly the airplane and knew all the foibles about it. I think we did a good job up there. We had a good syllabus. It happened that when I left Patuxent there was a reserve officer that was in service test at the time named Sig Bajack. I don't know whether you ever came across him or not.

---

* FASRON—Fleet Aircraft Service Squadron.
† Lieutenant Burton H. Shepherd, USN.
‡ Lieutenant J D Ward, USN—the letters are not initials; they comprise his first and middle names.

Paul Stillwell: No.

Admiral Shelton: I think he's dead now. Anyway he was a writer and a TV guy as well as a pilot. He got the contract from BuAer to do the fleet introduction film for the F7U-3, pilot introduction film.* He pulled me in as a technical advisor. By that time I was out at Miramar, and so we made the fleet introduction film for the F7U-3 at Miramar.

Meanwhile back, at the ranch at Patuxent, why, a guy named Williams, not the same Dave Williams but another Williams, had gotten into the post-stall gyration and ejected from the F7U-3, the first one. That put Chance-Vought on the horns of a dilemma. At that time they had not been required by BuAer to demonstrate stall and spin, but it put them on the horns to demonstrate whatever this was and how to recover. Tag Livingston down at flight test was designated to go down to Dallas and observe these flights, both airborne and from the ground.† I happened to be down there during part of that time.

They made a film of this, so I stepped in and got promised a copy of that film. Although I didn't know I was going to need it for TTU at the time, I wanted a copy of it. I did get a copy a little later on, just about the time that I went to Moffett for TTU. So in the syllabus up there we had the pilot familiarization film and the demonstration film of the post-stall gyration. We had four guys that had flown the airplane quite a bit, and we had the film of don't do it, post-stall gyration type thing. So we had a good syllabus, and I think they did a pretty good job of checking out the guys that were put through there. The idea, of course, was to put the senior people through, the three or four senior people of a squadron, and the key people from the maintenance group, engine, electric, hydraulics, so forth, through the ground course.

Paul Stillwell: Was this sort of comparable to the RAG concept that came along later?‡

---

* BuAer—Bureau of Aeronautics.
† Lieutenant Commander William H. Livingston, USN.
‡ RAG—replacement air group is a squadron that trains pilots and other flight crew members in a specific type of aircraft before the personnel report to a fleet squadron that flies the particular plane.

Admiral Shelton: Well, it was kind of the forerunner of the RAG. During the war they had had what they called Air Group 98, and that was sort of a training squadron also. So, if you wanted to look at it one way, they were all pretty much the same thing. But somewhere in the middle there, that had phased out, and so at that point Commander Ramage stepped in and got it going again as Transitional Training Unit and had the different types of airplanes. Then when that phased out then they set up the RAGs.

Paul Stillwell: Which was late '50s.

Admiral Shelton: Late '50s, yes. It was about early 1958, because in VF-124 we deployed with the Demons in April of '57 and when we came back from that cruise VF-124 became the RAG. So that's when the RAG was established. Air Group 12 became the RAG, and VF-124 became the fighter RAG.

Paul Stillwell: What do you recall about Schirra from that time?

Admiral Shelton: I think he had just come from China Lake, where he had been the Sidewinder project officer, so he was full of Sidewinders.[*] Wally obviously had talent. He had bagged a MiG in Korea on Air Force exchange duty and so, hell, he was nothing but a welcome addition to the outfit. Nobody knew anything about space at that time, of course. But good guy. He lives over here in Rancho Santa Fe. We see each other fairly often.

Paul Stillwell: What about Burt Shepherd.[†] What do you recall of him?

Admiral Shelton: Burt was a good guy. The process for getting an engine out the F7U was to make the F7U kneel down on that long, tall nose strut that it had and pull the engines out horizontally. But when they built the airplane, nobody thought to build an

---

[*] China Lake is another name for the Naval Ordnance Test Station at Inyokern, California.
[†] In the early 1970s, as a captain, Shepherd was executive assistant to the Chief of Naval Operations, Admiral Elmo R. Zumwalt, Jr., USN. As a rear admiral, Shepherd was Chief of Naval Air Training. In 2000, as an Episcopal priest, he preached the homily at Admiral Zumwalt's funeral.

engine removal stand. So there was another engine removal stand that could be altered fairly easily, and so Burt Shepherd went over to the other side of the field to the FASRON over there one night and brought back two of them. We modified those and drafted up a set of instructions on how you modify them, and we presented those to all the maintenance groups that went through the syllabus there. So I think we used those engine stands most profitably. They didn't sit there and rust. [Laughter] Burt later made rear admiral, retired, became a minister, and preached Admiral Zumwalt's funeral service.

Paul Stillwell: Anything on Jake Ward to recall?

Admiral Shelton: Oh, yes. Jake was a solid citizen, slow-spoken Louisiana guy. I'm not sure he was from Louisiana. That's where he lives now, but he might as well have been because he's that soft spoken. Tremendous guy. I don't think that he had flown the F7U up to that time, but it didn't take him long to get up to speed. Maybe he had flown it but nowhere that I know of. But he was good. We had a good time.

Paul Stillwell: He later came to grief with a so-called race riot on his ship.

Admiral Shelton: Yes. You know, I guess everything's been said about that, but I thought that was probably the biggest miscarriage of justice that I have ever seen. He should have made flag, and it's a pity that he didn't.

Paul Stillwell: What else do you remember about that introduction team?

Admiral Shelton: Oh, I remember Bud Sickel because Bud Sickel was a hell of a pilot. He had one notion that I couldn't get out of his head, which was that the F7U would spin just like other airplanes. I kept having to talk to Bud all the time to keep him from going up and demonstrating it. Well, as it so happens, at one point in the syllabus up there I happened to be down at San Diego at the time at AirPac.* There was a young jaygee

---

* AirPac—Air Force Pacific Fleet, the type commander for aircraft and aircraft carriers.

named Lindsey, I believe his name was, that got into post-stall gyration in the syllabus there on a tactics hop. He ended up ejecting. Bud hadn't felt that he gave it a full shot to recover, I guess. I don't know. But anyway while I was still down in San Diego Bud decided he was going go up and demonstrate that this airplane would stall and it would spin and you would recover just like any other airplane. So sure enough. I forgot who chased him on this thing. It might have been Don McCracken, who later worked for McDonnell, or it might have been Bob Baldwin.* One of the other TTU pilots anyway that I think chased him on this venture.

So, sure enough, he went up there, and he stalled it out. He got into the post-stall gyration, and sure enough he couldn't recover and sure enough he ejected. He was very fortunate in that, even though he got out at a low altitude. The seat got caught up a little bit in the harness when he ejected. Bud Sickel, the seat, and the airplane all came down pretty close to the same spot. He landed in a plowed field up there around Crow's Landing east of Moffett over in the valley. The field was plowed deep enough that when Bud hit as hard as he hit with that seat accompanying and all, that he went in about up to his knees. But it didn't break any bones, and didn't really hurt him that much. He was a little bit stiff and sore, but it didn't really hurt him.

Paul Stillwell: Very fortunate.

Admiral Shelton: He was fortunate. And I think about that time all hell broke loose. Commander Ramage decided about that time, I think, that he'd had enough of F7U-3s with that kind of a demonstration. And there had been some incidents elsewhere where in trying to get aboard and all this kind of thing it hadn't been too successful and all that. So he went down to AirPac and pretty much kiboshed the F7U-3. They did deploy some F7Us. I guess there were a total of maybe three or four squadrons that deployed. And later VX-4, I believe, deployed an F7U-3M squadron, which was a Sparrow missile squadron, Sparrow squadron. But other than that they weren't very successful. And, as I say, 90 major accidents in four years was enough to pretty much kill any airplane I think.

---

* Lieutenant Donald McCracken, USN; Lieutenant Robert B. Baldwin, USN.

It did have a lot of things going for it. It had a lot of advancements in it that were ahead of its time. But it did not have some of the things that you needed most, which was good flying characteristics all the way around and decent power. It had a lot of good ones, but in the clutch—when you were pulling and heaving and you got into the stall—that was not a good deal. We're lucky that we didn't lose more of them that way really.

Paul Stillwell: I'm guessing that Sickel didn't try that again.

Admiral Shelton: No, he didn't. [Laughter] I managed to keep my mouth shut. I'll put it that way. [Laughter]

Paul Stillwell: You didn't need to say anything.

Admiral Shelton: I didn't bring it up to him. [Laughter]

Paul Stillwell: Well, did you go from there then to 124?

Admiral Shelton: Yes, and we didn't have much time to get ready to deploy. We got the airplanes in about April or May of '56, and we were going to deploy the following April.

Paul Stillwell: Were you a lieutenant commander by that point?

Admiral Shelton: I made lieutenant commander about the middle of my tour up at Moffett. So came down here, and, as I said, we had some bad luck with Shannon McCrary and Shorty Ewing. We started flying the airplane quite a bit. We were having some of that engine problem that the J-71 had. I really can't describe it in detail at this point, even though I could at one time, but it had a fuel control problem so that under certain circumstances the engine would simply quit running.

Paul Stillwell: Now, this is the F3H you're talking about.

Admiral Shelton: Yes. And at the same time this was another one of the airplanes that the Navy has built that didn't have the power it should have had. We needed more power than that J-71 for that airplane even in burner. But it had a lot of good flying qualities. It had good radar, and it came aboard very nicely. And so we started flying it. In maybe late fall, we had gotten what were supposed to be the cream of the crop out of the training command, six or seven guys. And we had gotten a couple of lieutenants that had come back from shore duty into the squadron that were relatively senior lieutenants. But, given the deck time that we knew we were going to get, etc., etc., and the time that we felt that we needed to get people night qualified, field carrier qualified and everything, it became apparent that we didn't think we could qualify the whole squadron. So Paul Payne, he and I, the others, Wally, we got together, talked it all over with Ed Porter.* Talked it all over and Paul made his decision, and decided to only night qualify half of the squadron. Bob Elder, who was CAG, agreed. Not the kind of decision you really want to make.

Paul Stillwell: No.

Admiral Shelton: But we felt it was necessary, and I think in hindsight it was probably a good idea. There were a couple of the newies from the training command that in spite of being supposedly the best out of the chute, weren't really measuring up that way, and I can't blame them. They had never flown anything like the F3H. Coming right out of the training command, it was a pretty fair hunk of airplane to put your hands on, even though it did fly good and all that. So I can't really blame them, but I think it retrospect it was probably a good idea that we made that decision. So we set about it, and we finally, we deployed in April.

Paul Stillwell: What ship?

---

* Lieutenant Edward M. Porter, USN.

Admiral Shelton: We deployed on the Lexington.* Somewhere in there I had night qualified, but most of the squadron hadn't. We did not night qualify till we got to Hawaii, and we stayed in Hawaii for a couple of weeks. We were going to have an ORI that we used to have in those days.†

So the whole air group off-loaded to Kaneohe at the time, not Barbers Point but Kaneohe. We did all our night bounce and everything at Kaneohe and proceeded to night-qualify the guys that needed to be night qualified and then went into the ORI.‡ So we did fly at night through the ORI. We didn't have any accidents during that time and got through that all pretty good.

We did get one exercise that showed that we had a pretty good radar, and that is from Barking Sands they launched a Regulus missile.§ Four of us were up there to intercept it and shoot it down. So we got the intercept, and, as things go, CO gets first shot. [Laughter] So we got up, and I was calling the ranges for him on his wing out there, wide wing. Wally Schirra was over here, and somebody else was over there. So when we got inside of two miles, which was dependable Sidewinder range in those days, Paul Payne got the tone and he shot. The Sidewinder went apes. Didn't hit the missile.

So the next guy shot right away, because if the first shooter was in range the next guy was in range, too, and you don't want to argue about that. So I shot right away, being the number-two guy to shoot, and I got the missile. [Laughter] To this day Wally Schirra has never forgiven me, because he was the Sidewinder projects officer at China Lake. I wouldn't say he was hoping I would miss, but I don't think it would have disappointed him if I had. [Laughter] So I got the Regulus.**

---

* USS Lexington (CV-16) was originally commissioned 17 February 1943 an Essex-class aircraft carrier, then decommissioned 23 April 1947. She was redesignated as an attack carrier, CVA-16 on 1 October and the following year began modernization to the 27C version, including an angled flight deck. When she was recommissioned 15 August 1955 she had the following characteristics: standard displacement: 33,100 tons; length, 899 feet; beam, 103 feet; maximum width, 192 feet; top speed, 33 knots; armament, eight 5-inch guns; aircraft complement, 70-80.
† ORI—operational readiness inspection.
‡ Kaneohe Naval Air Station was on the eastern side of the Hawaiian island of Oahu. It has since become a Marine Corps Air Station.
§ Barking Sands is the name of a Navy missile range on the island of Kauai, Hawaii. Regulus missiles were designed to be fired from surface ships or surfaced submarines.
** This event occurred on 8 May 1957, confirmed by an entry in Schirra's logbook.

So we went ahead and deployed, and we had a pretty normal deployment after that. We off-loaded to Atsugi a couple of times.* Did a lot of night flying out of there and got a lot of education about strong winter winds out there and strong winds anytime really. But we did a lot of night flying, did a lot of instrument work out there.

Paul Stillwell: Were the night operations by now much more accepted than they had been, say, when you were in the Tarawa?

Admiral Shelton: Oh, yes. Quite a bit. In the first place, we were a night squadron or working on to be an all-weather squadron, not a detachment—a squadron with your place on the ship. There was still some of it left over. The ADs were night qualified, but VF-121, the FJ squadron, was not night qualified. Of course, they wanted their share of daytime flying, and you can't blame them on that. But we did get our fair share.

There are some like Charlie Brown in his book, Dark Sky, Black Seas, I think was a little bit critical of 124 because as the first Demon squadron we did not get as many night landings as he thought we probably should have gotten in a regular six-month cruise.† He's probably right. But if you look at it from the standpoint that we had a short training period relative to most turnarounds, a little less than a year, in a new airplane and a whole bunch of new pilots. The average for the guys that did fly from Kaneohe till we left Japan coming back, boiled down to about four months of flying time. And we didn't fly coming back from Japan, so that cut down on the time too. I don't know why we didn't fly coming back from Japan, but nobody flew. The guys that were night qualified each got 18 night landings during the four months, which wasn't that bad.

Three of us, Paul Payne, Ed Porter and myself were centurions on that cruise, which means we got more than 100 landings on the cruise. Wally got 98, and he's never forgiven us for that either. [Laughter] But all said and done, I don't think we have to apologize for the amount of night work that we did on the Lexington. As I said, it boiled down to about four months' worth because we didn't really get to night qualify until we were in Kaneohe. Maybe that was our fault, but we didn't have the training time.

---

* Atsugi is the site of a U.S. naval air station near the port of Yokosuka on the island of Honshu, Japan.
† Charles H. Brown, Dark Sky, Black Sea: Aircraft Carrier Night and All-Weather Operations (Annapolis: Naval Institute Press, 1999).

Paul Stillwell: What happened to the half of the squadron that didn't get night qualified?

Admiral Shelton: They flew during the day, and they did a good job. Did a really good job. They all averaged up in the 80s and 90s for total traps.

Paul Stillwell: Was this an adjustment for a carrier's operations to have this much night work?

Admiral Shelton: Yes, I think so. There hadn't been that much of a transition since the old days, if you want to call it that, of the Tarawa or the Korean War. The Korean War probably did more than any other thing that I know of to further flying around the clock, not in the same sense that we're doing today exactly. But there was none of this business we'd seen in the ready rooms in the Korean War: "Oh, why don't you guys go find someplace else to fly your time at night?" No, we flew at night. So I'd have to say that the Korean War was really a pretty big stepping-stone.

Unfortunately, for the most part none of the jets flew at night out there off the carriers. They did from the beach but not from the carriers, so you're still talking prop night work basically. So the jets hadn't really gotten into the day-and-night cycle business. So by the time we did it with the F3Hs, of course, the F2H-3s had been doing some. But there was a big gap to overcome there, and basically we didn't have any problem getting our time. I think everybody was probably a little bit more trepidatious than we needed to be, looking back at it—everybody meaning the ship's CO, the air group commander, who was Bob Elder, our CO, and myself. We were concerned with that airplane and the engine problem wasn't solved yet. At the time I didn't recognize that we were being trepidatious at all, but possibly we were.

Paul Stillwell: Bob Elder is regarded in reverential terms within naval aviation. What do you recall of him?

Admiral Shelton: Oh, I recall a lot about him. He's a good guy. I can go back to the first time I ever knew him, which was when I was in VF-1E, F6F-5Ns, and Dave Williams and I were out on the Valley Forge. We were qualifying and doing some touch and goes and carrier traps and all that kind of stuff. That was in the early days, when VF-51A was out there with their FJ-1s trying to get qualified on there too. The FJ-1s had been having some trouble with the tailhook coming out of the airplane.

Paul Stillwell: That's a problem.

Admiral Shelton: That's a problem. And I can remember that I saw this big, tall, lanky guy walk out there, and I didn't even know who he was. And I asked somebody, "Who's that?"

"Oh, that's Bob Elder," like I was supposed to know that was Jesus Christ. [Laughter] So I watched him. He went out to that FJ, and he went around there and he looked at that tailhook installation, which was a new one that they were getting ready to try. He turned around and walked away and came back and said, "It ain't going to work." Pete Aurand, who was a different breed of cat, just as smart, just as good a pilot maybe, everything, but he walked out to that same airplane and said, "Launch me." He was next seen with a tailhook coming out of the airplane and him going into the barrier. [Laughter] So that was my introduction to Bob Elder.

Paul Stillwell: When had that happened chronologically?

Admiral Shelton: Oh, that was in late '47 or early '48, before the Tarawa's around-the-world cruise, because I wouldn't have been there otherwise.

Paul Stillwell: How was he as a CAG?

Admiral Shelton: Great. Great. All he wanted to do was see you go fly. Yes, he was good. He was a centurion too. He had 129 landings. [Laughter] You know, we keep track of that sort of thing.

Paul Stillwell: Oh, yes. [Laughter]

Admiral Shelton: Yes, he was great. Back in the earlier days, as you probably well know, there had been some kind of—I think it was a myth myself—but there was a feeling that was promulgated around here and there that NavCads didn't like academy guys and vice versa.

Paul Stillwell: And Elder was a NavCad.

Admiral Shelton: And Elder was a NavCad. So was Don Engen.* So was Tom Sedaker. So was Dave Williams. So was Johnny Magda. So were a lot of people. I never felt that way myself, and I don't think that I ever felt any of it directed toward me. But I have to say I wasn't about to put up with it if it had been, because I honestly felt that I could hold my own with all of them. You could be just as good as Bob Elder and a few of those guys, but because they had been in World War II as aviators and had done one hell of a job, you don't gain that World War II leg on them—ever.

Paul Stillwell: And Elder has a Navy Cross, more than one.

Admiral Shelton: That's right, and you're not going to catch up in that kind of ball game. On the other hand, I had been catapult officer on the St. Louis, so I thought that wasn't too bad. [Laughter] I had been in the war. I didn't fly, but I'd been in the war, and I was certainly in the Korean War, and I was certainly in the Vietnam War, so I didn't really feel that I had to worry too much about my quals. But at a time there was that thing. I don't think it exists anymore. By now I think it's completely gone down the drain, at least I hope so.

---

* Ensign Donald D. Engen, USNR, received his wings in 1944 and was in combat in October of that year in the Battle of Leyte Gulf. He was in the first jet combat sortie in 1950, during the Korean War. Later in his career he became a vice admiral. After he retired he headed the Federal Aviation Administration and the Air and Space Museum. His oral history is in the Naval Institute collection.

Paul Stillwell: What sort of operations or exercises was <u>Lexington</u> involved in on that cruise? War games? Port visits?

Admiral Shelton: Well, we had port visits. We did the usual things in Yokosuka and Hong Kong, and that was about it, port visits. But I don't remember too many ship's exercises that we got involved in, but about every time we flew we were doing our business. We were making intercepts and so forth, day or night.

Paul Stillwell: Did you feel that you had really pushed the business of night flying along with that cruise?

Admiral Shelton: Yes, I did, and I had a lot of reason to feel one way or the other. I came back feeling that we'd made a little inroad. And I think mostly it was because that feeling of, "Why don't you guys go do it somewhere else on your own time?" was largely disappearing by that time.

Paul Stillwell: Were there counterpart squadrons in other carriers at that time bringing it along?

Admiral Shelton: Not in the F3H. The next West Coast F3H to deploy was roughly six months behind us. The first squadron to deploy on the East Coast was fairly close to the same time we deployed but about a month earlier. I think it was VF-141. We had a VF-124 squadron reunion, oh, about seven or eight years ago out here at Miramar at the Holiday Inn, and I wasn't sure how many of those folks would show up. Every one of them showed up, and it was really good. We had a good reunion. Bob Elder came down. We had a really good reunion. Norm Danielson was there too. I should have mentioned him earlier. He was our Allison engine rep on the cruise, and he was responsible in many ways for the overall lack of engine problems we had on the cruise and therefore for the success we did have. A good man and a real squadron mate.

Paul Stillwell: Anything else to say about the skipper except that his Sidewinder wouldn't work on that one intercept with the Regulus.

Admiral Shelton: No, but there again I kept my mouth shut. [Laughter] I wasn't going to say anything other than I had told him over the air, "You're in range," because that was my job to tell him that. He didn't want to have to keep track of all that, so as soon as he got the tone, he fired, and I don't know what happened to his Sidewinder. But even the Sidewinders in those days—as good as they were—they weren't 100% infallible either.

Paul Stillwell: You're smiling and chuckling. What are you thinking about to prompt that?

Admiral Shelton: Well, I'm just thinking that, once again, I was smart enough not to open my mouth. [Laughter] You know, you like to think it's all good sport and everything, but when you get right down to it, you want to be the one, so I lucked out. I was the one.

Paul Stillwell: Was that the first time that a missile had shot down another missile?

Admiral Shelton: I think it was the first time, certainly it was the first time an F3H had. I'm saying that "certainly," and I believe that's right. They obviously had shot down drones at China Lake. I don't think they had done it with an F3H on radar, but they had whatever they were using up there at the time, FJ or whatever, to qualify the Sidewinder, they had shot down drones with it.

Paul Stillwell: Well, Regulus was sort of a cross between a missile and an airplane.

Admiral Shelton: Yes. It flew pretty fast. It did about Mach .84. We were in burner, humping all we could to intercept that thing. We got a little bit of a too much tail-on intercept to begin with, so we were chasing that hummer for longer than you would like to do it. We started that intercept off out there south of Barbers Point, probably about 50 miles where we were, because we were simulating combat.

Paul Stillwell: You were orbiting waiting for it to go?

Admiral Shelton: Orbiting and waiting, yes, waiting for the intercept. When it finally went down, it was about 20 or 25 miles short of the Big Island so we chased that hummer a ways.* We were, as the old saying goes, balls out all the way. We had it in burner with everything we could get out of it.

Paul Stillwell: What was the top speed you could get out of that plane?

Admiral Shelton: Well, we were about an .86 airplane, .87. If we could get the advantage and get a little downhill, you could get up to .89 without too much of a problem. Actually, if you could get a little higher and go all the way down a little more, you could actually go a little bit supersonic, but it was pretty tough. You couldn't do that with any reliability and still shoot the thing down, because to shoot the thing down you've got to be looking at your instruments and at the radar and making sure. You had to have the tone and all that, so basically we were on a level intercept, and so we were doing about .86-.87.

Paul Stillwell: Are your back and vocal cords holding up enough to discuss another tour here?

Admiral Shelton: Sure.

Paul Stillwell: Okay. Well, where did you go from there?

Admiral Shelton: Well, let's see. From 124, '57, came back in January of '58, went to

---

* Hawaii is the name of the biggest island in the Hawaiian chain. Barbers Point is on Oahu.

Armed Forces Staff College in Norfolk, and that was where I met up again with my gunnery officer on the St. Louis. He was an admiral by then.

Paul Stillwell: Sarver.

Admiral Shelton: Sarver. I'm not sure whether he ever remembered me or not, but I didn't give him the chance to say he didn't, because I just introduced myself, and I said, "I was on the St. Louis with you when we got clocked." So that was good enough, and we went on from there. But I didn't make a point of trying to extend the thing all the way through staff school. First of all, I had a lot of studying to do, and he was in a sort of a different part of the curriculum. He didn't have much to do with me, and so I really didn't see him that much while I was there.

Paul Stillwell: So this was really the first non-flying duty you'd had since St. Louis.

Admiral Shelton: That's right. That is correct. And when I went to staff college I didn't know where I was going from there, so I had some reservations about that too. You always like to know where you're going to go, and you'd like to have some say in where you think you might want to go. Bob Baldwin by that time was in BuPers, and he called me up a couple of times and said, "Want to get you up here in OpNav or somewhere in Washington."[*]

I said, "Bob, I don't want to come to Washington." I wanted to go fly somewhere. About that same time Tag Livingston took over as director of the Test Pilot School. He called up one day and said, "You're coming up to Test Pilot School on the staff," so I did. I went up there. He was the director. A guy named Tiny Graning was assistant director.[†]

Paul Stillwell: Well, why don't we talk about what you did in Norfolk before you get back up there?

---

[*] Baldwin by then was a lieutenant commander. He eventually became a vice admiral and served as Chief of Naval Personnel from July 1978 to July 1980.
[†] Lieutenant Commander Leonard G. Graning, USN.

Admiral Shelton: Oh, staff college. At staff college it's six months of listening to all the services tell what they do best. An infantrymen gets up there, and you've got to listen to him say, "I'm proud to die as an infantryman." You've got to listen to a carrier aviator get up there and say, "There's only one thing in this world and that's carrier aviation." [Laughter] And you've got to listen to the Marines stand up there and give their pitch and the whole bit. It's six months of that. But you learn a lot. You learn a lot about infantry. You learn about tanks, and you learn about things that you don't know anything about. Whatever your line of work is, you're going to learn a lot about the other lines of work. And you do a few staff studies that are not very complicated, and you have to do the paperwork for those, so that's about it.

Paul Stillwell: We just had a little break to change tapes, and you told me a story that I think might be worth repeating to tell about another facet of naval aviation.

Admiral Shelton: Oh, yes. Another facet of naval aviation all right. One of the pastimes while you were getting your flight time in staff college was to take the SNB with another guy or two and fly all the way up to Brunswick, Maine. That filled up the four hours and more. While we were there, we'd take on a load of lobsters and bring them back to everybody that wanted some down at the staff college, as many as we could bring back. So that was fine, and that was just before graduation. We ate some of the lobsters, and we put the rest of them in the freezer part of the refrigerator in our apartment.

We had two weeks' leave when we finished staff college, and we went down to Myrtle Beach, my wife, two girls. Had a hell of a good time on the beach. Well, the little one caught impetigo. That wasn't so great, so we came back. Walked in the apartment and thought, well, we're going to have a Coke or something. So we opened the refrigerator to get some ice, and we got hit with the most god-awful smell that there is in the world, because the power had gone off. The refrigerator never did come back on the line, and so those lobsters were really rare. We could not get the smell out of the apartment. We could not get the smell out of the refrigerator. Public works came over. They tried all of the old things that you've ever heard about: charcoal, lemon juice, and everything else. Nothing worked. So they ended up replacing the refrigerator and taking the other one and doing something with it unknown to me, but I'm sure it's deep-sixed someplace. So that part of it was a little different.

Paul Stillwell: You've mentioned before that you were a bachelor during some of this traveling around, and now by this point you've got a wife and two daughters.

Admiral Shelton: Yes, that's right.

Paul Stillwell: Where did your wife come into the picture?

Admiral Shelton: Well, I was just going to say we forgot to get into that, but while I was at Moffett in the F7U-3 thing, why, a classmate of mine called me up one day from Alameda, Bob and Nicky Kasten.* He now lives down in St. Petersburg, Florida. Anyway, he called me up and said, "There's a young lady up here that I used to live next door to, and we're going to have the Army-Navy game class get-together at the O-club at Treasure Island.† How about coming up here and meeting this young lady?"

So I said, "Well, okay." I wasn't really too hot for the program at that point. In the first place, it was quite a ways up to Treasure Island, even if you want to go. But I decided I would. Went up. That's where I met Peggy Leaford, and that was the Army-Navy game, so that was early part of December.

Paul Stillwell: What year?

Admiral Shelton: Fifty-five. And so I started seeing her hot and heavy. I took her to the Claremont Hotel one time, and we watched Seguro and somebody else play tennis and had dinner there and danced a little bit. We went over to San Francisco, and we did San Francisco several times. On one of those occasions later, on about the first part of

---

* Lieutenant Robert I. Kasten, USN, who later retired in 1969 as a captain.
† Treasure Island is a man-made island in San Francisco Bay, located between San Francisco and Oakland. It served as the site of a world's fair in 1939-40, then was converted for use as a Navy base during and after World War II.

February, why, we went back to the Top of the Mark and had a drink, and I said words to the effect, "Why don't we get married?" [Laughter]

She had to think about that quite a while really, not immediately but several days later. One of the stumbling blocks I guess for her was that she had a four-year-old daughter at that time. Her first husband was an Air Force Reserve pilot who was an intelligence officer in Alaska and was flying back up to Alaska from Washington in a C-119 that managed to fly into the side of Mount McKinley. They never recovered any of them. Peggy had a daughter, Deborah, who was about three and a half years old at that time. Anyway, in about a week she said, "Okay." I credit her "okay" with being the best thing in my career; she has been great.

We managed to get things organized, and we were married down at Carmel at the little church there and spent our honeymoon at Highlands Inn, which we could barely afford in those days, and which I doubt I could afford under any circumstances these days. But we managed to afford it for about three or four days, and it was delightful. So then shortly after that, of course, we came down to Miramar. Had orders to VF-124, so we came down and started looking for houses here in the Del Mar area and found one that we rented on the beach. Then we bought a little house in Solana Beach. Paid $13,500 for it. Stayed in it 18 months through the time of VF-124. Sold it when we left to go to Armed Forces Staff College for $14,500 and thought we'd really made out like a tall dog. [Laughter]

Paul Stillwell: As indeed you had.

Admiral Shelton: We'd lived there for 18 months cost free and thought it was great. Donna, the youngest, was born in Camp Pendleton hospital while we were Solana Beach, just before we deployed in 124. She was born January 31, and we deployed the 16th of April I think it was. So when we got to the East Coast, Donna was not yet a year old really and not walking. She would sit on the beach in the water if you let her. Deb, the older one, was always throwing water on her. But, anyway, that was a good two weeks down at Myrtle Beach, and then we trucked on back up to staff college, and you got the rest of it from there.

Paul Stillwell: Well, that tour undoubtedly broadened your horizons as far as the services were concerned because you'd been very focused.

Admiral Shelton: Oh, yes, absolutely. And, as the old saying goes, I probably learned more about infantry than I wanted to know [laughter], but it was good for me, and I had an appreciation for what they did. I enjoyed it. It was a good six months. Not much aviation to it but a good six months, and I learned how to write again so not too bad.

Paul Stillwell: And then back up to Patuxent. What happened there?

Admiral Shelton: Well, I was the admin officer, being number three, and also a flight instructor. So along about that time we started getting up in the classes 20, 21, 22, and so forth and that's when people like Jim Lovell, Pete Conrad, Wally Schirra, and John Young started coming through the Test Pilot School.*

Paul Stillwell: Future astronauts.

Admiral Shelton: Future astronauts started coming through the school. And we had a pretty good bunch of airplanes there. We had the F4D Skyray and some other airplanes. We had TVs. We had TV-2, which was an F-80 in other words with two seats. And Tag Livingston was instrumental in finally getting approval to institute a spin program using the TV, in particular an inverted spin program. So everybody in the school spent quite a bit of time in a TV-2 up there upside down getting into inverted spins and learning how to get out.

So the tour was good, and we had outstanding pilots in there. Most of them probably better than the ones like me when we went through in class 7 because the school had grown and the curriculum had grown. The course was harder, I think. It was

---

* Lieutenant James A. Lovell, USN, whose story was later widely told in the Tom Hanks movie Apollo 13; Lieutenant Peter C. Conrad, USN; Lieutenant Commander Walter M. Schirra, USN; Lieutenant John W. Young, USN.

probably more professional, more in depth, more just about everything. So they had a good crop of people.

At this time, being at Test Pilot School, we were on the mailing list or distribution list for all of the test data that came from everywhere. NASA or anybody that was doing any kind of airplane or shape testing, we got a copy of it.[*] So we began to notice all these documents coming through that had test data on various shapes, reentry and all this kind of stuff. Not knowing what it was all about at that time, we read them with a certain amount of interest but didn't look like it was going to affect us right away, so we didn't pay that much attention to them.

But, lo and behold, one day I answered the phone, and it was Bob Gilruth from NASA up in Washington, D.C., and he said, "We're going to implement Project Mercury."[†] I didn't know what Project Mercury was at that point. I had suspicions, but I didn't know. Tag Livingston knew, but he hadn't said anything to anybody. Mr. Gilruth said, "We want to start screening all Test Pilot School graduates." And he gave us the parameters. They had to be, preferably, under a certain age. They had to be under 5-11. They had to be graduates of either Test Pilot School or an engineering school. And, like a lot of things, once they decided to do it, they wanted the list not tomorrow but yesterday. So there was a big scramble on to go through the files, pick out everybody that was in the categories that they established, and we ended up with 110 people that were screened.

Paul Stillwell: Was your name on the list?

Admiral Shelton: My name was on the list. What developed out of that was that I went in to see Tag, of course, and I said, "We just got this call."

He said, "Yeah, I knew something about it." So he went up to see the Commander NATC at the time and said, "We've gotten this call, and we're going to screen and list," which we did.[‡] As I said, we came out, as I recall, 110 names on the list.

---
[*] NASA—National Aeronautics and Space Administration.
[†] Robert R. Gilruth, an aeronautical engineer, became director of NASA's Project Mercury in 1958.
[‡] NATC—Naval Air Test Center.

A couple of weeks later, I guess it was, we got a call from Vice Admiral Bob Pirie, who was OP-05 at the time.* He said, "We got this crazy thing about to get started up here, and we want those 110 people up here on such and such a day to take three days' worth of tests." So the 110 of us showed up in Washington, D.C. Went down to the old NASA headquarters, which I think were on 15th Street at that time, not too far from the White House, and took a series of tests, both psychological and written and math and all that kind of good stuff. As it would happen, I was not one of the seven that were selected obviously. I knew all the ones that were except the Air Force guys. I didn't know them. As I look back at it now, it doesn't bother me too much that I wasn't selected. It bothered me then, but it doesn't bother me too much now.

Paul Stillwell: Why have you changed in your viewpoint?

Admiral Shelton: I felt that there were reasons that I wasn't selected. I was in the older category of the group anyway, and I was further away from the whole situation than the guys that were currently going through. So I felt they had the edge in the beginning. The only guy that was not in that category was Al Shepard, but he was kind of in a category by himself, I think. So it bothered me quite a bit at the time. As I look back at it now, I say, "Well, another one of those things that happened for the best." I didn't make it, but here I am. I'm not too unvarnished about where I am at this point, and I'm still on the right side of the grass and that helps. Some of them are not.

Paul Stillwell: I interviewed Admiral Thomas Hayward, who said there were initially 12 selected.† He was one of the 12.

Admiral Shelton: Yes, I think that's probably right.

---

* Vice Admiral Robert B. Pirie, Jr., USN, served as Deputy Chief of Naval Operations (Air) from 26 May 1958 to 1 November 1962. His oral history is in the Naval Institute collection.
† Admiral Thomas B. Hayward, USN, served as Chief of Naval Operations from 1 July 1978 to 30 June 1982.

Paul Stillwell: He said it was overloaded with naval aviators, and so five were knocked out. He was one of the five.

Admiral Shelton: I think you can get an even bigger number, depending on who you talk to, but I've also heard the number 17 mentioned, and that all 17 were Navy or Marine. Now, whether that's true or not I have no idea, and I don't imagine anybody'll ever be able to pin it down precisely, but I have that from a very good source—what I would call 100% good source, but nevertheless I'm not sure that that's true. Anyway, that's what they finally figured out, and as the numbers came out obviously there were there were three Navy, one Marine, and three Air Force.

Paul Stillwell: The impact on Admiral Hayward's career was enormous, because it's virtually certain he would not have been Chief of Naval Operations had he been an astronaut.

Admiral Shelton: Oh, yes. And you know which one would he rather have been? Maybe he can tell you. I don't know. I think under those circumstances, if you asked me, I'd rather be CNO. That's why I came in the Navy, to go as far as I could. I didn't know anything space or being an astronaut. I think it's great. I admire every damn one of them, and I've been pleased to know most of them, at least all the early ones I knew. So I don't have a problem with that. I can just say, "Well, I did what I wanted to do. I went as far as I could in the Navy."

Paul Stillwell: That is the important thing.

Admiral Shelton: Well, it was an important thing to me anyway.

Paul Stillwell: What happened then after you did not get selected as one of the seven?

Admiral Shelton: Well, my name came up for squadron command, and so we came back out to Alameda and that was in July. Took over that July the second, I think it was, or fourth of 1961 at Alameda. We scrambled around looking for a place to live. Found a little place that we could rent temporarily in the backyard of another place. [Laughter] It wasn't much, but it was a place. We deployed about a month later on the Ranger.*

Paul Stillwell: What was the squadron?

Admiral Shelton: It was VF-92, Air Group Nine. As soon as we deployed, of course, my wife and the two girls moved back down here to San Diego, to Del Mar. So we deployed on the Ranger, F3Hs again. Had a good tour. Centurion again on the Ranger. There was only one F3H squadron on there also. I've forgotten what the other fighter squadron was.

Paul Stillwell: Was yours a totally night squadron by that point?

Admiral Shelton: No. We still flew in the daytime, but it was a night squadron. Yes, the whole squadron was night qualified, and they did, I thought, a remarkably good job.

Paul Stillwell: Who was the carrier skipper then?

Admiral Shelton: Bill Leonard was the skipper and a Benny Sevilla was the CAG.† That's a sad story that I won't get into, but he ended up not being CAG for reasons not aviation oriented. But it was a good cruise.‡ The senior squadron commander, which was not me, moved up to be CAG for the rest of the cruise, and we had a good one. It was great. I enjoyed it.

Paul Stillwell: What do you remember about Captain Leonard as skipper? He was another Battle of Midway veteran like Elder.

---

* USS Ranger (CVA-61) was commissioned 10 August 1957. She had a standard displacement of 56,300 tons, was 1,046 feet long, 236 feet in the beam, an extreme width of 249 feet on the flight deck, and had a draft of 37 feet. She had a top speed of 34 knots and could accommodate about 80-95 planes. The ship had a long active career before finally being decommissioned on 10 July 1993.
† Captain William N. Leonard, USN, commanded the aircraft carrier Ranger (CVA-61) from 5 May 1960 to 7 May 1962. Commander Bernard Sevilla, USN.
‡ The deployment to the Western Pacific lasted from 11 August 1961 to 8 March 1962.

Admiral Shelton: Right. There are some things I shouldn't say, but of the things that I should say I thought he was an outstanding officer. Obviously a hell of a fine fighter pilot, and I'll stop with that.

Paul Stillwell: What can you say about the specifics of being a skipper? You were finally in command of a seagoing unit.

Admiral Shelton: I was finally in command, right, right. Oh well, I thought it was great. We only had one little problem when I took over. Two days before I took over, one of the guys took off in the F3H and managed to have that engine failure that I was talking about in the J-71, and he barely missed putting it in the middle of Candlestick Park.[*] He put it in the bay but not very far from being in the middle of Candlestick Park. So right away we had an accident investigation to complete while we were trying to deploy.

I don't know whether we were the first squadron, but we were one of the first squadrons to deploy with the Del Mar target, which was a trailing tow-wire target that you could tow and that enabled you to run head-on radar intercepts and live fire with Sparrows.[†] So we were going to deploy with that, and the Del Mar pod and all that sort of thing was brand new. You had to learn how to put it on the airplane. You had to learn what gimmicks there were to it and what made it not work sometimes and all this kind of stuff. So we had a lot to do to get ready to deploy just with that one thing. Fortunately, I did not have to worry too much about the night qualifications for all the pilots except for myself. I had to get night qualified again, which I did. But the rest of them were pretty well up to speed. Most of them were turnarounds in the squadron. Had some good outstanding lieutenants and so forth in there and so it was a good thing. An old Missouri boy was my XO.

Paul Stillwell: Who was that?

---

[*] Candlestick Park, near the Hunters Point Naval Shipyard, was then the home ballpark for baseball's San Francisco Giants.
[†] Since the late 1950s the Sparrow has been the U.S. Navy's major long-range air defense missile. The Sparrow I version entered fleet service in 1956 on board F3H Demons and F7U Cutlasses.

Admiral Shelton: Bob Ambrose was my exec.* But he basically liked horses better than he did airplanes. [Laughter] But he was a hell of a good aviator, and he was a good exec. I might sound like I'm running him down a little bit, which I didn't mean to do because he was dedicated. It's just that he was a, he basically was a farm boy from Missouri that wanted to get back to the farm, and he had a hard time deciding. He wanted to stay flying as long as he could possibly fly, but he wanted to get back to the farm while he was still able to farm, and that always causes a little bit of a dilemma. But that's what he did. As soon as he could after that tour was over, he got out of the Navy and went back to Missouri. He owned a big farm back there, and he had his horses and everything and I still hear from him, oh, about once a year. But he was a hell of a good aviator, and he was a good exec. The squadron was a good one, and we had a good time and we did a good job.

Paul Stillwell: What were some of the events of the cruise?

Admiral Shelton: Well, Tom Connolly was cardiv on that shot, and Bill McClendon was his chief of staff.† Admiral Connolly at that time wanted to find out about the Sparrow. We had a hard time getting the Del Mar target to do what it was supposed to do and a hard time getting the radar doing what it was supposed to do, and the Sparrow doing what it was supposed to do. When we finally got all that organized, we had several really successful shots right in a row so Admiral Connolly could come down off the overhead. He never made any noise about it. He was very good. He understood that there were those kinds of indoctrinational problems when we bring a new system in that way. And so we never had him leaning on us all the time. He just wanted to be kept informed of what the problems were and what we were doing to make it work, fix it.

Paul Stillwell: Did you get similar forbearance from Captain Leonard?

---

* Lieutenant Commander Robert W. Ambrose, USN.
† Rear Admiral Thomas F. Connolly, USN, served as Commander Carrier Division Seven in 1961-62; Captain William R. McClendon, USN.

Admiral Shelton: No problem. He left us alone pretty much. As long as we got on and off in pretty good shape, that was the bulk of his worry. And we did that quite well, so he wasn't worried too much about that. So, no, we didn't get any bad marks from him.

Paul Stillwell: That was the first big-deck carrier you had been in. How did that compare?

Admiral Shelton: Oh, I thought it was great. I mean, as you go up in size with that landing area you think it's pretty nice.

Paul Stillwell: Especially when you start in a CVE.

Admiral Shelton: Yes. That's right. That's right. And I've said that many times, when I was on the Ranger, I thought, "Boy, where have I been all my life? I should have been on one of these." [Laughter] But, yes, it was good. Going back, of course, I guess the Lexington was the first angle deck that I'd been on and then the Ranger was the next one. We off-loaded at Yokota, Japan, part of the time, Johnson Air Force Base. And we off-loaded at Atsugi part of the time and again did a lot of night flying there. Didn't have any accidents. I can't give you the specifics. I know I was a centurion. By that time, since we were a turnaround on that ship as well, there were a bunch of centurions. I was probably a latecomer as far as being a centurion in that squadron.

Paul Stillwell: Anything about the foreign ports you visited that sticks out in your mind?

Admiral Shelton: Well, as I told my wife early on, "You know, all the fighter pilots go to the Pacific, and all the lovers go to the Med."

Paul Stillwell: [Laughter] That's a good thing to tell a wife.

Admiral Shelton: Yes. That's sort of the way I looked at it. And there's been kind of a turnaround in that lately, but that's the way I looked at it then. We did the standard thing—Yokosuka, Sasebo, Hong Kong—and that was about it. But I've been in and out of those ports several times and enjoyed them every damn time I was there, so it was great.

Paul Stillwell: Were there any hints on the horizon yet about Vietnam or any unrest in the Far Pacific at that point?

Admiral Shelton: No, the waters were pretty calm out there at that point. I don't remember any ripples at all.

I did forget to mention when I was XO of 124, Peggy managed to take Donna, our baby and Deb, the youngest one, four years old, up to Glendale to stay with my cousin up there, and Peggy got on an airplane and came out to Atsugi. Bob Elder was nice enough to let me have the CAG hut, as it's known at Atsugi, so we had a nice little rejoinder there, and then she came on down to Hong Kong, which was the next stop. We had a ball down there too. She even got used to walking down the alleys at night without any fear. [Laughter] So that was good. You know, I loved all those ports out there, Japanese, Hong Kong. Don't know how Hong Kong is now. I guess we're going to find out soon.[*] The Stennis is going to make a port call out there, as I understand, so we'll find out.[†]

Paul Stillwell: What were the satisfactions to having command after being in subordinate positions previously?

Admiral Shelton: Oh, I think you kind of realize that you've been talking about all these things all this time, and now it's your turn to see if you can do something. I felt I did. I would have liked to have had a little different kind of tour as CO of VF-92, and I don't think I really should get into that. But I would have liked to have a little different kind of tour on there. But, aside from that, I felt that I had helped further the whole business of night and all weather. I had a bunch of guys that felt the same way, and we didn't have any lazy guys in the squadron. They all wanted to fly. They all did fly. I think we

---

[*] In 1898 Great Britain was granted a 99-year lease to the area known as the New Territories, including Hong Kong. The area reverted to China in July 1997.
[†] USS John C. Stennis (CVN-74), a nuclear-powered aircraft carrier commissioned 9 December 1995.

carved a slight niche there in the passage of time that helped get things going towards the 24-hour all-weather capability. Certainly we weren't to that point.

On that <u>Ranger</u> cruise, when I was CO of VF-92, the Sparrow was a new missile, capable of head-on intercept. I was eager to "train up" myself and the pilots in the squadron in its use. We used a towed radar target, called the Del Mar, which housed in a receptacle under the F3H's wing, and which could be streamed some 2,000-plus feet, as I recall, by cable. Utilizing the F3H's intercept and the carrier's intercept guidance, we could make head-on intercepts. Then, when the tow with the streamed Del Mar called "safe," we would be able to fire at the Del Mar. At first we had a lot of trouble with the Del Mar, which we could not get to stream properly and then also could not retract it. So we lost several Del Mars before we got that squared away.

We also had problems with the Sparrow not performing as advertised. Eventually, after a lot of hard work, we had a series of successful intercepts and shoots. The problems we solved were reflected in successful exercises of this type in later squadrons, on later cruises. I might add that a strong impetus to solve the problems was the fact that Rear Admiral Tom Connolly was the cardiv commander on the <u>Ranger</u> at the time, and he showed a strong personal "How-goes-it?" interest in our efforts.

Aside from other aspects of the cruise, I personally became a <u>Ranger</u> centurion during the cruise, as I had during the VF-124 cruise on <u>Lexington</u> back in 1957.

Paul Stillwell: Well, by the time you had your own squadron you must have been one of the senior evangelists for the idea of 24-hour, all-weather capability.

Admiral Shelton: Yes, I guess I was, although nobody ever let me say that. [Laughter] Nobody seemed to care whether I was or not at that point. I'll put it that way. Well, I could put it a different way. I certainly was not looked at in the way that Chick Harmer and W. I. Martin were looked at in their day as evangelists of the thing. Certainly I was trying to do my share, but there were a lot of other guys that were trying to do their share, too, and so I don't think I stood out at that point. I might have thought I did, but I don't think I did. [Laughter]

Paul Stillwell: Anything else on that tour that you'd want to mention?

Admiral Shelton: No. I think the Ranger tour, that's about all I want to say about it. It was a successful tour, and nobody got hurt. I think we advanced the cause a little bit. It was successful, and I enjoyed working both for Captain Leonard as the CO and I enjoyed having the opportunity under Admiral Connolly being on there and Bill McClendon, whom I also knew.

Going back a bit, because of the engine-caused accident a couple of days before I became CO, I went to AirPac and got permission for Norm Danielson, the Allison rep we had in VF-124, to join VF-92 on the Ranger cruise. As in VF-124, Norm played a significant role in our successful deployment on Ranger.

Paul Stillwell: Well, this is probably a logical breaking point. You've put in a marathon session today, for which I'm most grateful.

Admiral Shelton: So have you.

Paul Stillwell: Thank you.

Admiral Shelton: Yes, it's great.

Paul Stillwell: We got off to a magnificent start today, and I look forward to the next installment.

Admiral Shelton: Well, thank you.

Interview Number 2 with Rear Admiral Doniphan B. Shelton, U.S. Navy (Retired)
Place: Admiral Shelton's home in Del Mar, California
Date: Friday, 11 February 2000
Interviewer: Paul Stillwell

Paul Stillwell: Well, Admiral, it's really an appropriate place to conduct an interview here this morning. You showed me a den filled with seashells, which are treasures from the sea. And, as we look out the picture windows of this room, the sea is coming toward us in the background, and the surf is breaking on the beach a few hundred yards away. It's a beautiful sunny morning and a great atmosphere to talk about an oceangoing career.

Admiral Shelton: Right. And I have a frog in my throat from all the talking I did yesterday, which is more than I normally do. But, anyway, before we started this, you mentioned that the recorder wasn't on when I talked about the one big bomb hit that I got out there in the Korean situation up around Hungnam, so I'll repeat that.

As I recall, there were a couple of ADs and a couple of F4U-5Ns including myself in on this. And it was a dusk hop, as I recall. My logbook doesn't show whether it was a dusk hop or a 3:00 o'clock in the morning hop, but anyway it was dark whether it morning or early dusk. We got up to Hungnam, and we were surprised to find two long trains, obviously freight trains of one kind of another, sitting still, parked right there in the Hungnam rail yards and headed in opposite directions. Obviously, we couldn't tell what was on them, but it looked like a hell of a good target. So we started dive-bombing.

We were carrying either 250s or 500s, I've forgotten which—I believe 250s—but in any event after about one or two runs I was lucky enough to be the guy that got the hit.[*] And we were making about 80-degree dives, maybe 85 degrees. We didn't have any speed brakes on the F4U-5N, so we weren't quite as steep as we might have been otherwise. But anyway we were pulling out. That meant we were pulling out fairly low, because we were starting somewhere around 5,000-6,000 feet.

---
[*] The numbers refer to 250- and 500-pound bombs.

My bomb hit, and everything blew up down there, and by the time I pulled out it had hit just behind me, of course, and the stuff starting coming by me and the guy behind me, it started coming up around him. So the debris from those two trains was going up about, oh, at least 1,500 feet in the air, maybe more than that. As we learned later, one train was filled with ammo, and the other train was filled with fuel, so it made a pretty good combination. The explosion was such that it cast a pretty big glow in the sky.

Hutch Cooper, who was the intelligence officer on the cardiv staff on the Princeton, where we had taken off, had been following not only this hop but a lot of the nighttime hops where we were going after certain targets and all that kind of stuff.* And the carrier was roughly 75 miles away from Hungnam at that point. And this explosion was such that it was so big that we all of sudden heard this voice on the radio saying, "I saw that," and that was Hutch Cooper saying that he'd seen the explosion all the way back to the carrier. As it turns out, he sent a photo plane over the next morning, and, sure enough, there was a hell of a big crater right there at the train station, and both trains were pretty well obliterated.

Paul Stillwell: Were the trains moving when you attacked them?

Admiral Shelton: No. They were parked in the yard still so, no, they weren't moving at all.

Paul Stillwell: Did you use your radar to home in on the target?

Admiral Shelton: No. This was not a radar target and very little of the interdiction that we did over there depended on radar—little or none, really—because the radar we had on the F4Us was strictly an intercept radar, not much good for ground mapping. It did have a longer-range mode, where, for instance, if you were out over the ocean and you were looking for your carrier 15 or 20 miles away, you could certainly pick it up on the search mode. But as far as using it for interdiction purposes, it was of no use. You had to make your bomb drops visually anyway, so the radar was no help from that standpoint.

---

* Lieutenant Commander Damon W. Cooper, USN.

Paul Stillwell: Well, you must have had some light then to be able to see the target.

Admiral Shelton: Yes. We probably got there just as it was beginning to get dark, and so there was still a little light, but also at that time of the year there's a lot of snow on the ground and there wasn't much light around. Nobody was showing any lights of course, and most of the nights were reasonably clear. Some of them very clear. And so against the snow backdrop on the ground you really had better than average visibility, much more than you would think that you would have.

Paul Stillwell: Could you identify a time on that one chronologically when that incident took place?

Admiral Shelton: My logbook shows the date to be May 18, 1951, with a day cat shot and a night carrier landing.

Paul Stillwell: Another thing that we talked about, before the tape recorder started you had a few additional observations on R. Ritchie Robertson from your high school days.

Admiral Shelton: Yes, when I was talking about him I was a little bit caught up in trying to get started, and I probably forgot a number of things that I wanted to say. But, anyway, R. Ritchie was such an influence on the young people in Springfield and such a good influence I should say. He was famous for one of his sayings, which he liked to say quite often, and that is, "You teach a boy to blow a horn, and he'll never blow a safe." And I think that's a pretty good thing. He was quite a man, and he was certainly parental distance from all of us as Boy Scouts and in the Boy Scout band and in the high school band and everything. But at the same time he knew each and every one of our names and our parents and everything like that.

Paul Stillwell: And how good a musician you were.

Admiral Shelton: And how good a musician we were. As a matter of fact, he even saw to it that my first cornet was a gift from him indirectly through the Kiwanis Club there in Springfield.

Paul Stillwell: You told me that you talked to his daughter and the results of some parental distance there.

Admiral Shelton: Oh, yes. His youngest daughter, Doreen, was a half a class ahead of me in high school, and several years ago, a lot of us convened back there in Springfield for a dedication of the R. Ritchie Robertson memorial at the high school and a beautiful bronze bust. So I kind of singled out Doreen. I knew her quite well. I asked her what kind of a father he was. I said, "You know, we all know what kind of a man he was and all that kind of stuff but what kind of a father was he?"

She said, "Well, you know how fathers are. He was pretty strict with us and pretty tough. He was fair, but he was pretty tough."

I said, "Well, I guess that's about the normal way we all think about him in some respects." But he was a great man.

Paul Stillwell: But a lot of affection nonetheless.

Admiral Shelton: Oh, yes. Oh, absolutely. He had a beautiful wife that we didn't see very often. She sort of stayed in the background, but she obviously kept everything running in the household quite nicely.

Paul Stillwell: You just made a brief mention yesterday to being catapult officer in the cruiser St. Louis. What was involved in that duty?

Admiral Shelton: Well, what was involved in it was that they had to have somebody to be the catapult officer. I was a fresh-caught ensign on there, and that was one of those kinds of duties that the gunnery officer on there, I'm sure, thought that an ensign could be expected to handle. So I was designated as the catapult officer, and at that time we had the old SOCs on there, a biplane, Curtiss biplane, scout plane.* The two aviators on there that flew the airplane got me aside, as did the gunnery officer, and taught me the fundamentals of how you give the signals back and forth of when the pilot's ready and when you're ready and so forth and how you're going to launch him, and so we went through that. As I recall, those were all cartridge-type catapults. I don't think they were spring-loaded, so to speak. I think they were all cartridge-type, so when he gave the signal, why, you fired the cartridge, and that gave the impetus to the catapult to launch the airplane.

Paul Stillwell: It was essentially a 5-inch powder charge, wasn't it?

Admiral Shelton: I didn't remember whether it was a 3-inch or a 5-inch, but it probably was 5-inch, because I don't think you could get that much out of a 3-inch powder charge.

Paul Stillwell: And there's a very sudden impulse.

Admiral Shelton: Very sudden impulse. It put their heads back against the headrests. After we got hit by the kamikaze and came back to Long Beach, why, the SOCs were replaced with the SC-1, which was a low-wing airplane that looked quite a bit like a fighter.† In fact, had quite a bit more performance than the old SOC had had.

You know, it was a good deal for me. I was interested in aviation, and there I was back there launching these guys. I didn't have too much to do with the recovery. In those days they did what they called a Cast recovery, which was the ship would make a turn so that it provided a slick back there on the port quarter.‡ The deck division basically back there at the hangar area would rig out the crane that was on the stern, and

---

* The Curtiss-built SOC Seagull was a biplane that first entered fleet squadrons in 1935, primarily in a floatplane version to perform observation and scouting missions for battleships and cruisers. It served through World War II. The SOC-1 version was 31 feet long, had a wingspan of 36 feet, gross weight of 5,437 pounds, and maximum speed of 165 miles an hour. It was armed with two .30-caliber machine guns.
† The Curtiss SC-1 Seahawk was a monoplane that first went into fleet service in October 1944 to perform observation and scouting missions for battleships and cruisers. The SC-1 was 36 feet long, had a wingspan of 41 feet, gross weight of 9,000 pounds, and maximum speed of 313 miles an hour. It was armed with two .50-caliber machine guns.
‡ "Cast" represented the letter C in the phonetic alphabet of the time.

the pilot would land in the slick, hopefully as close as he could to the net without overshooting it. There was a net in the water, so that as he taxied up there was a hook on the bottom of the float, and this hook would engage in the net. Then the crane operators, without hitting the pilot in the head as he was standing up in the cockpit, would manage to get the pelican hook over to him so the pilot could engage the crane hook onto an apparatus on the airplane there. Then they would hoist the airplane back aboard. That was the trickiest part of the whole thing really, was that if the crane operator wasn't pretty good, why, he could have done some severe damage to the pilot, especially with the pilot standing up there essentially not in the airplane. More standing there trying to engage the crane hook in the apparatus to be hoisted back aboard.

Paul Stillwell: Well, there was a disadvantage going to the SC because there wasn't a rear-seat man to help out with the process.

Admiral Shelton: That's true. There was not a back-seat man. These two fellows on there were kind of frustrated carrier pilots anyway, so I think they welcomed the SC because they could do more with it. Not my recollection that either one of them ever got into any dogfights with either one of those airplanes, the SOC or the SC-1, but they did do a lot of search and recce and gun spotting, that kind of thing.

Paul Stillwell: You talked also when we weren't recording about some of the opposition of the higher levels of the hierarchy to the night fighter concept. Did you feel that you were shoveling against the tide in this project?

Admiral Shelton: I don't know of anybody that was in the night program that at times didn't feel like they were shoveling against the tide, so to speak. I think Korea was good in one respect, that it really was the first combat evolution where there was almost a 24-hour capability. There was a capability but not a 24-hour schedule. But for sure the ADs and the F4Us were flying every night that it was possible to fly. So I think in that sense the Korean War did a lot to further the cause of the night program and eventually the all-weather program and a 24-hour capability on the carriers.

There still was a hang-up as far as a lot of the people up the chain of command as far as the capabilities of the airplanes and the people that were in the night program. That filtered down to even my level on numerous occasions. I know that at one point there was a recommendation that had gone forward all the way up to who I think at the time was Admiral Beauty Martin, who I think is the same Martin that was later ComNavAirPac.[*] I'm not sure of that, but I think he was.

Paul Stillwell: Yes, he was.

Admiral Shelton: In any event, he was one of those that didn't think that the night program was all that valuable as far as interdiction was concerned and all that sort of thing and damage to the enemy. So the recommendation that had gone up to him was for some special recognition for the night people. It came back down with not only a "No" but a "Hell, no," so to speak, so at that time there was still that barrier with a lot of folks that just didn't think that it was worth doing at night, trying to do at night.

My personal conviction was that the night program in Korea was exceptionally rewarding in terms of damage to the transportation system out there and everything that we went after. And it was my opinion that we did as much or more damage to the enemy at night out there as the day guys did with flying at day because in many cases we found a lot of things that were travelling at night because they didn't want to travel during the daytime.

Paul Stillwell: Well, perhaps a legacy from that is that when Admiral Pirie was DCNO for Air we were bringing along what became the A-6. It was a dedicated plane for an all-weather attack capability, and that airframe in fact is still flying.[†]

---

[*] Vice Admiral Harold M. Martin, USN, served as Commander Air Force Pacific Fleet from 1 April 1952 to 1 February 1956. He had previously served as Commander Seventh Fleet from 28 March 1951 to 3 March 1952.

[†] The Grumman-built A-6 Intruder was the Navy's principal carrier-based bomber from the early 1960s to the 1990s. VA-75 and VA-196, the last two attack squadrons equipped with A-6 Intruder, went out of commission 28 February 1997. The airframe is still in service in the form of the EA-6B Prowler, an electronic warfare plane.

Admiral Shelton: Well, I just said, you know, the Korean War, I thought, had a really good effect on working towards the 24-hour all-weather capability. I guess really it takes a war almost to make something like that come about. Yes, the A-6 came along, and it was a tremendous boost to the all-weather capability, no question about that. And, of course, the next big one was Vietnam, and we certainly operated almost 24 hours a day there for the most part. So it was slow getting there, but it finally did get there, and, of course, we have a tremendous capability today.

Paul Stillwell: There has to be a lot of satisfaction for you in helping to bring that about.

Admiral Shelton: Yes. I thought I was there at the right time, and probably I was. Maybe I'd like to have stayed around a little bit longer to reap some the benefits of it. I don't know. But I like to feel that I did my little share in the whole thing.

Paul Stillwell: Well, we talked yesterday about your tour as CO of VF-92 on board the Ranger. Anything to add to that discussion?

Admiral Shelton: Not really.

Paul Stillwell: Did you get dragged ashore after that?

Admiral Shelton: Yes. Let's see. Actually, we had left from Alameda, but VF-92 became VF-52—I believe it was when we got back to Miramar, our new home base. It was still 92 as long as I had it, but I think right after that it became VF-52.

Anyway, I had orders to go to the Naval War College. As a matter of fact, I got the orders about a month before we got back. But, being at sea, I wasn't in a position where I could do anything early about finding a place to live in Newport. I got all the literature saying, "Now, it's important that if you want to find some quarters back here that you try to do something about it as early as you can." Well, it's pretty hard to do that when you're still halfway across the ocean. So we got back here and had the change of command, and I detached.

We got back to Newport, and the best we could do was to get into the cramped quarters at Breton Village, I think it's called. Pretty small. Still had the old steam radiators in it. Wasn't much to look at and wasn't much to live in but it was home. It was right next to the Hammersmith Farm, Jackie Kennedy's mother's farm I guess it is. And that in turn was right across the street from the Newport Country Club, which extended playing privileges to all the students at the war college, so that was neat.

Paul Stillwell: Well, again, this is another opportunity like the staff college to broaden your knowledge of the profession.

Admiral Shelton: Well, I really didn't look at it that way at the time. [Laughter] I drug my heels all the way back there, to tell you the truth. But that turned out to be one of the best years I had in the Navy. I'm not sure my wife would say the same thing, because it was her burden to have to type all of my papers because I couldn't type. That was one of the requirements at the college, and so you could easily seek out a person there at the college that would type your papers for five cents a page, or you could bang on your wife if she typed. And fortunately my wife, I don't think she was thinking too straight, but anyway she agreed to do all my typing.

Paul Stillwell: And the marriage survived.

Admiral Shelton: And the marriage survived. And it wasn't easy. But while I was there I signed on for the George Washington University course to get my master's in international relations, so that extended me one month beyond the normal time at the war college. But I really did thoroughly enjoy the year there once I got into it, and I wouldn't give anything for it at this point. It was great.

Paul Stillwell: What was the substance of the things that you were studying?

Admiral Shelton: Well, it was all strategy, and we had the benefit of listening to a lot of good powerful people. All the powers from Washington would come up and talk to us at various times through the year, fitting in with the various courses we were taking. And everybody had to pick a subject to write a paper on, and so I did that. I was able to use that same paper for my thesis in the GW program. So it ended up being a really fine year.

Paul Stillwell: What was the topic of your paper?

Admiral Shelton: At that time it was called "The Leapfrogging Soviets." It was kind of a combination of their military and merchant marine capability and what they were doing here and there in the world to baffle us and all that sort of thing.

Paul Stillwell: And in fact that capability really blossomed in the late '60s.

Admiral Shelton: It really did. That was '62, of course, and that's when the Cuban Crisis took place, so that was big news while we were there.* We were kept probably as well informed there at the war college about that situation as anybody, other than the people that were actually involved in it of course. We didn't know the minute-to-minute details on a timely basis, but we were kept pretty well briefed, and that was pretty good we all thought.

Paul Stillwell: Do you remember any of the guest speakers that came in?

Admiral Shelton: Well, no I really don't by name at this point, but they were people like the Secretary of Defense and chiefs of all the services and the Secretary of State and everybody.

Paul Stillwell: Did you get more of an idea how to do staff work?

---

* The Cuban Missile Crisis was triggered in mid-October 1962, when a U.S. reconnaissance plane photographed a Soviet nuclear missile site in Cuba and the presence of Soviet bombers. On 22 October President John F. Kennedy went on national television to announce a naval quarantine of Cuba, to be implemented on 24 October. On 28 October Premier Nikita Khrushchev of the Soviet Union notified President Kennedy that he was ordering the withdrawal of Soviet bombers and missiles from Cuba.

Admiral Shelton: It really wasn't a staff course. The junior course at the war college at that time was more of a staff situation, but the senior course that I was in was more thinking about the various strategic implications of any given situation, and we did a little war-gaming. Not as much as they did in the junior course, but we did some.

Paul Stillwell: Is this still on a tile deck, on the floor of a big hall?

Admiral Shelton: Yes, right. Still there. It was then.

Paul Stillwell: It wasn't yet to the electronic wizardry?

Admiral Shelton: No, no, this was with long handles and push the ship models around, you know.

Paul Stillwell: And throw the dice.

Admiral Shelton: But we didn't do a whole lot of that. As I said, that was more in the junior course. But the senior course was more of a read a lot, think a lot, listen a lot and try to make up your mind about various aspects of what was going on in the world.

Paul Stillwell: Geopolitical type things?

Admiral Shelton: Geopolitical type things.

Paul Stillwell: Was the Southeast Asia issue large enough yet to be discussed?

Admiral Shelton: Not really, not really. No.

Paul Stillwell: Did it have a benefit in acquainting you with more of your contemporaries of the naval profession?

Admiral Shelton: Yes, and also the other services. We had senior officers from the Army and Air Force there. As a matter of fact, the senior officer in our class was an Army colonel, and one of my roommates, Army Colonel Bob Studer, had been a POW in Manila during the war, so it was a good solid crossbreeding of a lot of information.* And there were various chairs up there at the college which were all filled by knowledgeable people. One of our classmates was a fellow named Frank Maestrone, who later became ambassador to Egypt and Kuwait.† He lives right here in San Diego, and I'm fortunate enough to see him once in a while. I also knew him out in Manila when he was in the embassy in Manila before he became an ambassador.

Paul Stillwell: Did you get exposed to Admiral Eccles, the guru of logistics?‡

Admiral Shelton: Yes. I don't think that anybody ever went through the war college at that point that didn't get exposed to that. I've got to say that that wasn't a favorite subject of very many people, but he made everybody understand that that's what won wars.

Paul Stillwell: And he's right.

Admiral Shelton: And he's right. Yes, he's right.

Paul Stillwell: When you were going against that rail yard in Hungnam, you had to have the bombs, you had to have the fuel, you had to have the spare parts for the radars.

Admiral Shelton: Yes, and what we were knocking out was the same thing on the other side.

---

* Colonel Robert L. Studer, USA.
† Frank E. Maestrone, a Foreign Service Officer, was U.S. ambassador to Kuwait, 1976-79, and in 1980 was director of the U.S. Sinai Support Mission. He also held several posts in NATO.
‡ Upon retirement from active duty in 1952, Rear Admiral Henry E. Eccles, USN, began a 25-year second career as head of the logistics department of the Naval War College; he was a prolific author.

Paul Stillwell: That's right. Any other of the staff members that you call to mind?

Admiral Shelton: No. Who was president at that time?

Paul Stillwell: It might have been Admiral Austin.

Admiral Shelton: Austin, Bernard Austin.* And he impressed different people different way, I guess. I think maybe some of them thought that he was kind of an old fuddy-duddy. My personal impression of him was that he was a pretty smart gent. He didn't force his way on the students, other than to try to make sure that they spent their time profitably and got something out of the course very profitably. But I thought he was a good man for the job.

Paul Stillwell: Some people have said it was useful just to take a break from the operational pace and have some time for reflection.

Admiral Shelton: Oh, I think that's true. You couldn't get me to admit it then [laughter], but after I got out of there and thought about it later on I would certainly agree with that. Yes, as I said, I drug my heels all the way back there, but in the end it was one of the most enjoyable years I've had.

Paul Stillwell: But, as I understand, it didn't have the competitiveness that it got later, that you pretty much could set your own pace.

Admiral Shelton: That's right. It was up to you to decide how much of it you wanted to absorb, and there was a little competition there because nobody wanted to look like a dumbbell of course. The only other competition, there was always an outstanding thesis paper, and I wasn't in that ballpark but I enjoyed it.

---

* Vice Admiral Bernard L. Austin, USN, served as president of the Naval War College from 30 June 1960 to 31 July 1964.

One of the things I enjoyed most at the war college, the GW course of course, but the old fellow that ran the GW course was a Professor Stout, and he was a typical professor who enjoyed having a pipe in his mouth all the time. I can remember that his idea of a good vacation was to go over to England and sit and watch the Parliament. Now, none of us at that point thought that that was much of a vacation, but that was his idea of a great vacation, go over to England and sit and watch the Parliament stew around.

Paul Stillwell: To each his own.

Admiral Shelton: To each his own. But he was a fine guy, and he would give his own little viewpoints on everything every now and then on this, that, and the other thing, and they were always to the point and well taken. And I think the body there, the student body, at the time sort of gave him something to think about because he'd never been around military people before. And there were some pretty sharp cookies in that class, and when it was all over he said one time that we probably had educated him as much as he'd educated us, and I think he meant it. He was a very sincere fellow, and I thought a lot of him.

Paul Stillwell: Are there any names of those sharp cookies that you remember?

Admiral Shelton: Well, yes. Frank Maestrone was one of them and my friend, William R. St. George, retired vice admiral, was one of them. And some of the others I don't remember by name right now. The Army guys basically had a free year because the Army system puts their people through a lot of schools, and so this was a hell of a fine school for them, but any of the staff work that we did they'd already done a hundred times. They didn't have to worry about that, so they could sit back and look into whatever they wanted to look into in more depth than most of the Navy guys could. The Air Force guys were pretty much like the Navy guys. They had not been introduced to too much of this, so they had to work at it too.

Paul Stillwell: What do you remember about the social life or just the life in Newport, for example.

Admiral Shelton: We generally limited that to the weekends and the ones that didn't have to work as hard to do well there, they would go to New York or go to Boston or go somewhere and do this and that and the other thing. Those of us, including me, that had to study harder didn't find that much time to go down to New York or up to Boston or whatever. We did get away once in a while to go to some of the places close by and do a little antiquing. My wife and I both love to go antiquing, and so we did a lot of that there. I don't know. It was really a good year all the way around. There was a different level of basic capability among all the students, and so you sort of adjusted your own effort to however much you had to do to satisfy yourself that you were doing as much as you should to learn what you should. But it was great.

Paul Stillwell: I'm sure it must have been fascinating to have that inside window on the Cuban Missile Crisis because that could affect the whole world.

Admiral Shelton: Yes. Of course we were all hanging there waiting to see what was going to happen. I think most of us were hoping we'd go down there and blow the hell out of them, but we didn't. [Laughter]

One of the things there was, as I said, we lived in Breton Village, and it was a pretty close community, these little old temporary structures that weren't much. But President Kennedy would come up there every once in a while, and when he did, why, the whole entourage came with him, of course, and they would move people out of a lot of those quarters. We were fortunate enough to be just outside the limit of where they needed to move people, but they would simply move everybody out of the quarters they wanted for as how long he was going to be there and put Secret Service people in there and all that kind of stuff. And he had his PT boat tied up at the dock down there, which is about a block from where we lived. So it was a little bit exciting just to know he was up there and see him and all that sort of thing. On the other hand, it was a great deal of inconvenience to a lot of people there in Breton Village.

Paul Stillwell: Where did they move to?

Admiral Shelton: Oh, they moved them over into dorms or whatever places they could find. They simply just moved them out literally.

Paul Stillwell: Tough if you've got a young family.

Admiral Shelton: Yes, that's right, and of course some of them went to school there on the base. There was a school right there in Breton Village, and others went into school out in town.

Paul Stillwell: What impressions do you have from seeing the President?

Admiral Shelton: I only saw him a couple of times, and my impression was, "Well, he's having a hell of a good time on that PT boat." [Laughter]

Paul Stillwell: He didn't get sunk this time.*

Admiral Shelton: Yes. Didn't get sunk this time, and otherwise I thought, "Well, you know, that's great." But that was my first introduction really to when somebody like that moves around into some area just how much disruption there is in that given area in order to accommodate that visit. That's pretty common these days, I guess, and everybody knows it and all that kind of stuff, but to us and particularly to me, I'd never been around anything like that so it was a little different insight into everything.

Paul Stillwell: I'm guessing that when it came time to move on to another tour you were ready to go.

---

* Shortly after midnight on 2 August 1943, while Lieutenant John F. Kennedy, USNR, was in command of PT-109, the motor torpedo boat was rammed and cut in two by a Japanese destroyer while operating in the Solomon Islands. Kennedy towed one of his crew members to safety after the collision and was awarded the Navy and Marine Corps Medal as a result.

Admiral Shelton: I was ready to go, and my wife was doubly ready to go. She was tired of typing my papers. I can remember to this day that one of the requirements for your thesis for the GWU thing was that each page had to be absolutely perfect. You couldn't have any erasures. No mistakes, no misspellings, no nothing.

Paul Stillwell: This is before word processors.

Admiral Shelton: That's right. Before word processors, and my wife was the word processor. It was very frustrating, of course, to get three-fourths of the way down a page and make some boo-boo that you had to go back and start all over. A long story of that was that we both stayed up all night the night before these papers had to be in. Finally got it finished about 5:00 o'clock in the morning. I went over there, and we had to give a little presentation. Five minutes was what it was, and I gave my little presentation. Went back home and we went to bed for two days, I think. I didn't give her five cents a page as I recall though. The only thing she got out of it was a little gold typewriter for her charm bracelet.

Paul Stillwell: Well, my wife very generously did the same thing for my thesis, and I remember that requirement about perfect pages.

Admiral Shelton: Yes.

Paul Stillwell: We had to take a break every once in a while just because she'd get so frustrated and tired of it. We had a child nine months later, so it had an additional benefit. [Laughter]

Admiral Shelton: Right. Well, I really couldn't believe that there were any kind of requirements like that in the world that a piece of paper had to be that absolutely perfect but there it was.

Paul Stillwell: Well, where to from there?

Admiral Shelton: Well, let's see. From there I got orders to be CAG-19. By that time they'd changed the name CAG to Commander Air Wing.* So I got orders to be Commander of Air Wing 19, which was again based out here on the West Coast at Lemoore.† By that time we had owned a house here in Del Mar on 15th Street, our second house in this area. So we moved the family into the house on 15th Street here in Del Mar, and I headquartered up at Lemoore. I wasn't going to be there very long, because I actually went out to Subic to take over command of the air group at Subic Bay so I didn't stick around.

As soon as we had time to get located and all that kind of thing, I went off and back out to the Western Pacific to Subic to take over command of Air Wing 19. A classmate of mine, Dick Alderton, had the air wing just before me, and I relieved him at Subic Bay.‡ By the time I actually went out there I had reported back here to Miramar and gone through the RAG and went through survival school, and so that used up three or four months, something like that, maybe more than that.§

Paul Stillwell: Could you tell me some more about the survival school please?

Admiral Shelton: Yes, it's up here in the hills not far from Ramona, and it's like anything that is a training device. Training devices are never like the real thing, but this gave a pretty good starting point for what you could expect if you were shot down.

Paul Stillwell: Part of it is to give you some incentive not to get caught.

---

* CAG—commander carrier air group. A carrier air group comprised all the planes assigned to the ship. The air group commander was the senior pilot in a flying billet, as opposed to being part of ship's company. In 1962 the Navy began using the term CVW, carrier air wing, in place of carrier air group, but the abbreviation CAG is still often used to denote the air wing commander.
† The Lemoore Naval Air Station, site of a master jet base, is in the San Joaquin Valley, ten miles west of Lemoore, California, and about 45 miles southwest of Fresno.
‡ Commander Dickson W. Alderton, USN.
§ Miramar Naval Air Station was near San Diego, California. It has since been turned over to the Marine Corps. RAG—a replacement air group is a squadron that trains pilots and other flight crew members in a specific type of aircraft before the personnel report to a fleet squadron that flies the particular plane.

Admiral Shelton: Not to get caught. That's right. I was the second senior guy. The senior guy going through at the time was a friend of mine named Jeep Streeper, and Jeep was a little guy about my size and about ten times as tough.* And he gave them all they could handle for a while while we were there. He lasted until the last day, and then the weather was so hot up there, and he got so antagonistic about what was going on that he actually had a heat stroke, and so they had to get him some medical treatment. But still, even that was an example of what can happen if you're caught in that circumstance.

The emphasis in those days primarily was getting everybody through there that were going to be involved in any kind of a squadron or air wing or whatever that had a nuclear capability, and of course they all had it at that time. So almost all the senior people were going through that school as well as a lot of junior people, primarily to see if they could withstand that sort of thing. There were a few that even under those training circumstances that didn't pass the course, and so they were transferred to other units, other squadrons, where nuclear capabilities weren't involved. But the emphasis was certainly on that. I wouldn't say they were trying to weed anybody out, but they were certainly looking for any evidence on anybody's part, particularly air crewmen, that might be expected to give in earlier.

Paul Stillwell: Was there training on how to resist interrogation and brainwashing?

Admiral Shelton: Yes. Basically it was name, rank, and serial number. There wasn't a whole lot of training beyond that as far as that. They said, "You know, all these things are a different situation, and there going to be different for each individual and it's the amount of whatever treatment you're going to get is going to be different." And so there wasn't a whole lot they could tell you as far as what to expect, I don't think, except there was a kind of an overhang thing saying there that, "You know, you're going to have a hard time being a winner in this situation, because they're going to do everything they can to make sure that you're not a winner." I think those that were unfortunate enough to be POWs in Vietnam certainly evidenced that philosophy. Hard to be a winner, but all except a few were.

---

* Commander Harold P. Streeper, USN.

Paul Stillwell: Well, the North Vietnamese demonstrated that everyone had a breaking point, and the idea was to push it farther and farther before you got to that point.

Admiral Shelton: That's right. Well, that's right. Bend as far as you can if you have to, but don't go the whole way. And I think for the most part they all succeeded in doing that there. I guess there were a few that didn't succeed, but that's pretty much true. If you take 100 people under any given circumstances there's going to be that percentage that, that 2%, as they say, that don't pass the course.

Paul Stillwell: Were you in the part of it that you go out into the wild and have to survive on whatever you can find?

Admiral Shelton: Yes. There wasn't very much of that. There was only about one day of that really, where they took you on about a seven-mile deal, and you had to exist as you could and then try to fight your way back. But most of it was right there in the camp, and they would put you in the black boxes and all that sort of thing. Put you in there without any clothes on, and then later on throw a bunch of clothes in there and tell you to get them on as best you could, and there wasn't much room in there to get them on. So it was a lesson in "Don't get too eager to do too many things too fast" because if you're in a situation where you are cramped up and everything, you kind of go hog wild about trying to do it. For instance, just the exercise of their throwing the clothes in there in a round tube or in a box telling you get them on. The box was not big enough for you to make very much movement, and so you had to do it very slowly, a little bit at a time. Don't get over-exercised. Don't get yourself all bent out of shape, all cramped up. Even the possibility of leg cramps, that kind of stuff.

Paul Stillwell: Don't panic.

Admiral Shelton: Don't panic. Do it a little bit a time and keep the goal in mind that you're trying to beat them, not the other way around. But it was worthwhile. I came back down out of there. I had a flight suit on, of course. That's what we all had on that were aviators, and it was pretty ragged by the time I came back down out of there, and then I had a pretty big beard by the time I came back down out of there. We were living down here on 26th Street on the beach at Del Mar at that time. I drove up. Somebody drove me up there, I guess, and I got out. My youngest daughter, Donna, was five years old by then I guess and, man, she didn't even know who I was, and she was scared of whoever this was [laughter] with the beard and the outrageous looking flight suit. She thought I was there to do some harm.

Paul Stillwell: The bogeyman.

Admiral Shelton: The bogeyman. [Laughter] And to this day she still remembers when I came back from survival school.

Paul Stillwell: You said you went through the RAG. Did they run you through all the planes in the air wing?

Admiral Shelton: They gave you gave a certain amount of time in them. I didn't get any time in the A-3, for instance, and I was based at Lemoore, so I elected to stay up there, and that meant flying A-4s mostly. And the F8U squadrons were down here, and 191 and 194, they were under the exceptionally capable hands of Jack Snyder and Billy Phillips, so there weren't any problems there.* And we had good AD squadrons. It was a good air wing all the way around. We left Subic and made what amounted to the first of the Indian Ocean cruises. It was called the Concord Squadron Cruise.

Paul Stillwell: What ship?

---

* The F8U Crusader was a jet fighter built by Chance Vought. It first entered fleet squadrons in 1957. In 1962 the aircraft was redesignated F-8. Commander Jack L. Snyder, USN, was commanding officer of Fighter Squadron 191; Commander Billy Phillips, USN, was CO of VF-194.

Admiral Shelton: That was the Bon Homme Richard.* And we went all the way to Mombasa. The Shah was still in power in Iran at that time, and we put on an air show for the Shah.† He flew his own airplane down to some little airfield there on the coast of Iran and then came aboard in a S-2 COD.‡ He spent the whole day, two days I guess, one day anyway. And it was pretty exciting to see him. He was a pilot himself. He loved to talk about flying, so he got around to all the ready rooms and talked to all the guys. Took a look at all the airplanes.

Paul Stillwell: So it appeared to be a genuine interest, not just an walkthrough.

Admiral Shelton: Oh, yes. There was no question about that on his part. It was not just a perfunctory walkthrough for him. I think the airplane that he had at the time in Iran was a Stinson Reliant, which was a pretty fine airplane [laughter] in the old days. I'm not sure of that, but I think that's the airplane that he had. He flew his own airplane all the time, but when he got out there on the carrier he was genuinely interested in everything that was going on and wanted to talk to people and look at the airplanes and got around the whole ship.

Paul Stillwell: Did you get into the Persian Gulf?

Admiral Shelton: No, we did not. We stayed just outside the Persian Gulf?

Paul Stillwell: The Gulf of Oman.

---

* USS Bon Homme Richard (CV-31), an Essex-class aircraft carrier, was commissioned 2 March 1946. She had a standard displacement of 30,800 tons, was 888 feet long, 93 feet in the beam, extreme width of 136 feet, and a maximum draft of 29 feet. Her top speed was 33 knots. Originally she had 12 5-inch gun mounts and could accommodate approximately 80 aircraft. On 1 October 1953 she was reclassified as an attack carrier, CVA-31. She went out of commission from 1953 to 1955 for a modernization that included installation of an angled flight deck, enclosed bow, and steam catapults. She remained in service until decommissioned on 2 July 1971.
† Mohammad Reza Pahlavi (1919-1980) became Shah of Iran (or Persia, as it was then known) in 1941 and held office until his regime was ousted in 1979 by the Ayatollah Khomeini. His visit to the Bon Homme Richard was on 2-3 May 1964.
‡ COD—carrier on-board delivery, an aircraft configured for carrier takeoffs and landings, dedicated to transporting personnel and cargo between ship and shore. The Grumman S-2 antisubmarine plane had a logistics version known as the C-1 Trader.

Admiral Shelton: Yes. And before that we had been to Mombasa, Kenya, which was pretty interesting.

Paul Stillwell: Please tell me about that.

Admiral Shelton: Well, it was just a nice stop and we had access to go into Kenya, to Nairobi, and so we got a chance to do a little bit of the safari bit. They had a nice golf course there at Mombasa, so we had a chance to play golf there. The shopping was pretty good there at Mombasa. Brought back a lot of printed cotton material for various people that had wanted some.

Paul Stillwell: I've heard that venereal disease is rampant there, so probably there were some lectures to the crew members.

Admiral Shelton: All kinds of lectures. Yes. And I think they were effective. I don't recall that we had much trouble there. We had been, I've forgotten now whether it was just before that or just after but we also went to Diego Suarez, which is a French island. And that was pretty interesting. There were a couple of destroyer squadrons there. And Diego Suarez itself is a rather French Foreign Legion type looking place, and so I couldn't say too much for that, but the bread was good and the wine was good so we had a lot of bread and wine while we were there. [Laughter] There was a little kind of an O-club there that they made available to us, and as I said there wasn't a whole lot of superb things, but the people were exceptionally hospitable and so we had a good time.

Paul Stillwell: Where did you get your logistic support when you were out in the Indian Ocean?

Admiral Shelton: We didn't take anybody with us, but we met here and there, as I recall. I wasn't really into that bag at that time, but as I recall we met coming and going and got whatever we needed. As far as the air wing was concerned, one of my highest priorities when I first took over was to get together with the squadrons and go down the lists and make sure we had everything on board that we were going to need because there weren't going to be many places where we could get it out there.

There was some argument in those days about the advisability of operating F8Us at night off the 27 Charlies, which was the class that Bon Homme was.[*] And I've got to say that Jack Snyder and Billy Phillips made it look pretty easy. They both were great COs, and they did a great job with their squadrons. But we kept everybody in the air wing night qualified all the way through the Indian Ocean without a bingo field and no accidents, so that was pretty good.[†] I'm not sure too many people at that time appreciated the significance of that, but it was a pretty good little trick.

Paul Stillwell: Was it becoming more of a norm that a whole air wing would be night qualified?

Admiral Shelton: Yes. Let's see, that was '64, so by that time they were getting around to that. As I said, the argument really at that point was kind of whether or not it was really a good thing to operate the F8Us at night on the 27 Charlie. And I think there were some arguments on both sides, and it took a pretty good, it took some doing for those guys to do that but as I said Billy Phillips and Jack Snyder. And they had some good guys in those two squadrons, Chuck Dimon and John Dixon, Tom Cawley, Dick Moseley, and some others.[‡] They were all gung ho and first rate.

Paul Stillwell: What do you remember about the considerations of having nuclear weapons on board, both from a security standpoint and then practicing the routes that you would fly?

---

[*] During the 1950s several of the carriers of the Essex (CV-9) class were modernized. The 27C package included improved arresting gear and catapults and an additional deck-edge elevator. Hull beam was increased to 103 feet and full-load displacement to 41,900 tons.

[†] "Bingo" is a slang term for an alternate landing field ashore in the event planes can't get aboard the carrier.

[‡] Lieutenant Commander Charles G. Dimon, USN; Commander John C. Dixon, USN, executive officer of VF-191; Lieutenant Commander Thomas J. Cawley, USN; Commander Richard E. Moseley, USN, executive officer of VF-194.

Admiral Shelton: We didn't get into that too much on that cruise, to tell you the truth. In the Philippines there were routes that you could practice all the low-level stuff, and for the most part the A-1s and A-4s were doing all that, and they had it pretty well in hand.* So I didn't have to worry too much about that. As far as the other aspects of the nuclear parts, that wasn't my concern. That was the ship's concern and other people's concerns, so I didn't really have to worry about that.

Paul Stillwell: Was the loft maneuver being used?

Admiral Shelton: Let's see. That was '64. Yes, the loft maneuver was being used then, and we had all gone through that.† I got my part of that in RAG before I got out there, both up at Lemoore and over at Yuma. And, of course, at Lemoore anybody with a nuclear capability and responsibility had to go through the targeting sessions that they had. You had to build up your own folder and know where it was that you were supposed to go and all that kind of stuff. It mostly boiled down to the fact that you had to realize you probably weren't going to come back [laughter] because if everybody went in that was supposed to go in and at the time they were supposed to go in, and if it wasn't any better coordinated than you might expect with all the B-52s and everything else, why, there were going to be a lot of things going off all around everywhere and your chances of getting back probably were slim. Even your chances of getting to where you were supposed to go probably weren't too really good. But nobody worried about that particularly.

Paul Stillwell: For a lot of reasons it's good that we didn't have a nuclear conflagration.

---

* Douglas AD Skyraider propeller-driven attack planes first entered fleet squadrons in late 1946. The AD-2 version was 38 feet long, wingspan of 50 feet, gross weight of 18,263 pounds, and top speed of 321 miles per hour. In September 1962 Skyraiders still in service were redesignated A-1s. The Douglas A4D Skyhawk jet attack plane first entered the fleet in October 1956 in squadron VA-72. The A4D was 40 feet, 4 inches long, wingspan of 27 feet, 6 inches, gross weight of 24,500 pounds, and top speed of 670 miles per hour. In 1962 the aircraft was redesignated the A-4.

† The loft bombing method was designed as a tactic to prevent airplanes from being damaged by their own nuclear bombs. The method called for the pilot to make a low-altitude approach to the target and pull up into the first part of a Cuban 8. The bomb would be released as the aircraft reached about 45-degree angle during the climb. The pilot then completed the half of the Cuban 8 and flew back in the direction from which he had made his approach.

Admiral Shelton: Yes, that's right.

Paul Stillwell: Well, being the CAG is the last pure flying job for a carrier aviator. You're at the top of the pinnacle.

Admiral Shelton: Yes.

We did have one incident there coming back out of the Indian Ocean. Coming out of the Malacca Straits, why, we were flying, and one of Billy Phillips's F8Us was trying to come aboard. He was putting her right in the wires every time, but he wasn't catching the wire. I happened to be up at PriFly at the time along with Billy Phillips, and after the pilot made about five or six passes we decided that he wasn't going to catch a wire. That whatever was wrong with the hook, and we ventured the guess that, I asked him if the hook point could be on backwards. The general consensus was that you couldn't put an F8U hook point on backwards. So anyway the captain of the Bon Homme made the decision. We launched all the tankers we had available, including the A-4s, and we escorted this guy, Bill Kiper, as I remember, and they escorted him out as far as they could and tanked him and he bingoed all the way to Cubi Point, which is some 1,000-1,100 miles.* [Laughter] So I think that may be one of the longest bingos on record.

Paul Stillwell: I would think so.

Admiral Shelton: And when he landed at Cubi Point and got a chance to look and everything, yeah, the hook point was on backwards [laughter], so he never would have caught a wire. But that's the only one that even came close to being a situation.

Paul Stillwell: Did you have group efforts in which more than one squadron would fly together, you as CAG?

---

* Lieutenant William D. Kiper, USN. Cubi Point Naval Air Station was at Subic Bay in the Philippines.

Admiral Shelton: Not really. It was pretty much all singled up kind of stuff in those days.

Paul Stillwell: Just proficiency flying?

Admiral Shelton: Yes, fighters would fight each other and the ADs would do their long navigation stuff and all that kind of stuff. But there wasn't much of a group-grope effort. The only thing that approached being a group-grope effort was the air show for the Shah of Iran.

Paul Stillwell: Who was the captain of the ship?

Admiral Shelton: Steve Morrison was the captain.* Good, able captain of the ship.

Paul Stillwell: You must have had interaction with him almost daily.

Admiral Shelton: Yes. More than daily, I guess you'd say. He was very supportive.

Paul Stillwell: It was a safe cruise from the standpoint of safety and incidents?

Admiral Shelton: Yeah. We came back out of the Indian Ocean and, let's see, we ended up going up to Japan. The "Bonny Dick" at that point went to Sasebo for a normal liberty port. The ship came out of Sasebo and hadn't gotten very far when she flung a high-speed turbine wheel, so we ended up going up to Yokosuka for the repairs. As I recall, they had to rob a high-speed turbine wheel from a similar carrier in Bremerton and fly it all the way out there to put it back together, because that's a rather unusual type of failure.† So that kind of put a little bit of a kibosh on the operations for longer than we wanted.

---

* Captain George Stephen Morrison, USN, took command of the Bon Homme Richard 22 November 1963.
† Puget Sound Naval Shipyard, Bremerton, Washington, was the site of the Pacific Reserve Fleet, so the turbine was cannibalized from a carrier that was in mothballs there.

Paul Stillwell: A little extra liberty there, though.

Admiral Shelton: A little extra liberty. And of course we got Hong Kong also and then back to the States.

Paul Stillwell: Was the incident in the Tonkin Gulf happening somewhere around this time?*

Admiral Shelton: Yes. When we came out of the Malacca Straits we were designated—that was when McNamara made his first visit over there and that was what, March or April of '64?†

Paul Stillwell: I'm not sure.

Admiral Shelton: Somewhere in there. Anyway, it was McNamara's first visit to Vietnam, and so we were designated to give him air cover while he was over there. That didn't amount to a whole lot at that point, because there wasn't really any fighting going on. And we flew over Laos and the Plains and all that kind of stuff, and there was nothing going on as far as we were concerned so we didn't get anything out of that as far as combat's concerned.

Paul Stillwell: But the ship would go back to Vietnam again and again.

Admiral Shelton: Well, yes. The air wing didn't, but the ship was. So the early part of Vietnam, that very early part of Vietnam we really didn't do much at all.

---

* On 2 August 1964, North Vietnamese patrol boats in the Tonkin Gulf attacked the destroyer Maddox (DD-731) in international waters. On the night of 4 August the Maddox and the destroyer Turner Joy (DD-951) reported being attacked by North Vietnamese craft. The question of whether the second attack occurred has never been completely resolved, though it now seems unlikely. The reports of attacks led to the congressional Gulf of Tonkin Resolution, which provided the legal basis for the commitment of U.S. armed forces in Vietnam.

† Robert S. McNamara served as Secretary of Defense from 21 January 1961 to 29 February 1968.

Paul Stillwell: I think the Hancock was in on some of those first strikes in August.

Admiral Shelton: Yes, and we weren't there.

Paul Stillwell: I talked to Spence Matthews.*

Admiral Shelton: I know Spence. Well, anyway, we came back from that cruise, and I got orders to OpNav. I had orders to OP-602C, and I got them in sort of an interesting way, to me anyway. I got a note from Admiral Hyland, John J. Hyland, who was either OP-60 or 60B at the time.† I got a note from him saying that I would be coming to work in OP-60.

Paul Stillwell: Had you known him at all?

Admiral Shelton: Yes, I'd known him at Patuxent River and here and there and never worked for him really.

Paul Stillwell: He'd been a test pilot.

Admiral Shelton: Yes.

When I was getting ready to leave the air wing, the person that was supposed to relieve me in Air Wing 19 was Jim Stockdale, and he had been through the RAG part of the way, all the way, and been to the survival school, et cetera et cetera.‡ And in our turnover thing, we spent only three four or four days, maybe a week. He had just finished being briefed by the ComNavAirPac intelligence people.§ But in our turnover we were

---
* At the time Commander Herbert Spencer Matthews, Jr., USN, was executive officer of the carrier Hancock (CVA-19). Matthews, who retired as a rear admiral, has been interviewed as part of the Naval Institute's oral history program.
† Rear Admiral John J. Hyland, Jr., USN, served as assistant director of the Strategic Plans Division of OpNav from 1963 to 1965 and in 1965 became division director. The oral history of Hyland, who retired as a four-star admiral, is in the Naval Institute collection.
‡ Commander James B. Stockdale, USN, eventually a vice admiral, was a prisoner of war in Vietnam from September 1965 to February 1973. He was subsequently awarded the Medal of Honor for his heroism while in prison.
§ ComNavAirPac—Commander Naval Air Force Pacific Fleet, the type commander.

just to the point where we were discussing the value of the survival school and what the hell would you do if you were actually taken prisoner. When we were right there in the turnover procedure when NavAirPac told us that BuPers had screwed up on the seniority process, and instead of Jim Stockdale it was going to be John Tierney that relieved me.[*] So John Tierney actually relieved me, and Jim Stockdale went to a different air wing.[†] I never really completely understood that part of the thing, but anyway it wasn't mine to quarrel with that. But anyway that's where Jim and I were when it was all terminated, and he went to a different air wing.

Paul Stillwell: Interesting to speculate on fate. What might have happened had he taken over Air Wing 19?

Admiral Shelton: Yes. I don't know what he has speculated on that because I never have asked him. But I do remember that that's where we were in the turnover process. We were just talking about intelligence and survival and what we figured would actually happen if we were shot down and taken prisoner, how good we'd be. Well, he found out, and I was fortunate enough not to have to.

But, anyway, I got this note and sure enough, I got orders to OpNav, and so I reported in back there. Right after I got there I found out some sad news about the ops officer that I had in Air Wing 19, a very capable gent named Hugh Loheed.[‡] He had gotten his own squadron right after I left the air wing. He promptly proceeded to get shot down in Vietnam and was never recovered. In fact, he was one of those that they finally, just not more than about two years ago, finally located his remains and brought them back. But he was gem of a guy and a great loss.

Paul Stillwell: And when you've flown with somebody like that and lived with them and served with them it's somewhat akin to losing a child, because you've invested to much into him.

---

[*] Commander John M. Tierney, USN.
[†] Commander Stockdale commanded Carrier Air Wing 16 from February to September of 1965.
[‡] Lieutenant Commander Hubert B. Loheed, USN.

Admiral Shelton: Yes. In his case I have to say that he probably had as much invested in me as I had in him because he was a sharp guy. His last tour of duty before he came to Air Wing 19 as ops officer had been down in the JCS, and I forget which job, but it was similar to my job in OP-602C there.[*] I didn't know anything about all that sort of thing at the time, so it was always interesting to talk to him, and he had a lot of good inputs. As I say, he probably had as much to do with educating me as I did with educating him.

That job in OP-602C1 was command relations and service roles and missions. It was not really command relations within the Navy but in all the services, so it was a good, hot job in those days. Still is, I think, because it has to do with all of the unified commands. It has to do with which services are going to have those unified commands. It has to do with whether or not you're going to establish a new one anywhere along the road, which service will provide the commander and what each service will do, and all that. Pretty interesting and pretty heady stuff that I'd never been in before.

My boss was John Dick, who was OP-602C, and I was OP-602C1.[†] He was a pretty smart guy, a lawyer of sorts, and he was an aviator. As soon as I got there, he pointed to the files and said, "Your first job is to take about six weeks. Go through every file in those drawers over there until you think you know what's in there and where to put your hands on it." That's probably the best piece of advice I ever had, because there was an instance later on when I was OP-602C myself, and we got a tasking to put together a piece of paper for Senator Margaret Chase Smith.[‡]

She didn't like something that McNamara had proposed to do, and so she leaned on the Navy to give her a piece of paper to argue with him about. That tasking came down to me. I think that was a Wednesday or a Thursday, and—like everything that ever concerned McNamara—you had to have it back by 8:00 o'clock Monday morning. It had a lot to do with things that I had read up on in detail, and so I was able to sit down there on Thursday and Friday and put together a piece of paper and send it on up. She was able to offset what McNamara had in mind. In any event, they all thought that was a pretty good piece of paper that I did.

---

[*] JCS—Joint Chiefs of Staff.
[†] Captain John Dick, USN.
[‡] Margaret Chase Smith, a Republican from Maine, served in the U.S. Senate from 3 January 1949 until 3 January 1973.

But it goes back to John Dick and the fact that he had told me to sit there and go through those files for six weeks and know everything that was in there and be able to put my hands on them and be able to put together various pieces of paper from that. Because those things have a habit of not changing too much over the time. You know, those things don't change on a daily basis or monthly basis or anything like, so once all those principles are pretty well established in command relationships why they don't change too much.

Paul Stillwell: Who was OP-06 then?

Admiral Shelton: Andy Jackson, and I thought he was a great guy myself.[*] He was typical—I don't know how to put this exactly—certainly set in his ways, and fortunately they were good ways as far as I could tell. [Laughter] He was kind of a barnacled guy, but he knew that OP-06 business. He really knew it, and so I had a lot of appreciation for him. After he left, W. F. A. Wendt was OP-06.[†]

Paul Stillwell: What do you remember about him?

Admiral Shelton: Great guy. One of the best black shoes I ever knew.[‡] He had the capability of putting his finger right on the button every time. My times really to go up and be in front of him weren't too many, because I was still a little bit down in the hierarchy. I would give the paper to my boss, and my boss would go up there and be in front of him. But the few times that I did get to talk to him personally I just thought the world of him. I thought he was great.

Paul Stillwell: I've heard him described as low key and a real gentleman.

---

[*] Vice Admiral Andrew M. Jackson, Jr., USN, served as Deputy Chief of Naval Operations (Plans and Policy) from 13 July 1964 to 17 April 1967. His oral history is in the Naval Institute collection.
[†] Vice Admiral Waldemar F. A. Wendt, USN, served as Deputy Chief of Naval Operations (Plans and Policy) from April 1967 to June 1968.
[‡] In the early days of naval aviation, the aviators wore brown shoes with their khaki uniforms and green uniforms. They thus acquired the nickname "brown shoes" to distinguish them from the traditional surface ship officers, who are known as "black shoes."

Admiral Shelton: Yes. Admiral Smith was OP-60 at the time, so he was my more or less immediate boss.* That's Howlin' Mad Smith's son.† He lived here in La Jolla at one time, but he's deceased now. J. Victor Smith.

Paul Stillwell: We have his oral history.

Admiral Shelton: Well, he was a great guy to work for too. He was a black shoe, of course. That whole OP-06 organization was a pretty sharp outfit. I'd been in a lot of outfits here and there, and that was one of the best if not the best. I mean, all the way up and down the line the requirements were quite high as far as knowledge is concerned. And the requirements were quite high as far as being able to put it on paper promptly and in a manner that made sense and that you could read and make sense, you know. But that was a great organization.

Paul Stillwell: How much of a factor was McNamara in your dealings?

Admiral Shelton: In my personal dealings not very much, other than the fact he caused me a lot of hard work. [Laughter] He caused everybody a lot of hard work. But, you know, he was famous for on about a Thursday or a Friday sending a note down to one of the services saying something that he proposed to do and that he wanted to give them a chance to respond with their viewpoints and would they please have it back to him by 8:00 o'clock on Monday morning, you know, over the weekend. And then on Monday, why, he was equally famous for sending a note back saying, "Well, thank you very much for your input, but I've decided we're going to do it my way." So there was a lot of appreciation of McNamara but not very much good appreciation as far as I'm concerned.

Paul Stillwell: Well, and that's the kind of approach that does not build morale below him.

---

* Rear Admiral John Victor Smith, USN. The oral history of Smith, who retired as a vice admiral, is in the Naval Institute collection.
† Lieutenant General Holland M. Smith, USMC, commanded the landing forces in several amphibious assaults in the Pacific during World War II.

Admiral Shelton: Yes. He did not have the willingness of the working body to respond to him very much. He had a lot of what you might call bright guys working for him, Enthoven and so forth, and even in my place I wasn't high enough to really see the effects of that as much as a lot of the people above me.[*] But the work eventually drifted down to my level. [Laughter] I thought the job was absolutely great but I spent a lot of weekends there that I thought were absolutely useless.

Paul Stillwell: Make-work?

Admiral Shelton: Yes, just make-work and because it was not going to come to anything. McNamara had already made up his mind. In most cases that's who we were dealing with. He had already made up his mind, and it wasn't going to make any difference. But, still and all, I loved that job. It was a great job.

Paul Stillwell: What about it made it good? What were some of the issues that you worked on?

Admiral Shelton: Well, command relations. As I say, this had a lot to do with who was going where particularly in the war out in Vietnam, and so all of the services had a lot of inputs to make on various aspects of who was going where out there. There were a lot of issues having to do with service roles and missions to be decided on from time to time, and so you had an opportunity to work on all that.

Paul Stillwell: Do you remember specific issues?

Admiral Shelton: Well, the one I remember the best of course was that one and that had to do with whether or not a separate unified command needed to be established on the

---

[*] Alain C. Enthoven served as Deputy Comptroller and Deputy Assistant Secretary of Defense, 1961-65, and as Assistant Secretary of Defense for Systems Analysis, 1965-69.

Asian continent. McNamara wanted to, and everybody else did not want to basically, and that's what my paper was about.

Paul Stillwell: Well, was this the Military Assistance Command, Vietnam that came from that?

Admiral Shelton: No. That stayed intact there. If anything had come of it, why, you would have had another separate unified command in Southeast Asia, and it would have only lasted a couple of years anyway. There were plenty of commands to handle the situation. You had CinCPac, and you had MACV, and you had all the rest of them.[*] And so all the methods that were in existence for handling the situation were perfectly capable of handling it.

Paul Stillwell: What was the theoretical designation of this new command he wanted?

Admiral Shelton: I never knew. I never knew, except that it would be another unified command such as CinCPac, CinCLant, etc.

Paul Stillwell: Did you deal with individual people who would go into these commands?

Admiral Shelton: We normally briefed most of them that went out there, including Admiral Zumwalt and Stansfield Turner [laughter] and people from other services, too, that went out there.[†] We had a lot to do with the papers that went forward to the various chiefs. All the services had an OP-60 of one sort or another. So the papers that ended up before the Joint Chiefs of Staff were normally prepared by that chain so a lot of the papers that went forward went through the 06 chain. So it was working on all that sort of thing, papers that the chiefs were going to consider. Almost any variety of issues.

---

[*] CinCPac—Commander in Chief Pacific Command.
[†] Vice Admiral Elmo R. Zumwalt, Jr., USN, served as Commander Naval Forces Vietnam/Chief of Naval Advisory Group Vietnam from 30 September 1968 to 14 May 1970. Captain Stansfield Turner, USN, commanded the guided missile frigate Horne (DLG-30) during operations off Vietnam.

Paul Stillwell: Was it a demanding job in terms of hours?

Admiral Shelton: Yes. I don't know of a job in the Pentagon that wasn't demanding in terms of hours back in those days and probably still today. My normal situation was to get there about 7:00 o'clock, 7:30 in the morning, and my normal situation was to try to start leaving there about 5:30 or 6:00 in the evening and normally get out by about 8:00 o'clock. So it was a 12-hour day, and about the only break you had really was if you managed to go down to the athletic center or for lunch, something like that. But otherwise you were there for 12 hours basically. And, as I said, there were a lot of weekends when there were just kind of useless drills as far as I was concerned.

Paul Stillwell: Were you a captain by then?

Admiral Shelton: I was a captain. Let's see. I made captain right after I got there. I was a commander when I reported in, and I made captain right after that.

Paul Stillwell: Any observations on Admiral McDonald, the CNO from that period?[*]

Admiral Shelton: Yes. I liked him. There again, I remember one of the responsibilities I had was to review and overhaul NWP-31 or 32, whichever it is, the amphibious doctrine.[†] This effort was to try to bring the Air Force into the picture, and the Air Force basically didn't want to be brought into the picture. So on that one thing alone I spent a number of briefing sessions in front of Admiral McDonald on the pros and cons of this, that and the other thing, and why they wouldn't and why I thought they should and all this kind of stuff. We eventually did get them into the picture, and today they're incorporated in it. I don't know whether they're glad or sad at this point but they are.

Paul Stillwell: Well, jointness has now become such an important watchword.

---

[*] Admiral David L. McDonald, USN, served as Chief of Naval Operations from 1 August 1963 to 1 August 1967. His oral history is in the Naval Institute collection.
[†] NWP—naval warfare publication.

Admiral Shelton: Jointness is the word these days and it wasn't then.

Paul Stillwell: And the Navy was the one that was most often accused of foot dragging.

Admiral Shelton: That's true. We were even accused of foot dragging on that drill, but it wasn't us really. I can't say that we were all that eager to have the Air Force in the normal thing for amphibious operations, for instance, or anything like that. But on the other hand if you were going to do it somewhere, and if you had to use them, it was important that they be used in the right sort of way. So we had to get them in on the act and we finally did and we got the whole thing down. God, I think I took a year and a half to get that done. So I did spend a fair amount of time up with Admiral McDonald in the briefing sessions. I don't ever remember that it was just he and I, one on one; it was always in a briefing session. And OP-06 would always be there, of course, and other people, 03 and the Marines and so forth.* Many, many watch days!!

It just took a lot of wearing down hard work. You know, you'd say it and you'd say it and you'd say it again and you'd say it again. And eventually you'd get somebody's attention. That's about what it amounted to. As I said, the Air Force was reluctant to do anything about it, but I think after about a year and a half they finally agreed that it was to their benefit to understand if they were called upon how to do it.

Paul Stillwell: Well, most of the people who will eventually read this probably have not prepared an OP-06 type paper. Maybe you could go into a little of the mechanics of that please.

Admiral Shelton: Well, I can talk about this particular piece of paper I referred to earlier that I did for Senator Margaret Chase Smith. I would have to say among the many pieces of paper that came out of that shop, that one was significant. And so therefore it was important that it be done properly. Not be a volume; nobody's going to read a book. You've got to put it together in short form so that the points you want to make stick out and in a logical sequence. And so that takes some; you have to understand what it is that

---

* OP-03—Deputy Chief of Naval Operations (Fleet Operations and Readiness).

you're trying to do. My boss at the time was Captain James Conger, fine guy, and he simply said to me, "Do you need any help on this?"[*]

I said, "No, just let me have these two desks out here in the hall and a secretary whenever I need it." This was on a Thursday morning and I said, "I'll have it done by Friday night." I don't think I quite made that mark. I think it was actually sometime Saturday before I had it done. But, anyway, I simply sat down at that desk, and I broke out the files that I knew had the information that I needed to get at, and so for about the first six or eight hours I guess I had papers all over those two desks. But eventually that mass of confusion went away, and it boiled to one or two pages that I think turned out to be a pretty good piece of paper. And it did turn the tide, at least as it turned out on the particular issue at hand.

Paul Stillwell: Well, probably part of what you did was to go back and demonstrate what the existing structure was in Asia and how that could serve the purpose.

Admiral Shelton: That's right. Essentially the paper reviewed briefly the history of the commands in the Far East, their reason for being, how they had successfully interacted in the past, were handling the present situation just as successfully, and that there was no need to mandate another unified command. You know, there's always those that want to tinker with the unified command system, and perhaps one of these days there'll be some more tinkering with it, and there probably will be. But, for the most part, the system doesn't need any tinkering with. There are command systems set up that are perfectly capable of handling any job that's thrown their way, and every now and then there's always somebody that wants to introduce something new to the whole system, and that's what this boiled down to.

McNamara simply wanted to establish a whole new unified command out in Asia, not only just for the Vietnam thing but for anything else. At that time there was a lot of consideration that it might grow in aspect and be something bigger than the Vietnam War just itself. So it was one of those Thursday afternoon decisions of his that he wanted an answer to by Monday morning, and we were lucky to be able to put together this piece of

---

[*] Captain James W. Conger, USN.

paper. A significant person in the Senate was on our side and argued the point with him, and it didn't happen. So it's those kind of things that come about every now and then, and if you happen to be the guy that's on the spot, why, you feel good if you're able to do something that's worthwhile, and that was the case in my case there.

Paul Stillwell: Anything more on your time in the OP-06 organization?

Admiral Shelton: No. I did get back there later, not quite in the same thing. I went back to OP-61 later, but that's still down the road a little bit. Well, let's see, from OP-602C it was time for me to get a boat. So I left there, came out to Treasure Island, and I took command of the USS Paricutin, which was AE-18 and which was one of the oldest still-floating Kaiser hulls in the inventory.* That was my deep draft, as they say.† I've said that a lot of years were very interesting and one of the most interesting years and all that sort of thing, but that tour on the Paricutin was probably the best, pretty close to the best tour that I had as far as just duty is concerned.

We left Treasure Island, I think on July 1 or July 2, 1967. Our first trip was to Ketchikan, Alaska, for the Fourth of July weekend, so it must have been just before that. In those days people loved to have Navy ships come in here and there, and Ketchikan has always loved to have Navy ships go there. I think we still send one up there. And when you go in there of course you go up the Inland Passageway, and then you come down part of the Inland Passageway on the other side of the island. We tied up right at the foot of Broadway, so to speak, and it literally was right at the foot of Broadway.

I remember the dock there that we tied up to was one of those docks that had these huge wooden planks where they were so worn that the wooden knots stuck up five or six inches you know. And so if you looked down there at that dock it was as uneven as anything you can think of for something that's supposed to be part of a street or

---

* USS Paricutin (AE-18), a Mount Hood-class ammunition ship, was commissioned 3 March 1945. She displaced 15,295 tons, was 459 feet long, 63 feet in the beam, and had a maximum draft of 28 feet. Her top speed was 16 knots. She was originally armed with one 5-inch gun and four 3-inch guns. She was in mothballs from 1948 to 1950. After being reactivated she continued to serve until 23 April 1971, when she was eventually decommissioned for the last time.
† The practice is to give an aviator captain slated for a subsequent carrier command an intermediate command of a deep-draft ship to provide experience.

something like that. But the people there were tremendous. They took that whole crew in hand, and I'm telling you, for that whole Fourth of July weekend it was one great time. And I don't mean it was out of hand or anything like that. It was just that everybody had people out to dinner, had the whole crew out to dinner and all that sort of thing.

Paul Stillwell: Mutual good feeling.

Admiral Shelton: Mutual good feeling. And I remember the fish cannery there at Ketchikan at that time was owned by a fellow named Pendergast, same name as Kansas City Pendergasts.

Paul Stillwell: Harry Truman's crowd.

Admiral Shelton: Harry Truman's crowd. And I can tell a story about that, too, just very quickly. As I mentioned earlier, Harry Truman and my grandfather were both haberdashers at one point and good buddies, but anyway I'll go back to this. Mr. Pendergast wanted me to come over and go through his fish cannery. Well, I didn't really have that much interest [laughter] in fish canneries to be very truthful, but I said, "Yeah, sure. I'll do it."

So I went over there, and it turned out to be a pretty interesting operation, and they were happily unloading a lot of fish right at the time, so he went through the whole process with me. How they unloaded them right there on the dock and then they'd quick freeze them and take them in and then how they literally stock them in bins by size. So it was pretty interesting, and, lo and behold, the next day back on the ship, or at least before we left, why, here came two great big boxes of frozen fish, salmon and halibut. I was not a great fish eater in those days, although I liked it at times, but I had two stewards that loved it. I kept wondering why those boxes of fish were diminishing all the time, and I had made the mistake I guess of telling them that, "Well, you know, I'm not a big fish eater. I'd like to have some of it, but you guys take what you want of it." Well, they did. [Laughter]

Paul Stillwell: That's what you told them.

Admiral Shelton: That's what I told them, and they understood that. They did that. But it was great. One of my stewards was a young fellow named Bautista, and he had ambitions beyond being a steward. At that time Filipinos weren't looked upon as candidates for electricians or boatswain's mates or anything like that. But anyway I liked this young fellow. He had some ambition. We had a chief petty officer on there, a chief electrician on the ship, that was an outstanding chief. And so, unbeknownst to me, really, up until then, why, Bautista had kind of gotten next to him and had been kind of going to school and this sort of thing. So by the time they came to me, why, you know, I wouldn't say I was trapped, but I was behind the power curve.

Paul Stillwell: The only gracious thing to do was say, "Yes."

Admiral Shelton: Say, "Yes." Well, I couldn't unfortunately at that time, so the best I could do was to write a letter to BuPers saying that I would like to change this fellow over to being an electrician. I got the standard BuPers answer in those days: "Well, we don't do that and sorry about that," and a few other things.

So that didn't sit very well with me, and so I wrote back another letter that was quite a bit more pointed. And I said among other things, "What I intend to do with this young man is to put him in the electrical crew for six months. And if he can pass the third class exam by that time, I'm going to write you back and you're going to make him a third class electrician." And that's what we did. The last I saw of him he was an E-8 electrician, and so there you are.[*] We've come a long way since then. Filipinos are doing a lot of things in the Navy these days, but in those days it was just one of those things.

Paul Stillwell: I was in an LST at that time and we had a shipfitter who was a Filipino, and he had had to break out of the steward mold to get into that.[†]

---

[*] In the Navy the pay grade of E-8 denotes a senior chief petty officer.
[†] The interviewer served in the tank landing ship Washoe County (LST-1165) from 1966 to 1969.

Admiral Shelton: Yes, very difficult. First of all the individual had to really have some moxie, and he had to have some ambition.

Paul Stillwell: And he had to have some help.

Admiral Shelton: And he had to have some help. Above all, I guess, some help. And not enough of them in those days got that kind of help, partly because I think to give a guy help you have to know about it. A lot of them were reluctant to come up the chain of command and try to get that kind of help, but he did. Of course he didn't have to go up the chain of command. I was standing right there. [Laughter] He was one of my stewards, so he didn't have to go through anybody. But he did a great job.

And, you know, one of the reasons that BuPers always gave that they didn't want to do this was because at GQ his voice communications and his ability to speak proper English wouldn't be understood over the sound-powered phones. And I thought, "That's the biggest bunch of crap I ever heard in my life," because this young fellow could make himself understood very easily. That conceivably is a valid argument with some people but not with him. He was able to make himself understood quite easily. So anyway, as I said, we finally got that done. We came back from Ketchikan and went in the yard right under the Oakland Bay Bridge for a couple of months and then went right on out to Vietnam. During that one year that I was on there, I spent about nine months out in Vietnam.

Paul Stillwell: What was the material condition of the ship?

Admiral Shelton: It was good. You know those ships were all old DC ships, DC electric ships.*

Paul Stillwell: Converted merchant ships.

---

* DC—direct-current electricity.

Admiral Shelton: Yes, which means that you automatically had all kinds of electrical problems every day. As long as you could stay on top of that, the rest of the ship was pretty good. It was a single-screw ship, but the power plant was pretty old, so you had to pay a lot of attention when you were going to anchor. For instance, if you were going to tie up to a buoy you wanted to get it done pretty fast because when you were running all the gears and stuff down there at low speeds they heated up pretty badly. And if you didn't watch out, why, you'd lose your ability to go forward or aft either one. So as long as you understood those things and worked with it, not against it, why, you could be successful, but there were times when we were pretty close.

Anyway, we went in the yard and we were there for a couple of months. Came out and then we came down to San Diego to run a sort of a little modified ORI for ships going west. We got down here, and they were having one of these situations, pretty unusual even for San Diego, where a cold front was going through one way, and then it would reverse itself and go back the other way right there in San Diego Bay.

Well, if you look back, maybe we shouldn't have even been trying to tie up to the buoy, but we were trying to tie up to a buoy right down there by the Coast Guard station. That was as close as we ever came to really getting in trouble because we did get everything heated up down there in the engine room, shafts and everything, and we just got it tied up in time basically. But we got through that and went out and did our business with running the minefield, all that sort of thing, which was our part of the ORI, and went on out to Vietnam. And our normal routine out there was to go into Subic, over to Kalayaan Pier, the ammunition pier there, and we would take on 4,700 tons of ammunition.* And in those days the bulk of it was 5-inch/38. There were a lot of 6-inch stuff as well and even some 8-inch stuff, but most of it was 5-inch/38.

Paul Stillwell: So did you take on bombs as well, rockets?

Admiral Shelton: Oh, yes, bombs up to 2,000 pounds. We had a lot of those, because we went alongside everybody out there, or they came alongside us really. But we would

---

* During the Vietnam War, Subic Bay in the Philippines had a strong role as a support base for the U.S. Navy. Included were a naval air station, piers, ship repair facility, supply depot, and recreational outlets for ships' crews.

leave there with 4,700 tons of ammunition, and that would be in the hold and all over the topside. And then we would trek across the China Sea. The China Sea fortunately in most cases was pretty calm, but even then, that ship was never level. It was never on an even keel. There would be about a degree and a half list one side for mile after mile. And then gradually something would cause it to roll slightly the other, and you'd go a degree and a half the other side and list and you'd steam that way for 15 or 20 miles.

That was when I learned how long it takes to stop a ship on the open sea when it's well loaded. That ship, if you put it into reverse with 4,700 tons of ammunition on it and you'd been going at 12 knots, which is about what we did, it would take you about 15 miles to stop. I didn't believe that, and so my exec, Lee Wells, who was a hell of a seaman, kept telling me that, and I said, "Jeez, I just can't believe that, Lee."[*]

He said, "Well, let's try it." So we did. And he was right. Well, it proved to be good because the north-south traffic lanes from Singapore to Japan, Okinawa and so forth go right down through there by the Triton Islands. Most of them were merchant ships that were on automatic pilot, and there were times when they simply would not respond. We had the right of way in almost all the cases, because most of the traffic we happened to run into was coming from south to north rather than north to south. So we had the right of way in most cases. And you could give them an Alfa Alfa, which is you know, "Who are you and where are you going?" basically.[†] And you could give the five long toots on the horn or anything you wanted to do.

It didn't seem to bother them very much, and we've had more than one of them just come up as far as they dare and then go right down our port side and underneath our stern. Well, you get a little nervous when you've got 4,700 tons of ammunition on there. You don't want to have a collision. On the other hand, you've got the Rules of the Road that you've got to obey very strictly, or then they turn around and it's going to be your fault. So we had a lot of what I would call little adventures out there with the Rules of the Road and with the merchant ships.

But once we got out to the Yankee Station basically, why, we would start up north, and we would work our way south, and that would basically take about a 16-day

---

[*] Lieutenant Commander Aaron Lee Wells, USN, was a mustang officer who had been a quartermaster when he was an enlisted man.
[†] "Alfa Alfa" was a signal sent by the ship's flashing light in Morse code.

trip.* At various times we would do what we called consols, which meant that we would get together with another ammunition ship, and we would either give them some of our load or they would give us some of their load and then go on about our business. It would depend on who the customers were going to be and what they needed. But it would take basically about 16 days to make that route, and then we could beat back to Subic, pick up another 4,700 tons of ammunition.

Paul Stillwell: How did you determine that 15-mile stopping distance? Loran fixes?†

Admiral Shelton: Basically we had a pretty good pit log and all that kind of stuff, and it was a good guess basically.‡ It was not anything scientific as far as 15 miles is concerned. But we could reasonably ascertain that it was pretty close to 15 miles, 12 miles or 15 miles.

Paul Stillwell: Please describe what was involved for you and your deck crew and your bridge crew in doing underway replenishment with a carrier, let's say.

Admiral Shelton: Well, in nearly all cases whoever we were going to replenish came alongside us. Our job was to be in the right place at the right time and time our turn into the wind, so to speak, so that the ship being replenished could come right up and not waste time. We would be settled out on the replenishment course at 12 knots, which is what we normally did. Then they could come alongside without dilly-dallying around and take a lot of time. Most of the time we weren't alongside very long, maybe an hour or two hours, sometimes three hours.

And, you know, we transferred all kinds of ammunition. We took back all kinds of empty shells and all this kind of stuff. We rigged the highlines just like the

---

* During the initial stages of involvement in the Vietnam War, the U.S. Navy maintained aircraft carriers on two stations based on Civil War designations—Yankee Station off North Vietnam and Dixie Station off South Vietnam. The latter, which began on 16 May 1965, was dropped 15 months later once airfields were available ashore in South Vietnam.
† Loran (long-range aid to navigation) is a system of electronic navigation that involves the reception of pulse signals transmitted simultaneously by paired stations ashore.
‡ A pitometer log provides the speed and distance of a ship's travel through the water by measuring pressure on a pitot tube that extends from the hull.

replenishment book says, and at times, why, you could watch those 2,000-pound bombs go across there and do a big full loop by the time they got it over to the other side. It was exciting at times, but we did it.

The longest time we were ever alongside anybody was the Newport News, which was a heavy cruiser commanded by Ted Snyder.* We had a lot of fog to contend with out there off the coast of Vietnam at times, and so we did a lot of getting together by radar. You'd be in a spot at a certain time, and you'd make your turn, and then whoever was being replenished the first time you'd see him was when he came up past your stern. And he would make his approach on radar, and of course we could watch him on our radar. But this one time with Newport News we got together in the fog and we set out on a course, and we went way to hell and gone down south on this thing. Made a 270-degree turn to go back north, still connected. We started about 10:00 o'clock in the morning, and we finally finished that replenishment on the stroke of midnight. And that's the better part of 14 hours alongside.

Paul Stillwell: Why so long?

Admiral Shelton: Well, they had a lot of stuff to transfer to us, and we had a lot of stuff to transfer to them. And basically the Paricutin was not one of the new ones, like the Camden or Sacramento or any of that. So we had to find places to put this stuff, and you had to do it pretty much manually, you know, with forklifts and people. We didn't have the automatic elevators and handling equipment, so by mandate we were slower than the newer ships, and you'd have to believe so because otherwise, why, you didn't need the new ships.

But, yes, they were alongside us, and we did that one 270-degree turn tied together. I hadn't done that before, and that was pretty interesting. Basically I set my turn, and he was a longer ship than I was, so he kind of went in and out a little bit here and there. We got pretty close back at the stern a couple of times, pretty close at the bow a couple of times, but basically not a big problem. We got through the 270-degree turn no sweat. And the only reason we quit at midnight I guess was we got up in the area

---

* Captain Edwin K. Snyder, USN, commanded the heavy cruiser Newport News (CA-148) in 1968-69.

where there were a lot of other ships, and the USS Princeton, which by then was back out there.

Paul Stillwell: LPH.

Admiral Shelton: LPH. And my friend Paul Payne, who had been CO of VF-124, I'd been his exec, and here he was sitting right in front of us, and he was not in a position to move too much and all that sort of thing and visibility wasn't all that great.* So at something less than a mile, we had an emergency breakaway and managed to avoid catastrophe.

Paul Stillwell: Your line handlers must have been really fatigued after a 14-hour replenishment.

Admiral Shelton: Well, the situation on the ammunition ship like that was that basically, when you got there on the line, it was nothing unusual to go for about 36 hours at a time. Pick up one ship, get rid of it, get ready for another one and go for about 36 hours. Then if everything went your way, why, you'd have a break for maybe eight or ten hours and that's when you got your sleep. Other than that, you let a few people go as you could and get sleep. But basically it was on the job for about 36 hours at a time.

But it was interesting and everything was moving and so you never felt too much about the need for getting sleep. Everybody got tired, tired as hell. I was very pleased really that we got through that whole cruise, and we only had one man injured. And he was the best boatswain's mate that I had on the whole ship; his name was Clark. He was up in the first or second division, I've forgotten which. We had the old-fashioned hatches that had the high coamings you know, about, oh, almost two feet high, maybe more. The biggest problem you had to guard against was don't get between a load and the hatch when you had a load coming or going.

He got caught one day and didn't quite get out and the load hit him and hit him right in the leg against that hatch. Well, I thought sure as hell it just smashed the hell out

---

* Captain Paul E. Payne, USN, commanded the amphibious assault ship Princeton (LPH-5).

of him. It did hurt his leg, and we got him off there and got him to the hospital at Subic, and a month later he was back aboard. That's the only guy we had hurt. I'm not saying we didn't have a bunch of scratches and all that kind of thing, but we didn't have anybody with any injury to speak of except for him.

Paul Stillwell: You must have had a good ship's boatswain.

Admiral Shelton: He was great. He really was. And, you know, he was great not only for knowing how to do things but he was great for morale. Along with Lee Wells, the XO, he kept those guys alert and knowing what to do, et cetera, et cetera.

Paul Stillwell: That's a real challenge.

Admiral Shelton: Yes. And, you know, as I say, it wasn't unusual to be going for 36 hours at a crack before you got any real rest. But the whole thing would last about 16 days, and then you'd get back to Subic. The first thing that happened, of course, when you got back to Subic to the ammunition pier was you had a hell of a mess on your hands down there in the hold with all the wood dunnage. So you had to clean all that out. Hell, that took about three days just to do that. Then you'd start all over loading it back.

Paul Stillwell: And one of the other things that happened is that the crew would head for Olongapo.*

Admiral Shelton: Yes, they did that all right, and I let them. [Laughter] I figured they'd earned it.

Paul Stillwell: Well, did you have to learn some things about ship handling when you took that job?

---

* Olongapo, the town right outside the U.S. naval base at Subic Bay in the Philippines, was noted for its raunchiness during the Vietnam War period and later.

Admiral Shelton: Yes. I think I'm probably a heretic, but I'm among that group of aviators that doesn't think that ship handling is as difficult as some people make it out to be. Now, I'm not saying that there aren't times when it's difficult because there are. But if you have a really good knowledge of relative motion and if you've done any maneuvering of any kind in the air or otherwise, it comes fairly natural I think. And, oh, there were times when I was nervous. I didn't like that 270-degree turn that we made there tied up to another ship.

Paul Stillwell: Well, two other handicaps are you didn't have that much power and you had only one screw.

Admiral Shelton: That's right, so you learned to avoid those positions where you didn't have to go astern because you were only going to go one way astern. [Laughter] But I really enjoyed that tour. It was just about exactly a year to the date.

Paul Stillwell: I would suspect that your experience in the St. Louis had been useful when you took that command too.

Admiral Shelton: Oh, yes, yes. Sure.

Paul Stillwell: Any other things to say about the crew, discipline, morale, liberty ports?

Admiral Shelton: No, we didn't get much liberty ports except Subic, so there wasn't much to say about that whole thing. We went out there and we came back. When we came back we went to Treasure Island again. My homeport was Concord actually. I never saw Concord the whole time I was on there. So I came back to Treasure Island. I'm not sure whether the Paricutin ever made another cruise back out there or not. I don't think it did. It may have.

Paul Stillwell: Well, some of those AOEs were coming on the line.

Admiral Shelton: Camden and Sacramento of that class. Of course they had tremendous capability. And you at the time I thought, "Jeez, I'd sure like to be CO of one of those. You know, what a dream." But on the other hand I think the Paricutin was a bigger challenge, and I think I really enjoyed it more because there was a lot to do on there to keep things going straight.

Paul Stillwell: I interviewed Admiral Hal Shear who was the second skipper of Sacramento.* He just loved that ship.

Admiral Shelton: Oh, yes. Well, Joe Moorer had the Camden.†

Paul Stillwell: Yes, he did.

Admiral Shelton: Yes. And he loved it. A classmate of mine, Warren O'Neil, who had been CO of VF-92 when I relieved him, he had the Sacramento or the Camden also. Sacramento I think. So I was kind of gnawing my teeth. I thought, "Goddamn it, I sure would like to have one of those," [Laughter] you know, but looking back at it I really appreciated the tour on the Paricutin. The thing I liked most about the Camden class and all that sort of thing was the extra capability it had. It had oiler capability as well as ammunition and all that sort of thing and so much automatic. You didn't run quite as many risks with the people as you did with ships like the Paricutin.

Paul Stillwell: Well, they had those constant-tension rigs, for example.

Admiral Shelton: Yes.

Paul Stillwell: What about the quality of your crew? The service force traditionally didn't get the handpicked sailors.

---

* See the Naval Institute oral history of Admiral Harold E. Shear, USN (Ret.).
† Captain Joseph P. Moorer, USN, a Naval Academy classmate of Shelton.

Admiral Shelton: No. Well, that's probably right. My exec was a guy named Lee Wells, and he was a mustang. If you would put him education wise up against his peers he wasn't there. But if you put him up against his peers seamanwise he was all there.

Paul Stillwell: And that's what you needed.

Admiral Shelton: And that's what I needed. He had his master's license, for instance. He had his ship pilot's license, all that kind of stuff. So he taught me a lot. I didn't teach him very much, I don't think, but we managed to stay out of trouble a lot of times when we might have been in trouble otherwise because he really knew his seamanship. The gunnery officer on there was a Marine and he was great. My engineer was an old fellow that just knew how to keep the goddamned gear stuff running down there. [Laughter] He would have been out of place on any other ship, but he knew how to operate that one. The IC, the intercommunications thing, gave us a fit on there all the time. Anything that had to do with electricity or sound gave us a fit on that ship, so the electricians were busy 24 hours a day on that ship.

Paul Stillwell: Any disciplinary problems in the crew.

Admiral Shelton: No, we didn't have a single one that I can remember. I don't remember that I ever had to bring a guy to mast for instance, and that's pretty unusual.[*]

Paul Stillwell: They were too busy to get in trouble.

Admiral Shelton: Too busy to get in trouble. And they had my blessing to go ashore and try to get into trouble on occasion. I figured they rated that.

Paul Stillwell: Did you take extra safety precautions for a night replenishment?

---

[*] Captain's mast is a sort of court in which the commanding officer of a unit listens to requests, awards non-judicial punishment, or issues commendations. Most often captain's mast is used for punishment of lesser offenses than those that merit courts-martial.

Admiral Shelton: Yes and no. The routine was pretty standard, whether it was day or night, and the other situation we encountered a lot of out there was fog, so visibility was whatever you had, day, night or in the fog. But I don't recall that we spent that much time worrying about night just because it was night. Not all the ships had it, but we were lucky enough to have one of the little Raytheon pathfinder radars on there, and that was great. Boy, you know, you could make approaches with it. You could do a lot of things with it. And so that took away the sting really of a lot of things. But I thought the world of that crew, and I really enjoyed that year on there. I thought that was probably as productive a year as I ever spent in the Navy. [Laughter]

Paul Stillwell: You've got to have some good, reliable helmsmen for that kind of a job.

Admiral Shelton: Oh, yes, and that's where my exec came in. I mean, he watched that helmsman like a hawk. [Laughter] And, you know, on older ships you always wonder—not whether it's going to happen but when you're going to have a failure of some kind, and we were lucky we didn't have any that gave us real problems. But we had to have two or three helmsmen well qualified, because a lot of times you'd be alongside long enough that you had to have somebody to give somebody some relief because you can only stand there and be exact so long as a helmsman. So we had two or three really well qualified helmsmen, and so we would spell them every once in a while.

Paul Stillwell: I would think a concern with that electrical system would be that you'd get a steering casualty or problem with the gyro.[*]

Admiral Shelton: Well, we had them all, but fortunately we didn't have any of them when we were alongside like that. I could give you another one later on when I had the Tripoli, but we'll get into that I guess a little later on. But as far as the Paricutin—old ship, old systems, old everything, but it did a job.

---

[*] A gyro compass is based on one or more gyroscopes torqued to true north in order to provide true compass readings. Typically, gyro repeaters are in various locations throughout a ship so that compass bearings may be taken at places other than the master gyroscope itself.

Paul Stillwell: Anything more on that tour?

Admiral Shelton: No. I think that's about it. I came back from that, and I was in Subic when I got a telephone call from the detailer in BuPers saying I was going to get orders to be CO of the Tripoli, and that didn't sit well with me at all. I had no doubt about getting an attack carrier, CVA. I found out later that Admiral Clarey wanted someone off the carrier list and junior to the phibron commander to be CO of Tripoli.[*] Certainly the timing and availability were right for me to be the one. So there went my carrier, and I got the Tripoli instead.

Anyway, I left Subic and came back to San Diego. Incidentally, Tripoli was out there off Vietnam, but it wasn't time for me to take over yet, so I came back to San Diego and went through amphibious school basically for about three weeks. Maybe six weeks, I guess. Then I turned right around and went right back out to Vietnam and relieved off of the coast of Danang.

Paul Stillwell: What month did you take over Tripoli?[†]

Admiral Shelton: August of '68. I flew back out there and flew into Danang, and then they picked me up by helicopter and went out to the ship. Very fortunately, I had known Admiral Moorer a little bit here and there, and I had known Bush Bringle fairly well.[‡] He was Seventh Fleet at the time. They both were at the change of command on the Tripoli. I thought that was pretty nice.

Paul Stillwell: Very nice.

---

[*] Admiral Bernard A. Clarey, USN, served as Vice Chief of Naval Operations from 17 January 1968 to 30 October 1970. His oral history is in the Naval Institute collection. Phibron is short for amphibious squadron, the commander of which is generally a senior captain.

[†] USS Tripoli (LPH-10), an Iwo Jima-class amphibious assault ship, was commissioned 6 August 1966. She was 602 feet long, 84 feet in the beam, extreme width of 105 feet, maximum draft of 29 feet, had a standard displacement of 18,000 tons, and a top speed of 24 knots. She remained in service until decommissioned on 15 September 1995.

[‡] Admiral Thomas H. Moorer, USN, served as Chief of Naval Operations from 1 August 1967 to 1 July 1970. His oral history is in the Naval Institute collection. Vice Admiral William F. Bringle, USN, served as Commander Seventh Fleet from 6 November 1967 to 10 March 1970.

Admiral Shelton: Yes, two of the guys I respected the most in the whole world. So I relieved Pinky Adams in August and stayed out there for another ten months, which meant that out of those two years, I spent 19 months deployed.*

My boss was Art Battson, who still lives here in Coronado and a very fine boss. Couldn't ask for a better one.†

Paul Stillwell: Was he a phibron commander?

Admiral Shelton: PhibRon 5, I believe it was. He was the squadron commander, and he was based on the Tripoli.

Paul Stillwell: And probably dual-hatted as commander of the amphibious ready group.

Admiral Shelton: Yes, although Admiral Behrens was out there in those days, and he was in the amphibious hierarchy.‡

Paul Stillwell: Well, I think it was one of the phibgrus as they called them then and the squadrons reported to the phib group.

Admiral Shelton: I know later on the one big administrative landing that we made there Admiral Behrens ran that. We were talking about steering casualties and all that sort of thing. The Tripoli class of ship had a throttle mechanism down in the engine room that was not very good. Every once in a while it had a tendency to go silent, so to speak; it would go dead. You had no throttle control. And here we were in the middle of this amphibious operation, trying to be as silent as we could possibly be, and make no noise over the radio or anything else. Steaming along at not very much, maybe about five

---
* Captain William L. Adams, USN, commanded the amphibious assault ship Tripoli (LPH-10) from 7 September 1967 to at August 1968.
† Captain Arthur L. Battson, Jr., USN.
‡ Rear Admiral William W. Behrens, Jr., USN, Commander Amphibious Group One.

knots, in formation with a whole bunch of amphibious ships. Throttle failure. So there we were dead in the water.

Man, we'd had enough of this by then. We'd even had it worked on in Subic two or three times by then. So I hesitate to say that what you did was to use a bigger hammer, but it something pretty close akin of that. [Laughter] That you hit one of the mechanisms down there a certain way with a certain amount of weight, and generally speaking things got back on the line. Fortunately that's what happened in this case. But, anyway, that kind of got my attention for the last time, and I sent a message in to Subic and to NavShips that was fairly strong language as far as this throttle control business on Tripoli.* So they sent some people all the way out from Washington to fix the damn thing. I'm not sure whether they ever got it fixed, because I think there was something inherent in that system, in the mechanism of that system, that every now and then you were going to have that whether you wanted it or not.

Paul Stillwell: When it's a single-screw ship, you didn't have any redundancy.

Admiral Shelton: Didn't have any redundancy. So it was always a little concern, and, as I say, this had happened to us several times. We'd had it worked on in Subic, and we'd had people come out from Subic to work on it, and it still happened. So finally we got somebody out there from Washington and Subic that managed to fix it for as long as I was on there anyway. I'm not sure what happened after that.

The other thing that that system had was what they called the flume system of stabilization. I don't know who the guy was that thought this up, but [laughter] the way it was supposed to work was that when you rolled all the water down in these flume tanks was supposed to roll the other way and stabilize you. That didn't happen that way at all. You rolled one way and all the water went that way.

Paul Stillwell: Made it worse.

---

* NavShips—Naval Ship Systems Command.

Admiral Shelton: Made it worse. And I complained about that too. I sent several messages about that, and we got several messages back basically saying, "Well, it is a problem, but you just have to handle it the best way you can." So that's what we did, which meant that we were able to handle it hardly at all.

Paul Stillwell: And that's a high-freeboard ship, so you've got a lot of sail area.*

Admiral Shelton: Yes, and you needed that ballast, so it wasn't a question of just pumping all the water overboard. That would have been easy, but it wasn't exactly a question of that. We tried most everything, filling the flume tanks all the way and everything else. I think we finally ended up doing that rather than having the water sloshing around no matter what.

Paul Stillwell: Cuts down the free-surface effect.

Admiral Shelton: Yes. I remember after we left Vietnam and went up to Yokosuka on the way home, we knew that we were going to have quartering swells all the way back to Hawaii because it was that time of year, February and March. You had the jet stream, and you had the quartering swells going that way. Commander Don Perry was my exec; he and I and the ship's engineer and everybody else, damage control and everybody else—most of our time in Yokosuka that we weren't shopping, we spent inspecting that ship to make sure that everything was secured.† And, of course, you had to do it almost on a daily basis because people were bringing back things, some heavy things. So you had to make sure that everything, everything, everything was really secured and in place and it wasn't going to go skating across the deck some place.

Sure enough, when we left Yokosuka we started rolling. We rolled and we rolled and we rolled and we rolled. Even Art Battson finally called one day and said, "Isn't there anything you can do to stop this hummer from rolling?"

---
* "Sail area" is a term for the vertical hull surface of a ship on which the wind exerts force.
† Commander Donald W. Perry, USN.

I said, "Yes, sir. You can turn it and go to some other port [laughter] or go in any different direction, but as long as we're going to go where we're supposed to go we're going to roll." And we did until we got about a day out of Hawaii. But there was nothing to do. You'd just sit there and rode it out.

Paul Stillwell: How big a roll period?

Admiral Shelton: Oh, it was 10 or 12 degrees, maybe 14 degrees. I forget who I was talking to here recently, but somebody who had been on the same type ship, the Iwo Jima, the Guam, Tripoli, New Orleans. They had had a similar experience, and they had finally put together a barnburner blast to NavShips like I did, and they got a similar answer. But by that time that class of ship was pretty close to going out of business, so I don't think anything ever happened to that flume system.

Paul Stillwell: Well, please tell me more about your deployment period over in Vietnam, the types of operations you were involved in.

Admiral Shelton: Well, our operations basically were supporting the Marines of course, so we had CH-53E, we had CH-46s coming and going, all day, all night.[*] We were operating right off the beach for the most part, not very far out, a couple or three miles. Our biggest business was bringing casualties back and getting them into our operating rooms—on the ship we had two full-fledged operating rooms—and then being able to get them over to a hospital ship.

Most of the kinds of injuries that we were getting in those days were landmine kind of stuff, and that's pretty bad. I had never been next to that sort of thing. I wasn't sure I wanted to be next to it then, but we gave them good support in the sense that we were right there. It wasn't very far out there, and it was better than the kind of medical treatment they were able to get where they were. So as soon as you could get them back out there and then get them over to the hospital ship, that's what we did. But it was pretty constant, going and coming. Then there would be a certain number of Marine

---

[*] CH-53s and CH-46s were different types of helicopters.

platoons or whatever that would be brought out of there for a day's rest or something like that. But that's what we did. We supported all the Marine involvement in that part where we were.

Paul Stillwell: Probably saved some lives from people who got stabilized till they could get aboard.

Admiral Shelton: Undoubtedly that was the case, because the medics we had on there were first class and so were the operating rooms, and so was the hospital ward that we had on there within the limits of what it was. So if we could get them over there, we had a triage area right there before you even got to the operating rooms. So basically it was a question where you landed a helicopter back there at the aft elevator. You took them down the elevator right to the triage area. Then the operating rooms were back up again, so we had an elevator that took them right back up to the operating room, and so forth and so on. Then as soon as you could if they needed it, why, we would get them on over to a hospital ship.

Paul Stillwell: That was a period that the antiwar movement was really beginning to bubble up.

Admiral Shelton: Yes, that's right. We didn't get much of that on there. You know, I've always been surprised that we didn't either by mail or otherwise, but we really didn't get—at least I was not conscious of getting that kind of communications.

Paul Stillwell: Well, I was out there at the same time, and you really felt isolated because a lot of the news came from Stars and Stripes, which was pretty well digested before you get it.*

Admiral Shelton: Before you get it.

---

* Stars & Stripes was a daily newspaper produced by the U.S. armed services mainly for reading by service members. It had separate European and Pacific editions.

Paul Stillwell: For example I heard about all the disruption at the 1968 Democratic convention in Chicago, but it wasn't till years later that I saw the TV tapes that I really had a sense of it.

Admiral Shelton: You had a sense of it. Well, that's about right. Certainly where I was we didn't have any real knowledge of that kind of thing. We were there doing a job, and that's what we were doing.

Paul Stillwell: There's another factor—that when people are doing a real job it means more than just going through all the training cycles.

Admiral Shelton: All the training cycles, that's right, for sure. So it was a question of staying right there and being into the wind most of the time as far as landing the helicopters a little bit. A lot of times we weren't steaming very much; we were almost dead in the water.

Paul Stillwell: A floating airport.

Admiral Shelton: A floating airport. That's what it was.

Paul Stillwell: Did you get any good port visits in the Far East?

Admiral Shelton: We went back through Hong Kong and Yokosuka. That was it. Of course, in Hong Kong we tied up at a buoy again right there at the foot of Broadway, so to speak. I was remembering my occasion on the Paricutin when we had had so much trouble trying to tie up to that buoy, single screw and all that kind of stuff. This was no different except it went a lot easier. [Laughter] We were able to get somebody on the buoy and get tied up without a whole lot of trouble. The thing that helped us the most was that you have a pretty steady current one way there, and even though it was a fairly swift current when you got lined up, why, all you had to do was steam up there steady enough to get hooked up. Not like it was in San Diego with the Paricutin. So once we got there there we were. We were sitting, you know, spitting distance to the beach.

Paul Stillwell: The China Fleet Club and the Hong Kong Hilton.

Admiral Shelton: The China Fleet Club and the Hong Kong Hilton, and they were right there. You could see them. And so, yes, we had a good port visit to Hong Kong, and then we went on to Yokosuka and had a good port visit there. We had a long rolling ride back to Hawaii and then on back to the States.

Paul Stillwell: Another trend of that time was racial unrest. Did you see any evidence of that on board?

Admiral Shelton: I didn't remember having any of it on either the Paricutin or the Tripoli. I sometimes ask myself if I was blind to the situation, but I don't think I was. I think some if it would have been reflected one way or other in fisticuffs or mast cases or something like that, but I didn't have any of that.

Paul Stillwell: If there was, it got settled at a lower level.

Admiral Shelton: Yes. If there was, it got settled at a lower level, and I never knew about it.

Paul Stillwell: Did you feel a sense of disappointment that you got the LPH instead of a CV?

Admiral Shelton: Definitely. A tremendous sense of disappointment there. Once I found out at least to my satisfaction why I was on the Tripoli instead of otherwise, why, it took some of the sting out of it but nevertheless I'd been brought up in carriers.

Paul Stillwell: You were a tailhooker.

Admiral Shelton: I was a tailhooker, and I'd been brought up that way, and that's what I expected to do. It was quite a shock to me basically to find out that I was not going to get a carrier. I really considered calling back to the detailer and saying, "Take it and shove it," you know, but I didn't do that. I guess, looking back, a good thing I didn't. For one thing, I didn't know the detailer, and no telling what he might have said to me.

Paul Stillwell: Well, I would guess that that would be a hard job for a detailer to sell to a captain who wanted and expected a carrier.

Admiral Shelton: I don't think he was particularly worried about whether he was going to sell it to me or not. It was a, "You know, here it is, and this is what's you're going to do or else." Well, the or else part was that the war was still on, and I sort of felt like it was an opportunity to come back out here, so in the end I think that's what turned me around, that I would have an opportunity to get back out here again, and even though it wasn't on a carrier, why, I kept getting a lot of sympathy from my other CO buddies that were on carriers at one time or another, either in the O-club or when I was on the Paricutin.

Paul Stillwell: What might have been the "or else" if you had just said, "I won't do that job?"

Admiral Shelton: It meant get out.

Paul Stillwell: That was the only other alternative?

Admiral Shelton: That was the only other alternative. I suppose he probably could have given me a set of orders somewhere, but it wouldn't have been a set of orders that I would like, I'm sure. And it would not have been a set of orders where I'd be doing what I thought I should be doing. So in the end the only answer for me would have been to get out, because I probably wouldn't have been willing to accept what the other orders would have been.

Paul Stillwell: What do you recall about your relations with the Marines on board the Tripoli?

Admiral Shelton: They were good. I let them do their business basically. I let a few of the senior ones know that I knew what NWP-31 was [laughter] and that whatever they wanted to do, I would be familiar with it. Basically, I told them, "I'm your guy to support you. Tell me what you want, and I'll do my best to make it so." I think that's the way we operated, and I don't recall that we had any big problem with the Marines. I didn't have any personality problems with them. You know, Marines are Marines, and you've got to learn what Marines are. Once you learn that, why, then things go better.

Paul Stillwell: It's interesting, though, from what you're saying that you apparently enjoyed the ammo ship more than the Tripoli.

Admiral Shelton: I did. You know, it was really a more interesting job, and it was closer to the action basically. When I had the Tripoli, I wasn't flying over there and I wasn't flying in combat. I wasn't doing any of that. Basically I was a support platform for the Marines. But when I had the Paricutin, I was a lot closer to it, and you could see a lot of the results of what you were doing.

Paul Stillwell: Anything else on Tripoli before moving on?

Admiral Shelton: No. Came back, and I was fortunate enough that Vice Admiral J. Victor Smith by that time was ComPhibPac, and so he officiated at the change of command.[*]

---

[*] Vice Admiral John Victor Smith, USN, served as Commander Amphibious Force Pacific Fleet from May 1968 to July 1970.

Let's see. Then I went back to OP-506, Aviation Military Requirements. There was some noise made that—in fact, I had one set of orders that I was going to go to Tufts College for a year, and I didn't care much for that. I had already been to the Naval War College, and I didn't think I needed to go to Tufts, although it did tie in to my previous duty in OP-602. While I was mulling over the Tufts possibility, I received a surprise phone call from my classmate and friend Bob Baldwin, who was in BuPers at that time. I told him that I wasn't really too interested in the Tufts job. As I recall, he said, "That's why I'm calling you, because I want you to go to OP-506." It turns out there was a vacancy there, and they needed a guy with carrier aviation experience in the right seniority to fit in. Bob thought I fit the bill, so I went to OP-506.

Paul Stillwell: You got to work for Admiral Connolly again.

Admiral Shelton: I got to work for Admiral Connolly again.[*] And it was good. I didn't mind that.

Paul Stillwell: What specifically did the job involve?

Admiral Shelton: We had the job of basically buying airplanes, what kind of airplanes we wanted. Now, you know, NavAirSysCom basically had the job of buying airplanes as such, but we had the job of saying what the requirements were and what kind of airplanes we were going to buy.[†] At that time we were trying to buy the F-14, so there was a lot of emphasis on the F-14.[‡] Scotty Lamoreaux was my F-14 detail officer.[§] I knew Admiral Connolly's interest in the situation, so I said to Scotty, "I know that I don't have to tell you this because Admiral Connolly's going to tell me and you both, but your job is to see Admiral Connolly whenever he wants to see you and to keep him informed and to do

---

[*] Vice Admiral Thomas F. Connolly, USN, served as Deputy Chief of Naval Operations (Air) from 1 November 1966 to 31 August 1971. Admiral Connolly's oral history is in the Naval Institute collection.
[†] NavAirSysCom—Naval Air Systems Command.
[‡] Grumman F-14 Tomcat fighters first entered training squadrons in late 1972. The F-14A version was 64 feet long, wingspan of 38 feet, normal takeoff weight of 55,000 pounds, and top speed of Mach 2.34. It was equipped with a 20-millimeter cannon and was designed to carry a variety of types of missiles—Sparrow, Sidewinder, and Phoenix—and later equipped to deliver bombs as well.
[§] Captain Lewis Scott Lamoreaux, USN.

what he says." [Laughter] "And don't worry about me. Just keep me cut in." And that's basically what happened.

But with all the other guys it was a little more regular business. I had Charlie Hunter and Lyle Bull in there from A-6 days.* They're both Navy Cross guys. I had Boyd Muncie back there in the air weapons business.† He and guy named Jim Foster were just completing about a year-long study on what needed to be done to update our weapons and weapons delivery systems, and that's when we first started getting into Walleye, laser systems, et cetera, et cetera.‡ So that was pretty interesting. I had a guy who was my deputy whose name was Bing Crosby, and his dad was the guy that built the Lake of the Ozarks.§ They were from Warsaw in Central Missouri. So at times when we didn't have anything else to talk about, we could always talk about that.

It was a good job. Basically I was keeping a hat on everything that was going on in the aviation requirements thing. I had some 35-36 guys working in there, all first-rate people that didn't need to be told all the time what to do and knew how to do it. And almost everything they did came and went through me, so we had a handle on everything. But my job was to pick out the idiosyncrasies in things and point them out to people up the road that they might not catch otherwise and make sure that everything was pretty much trying to stay on track. Try to point out any areas where attention was needed in any of the airplane systems or anything like that. We had a lot of junior meetings up there in Admiral Connolly's office about buying airplanes and whether we could replace the C-2 and the E-2 and everything else.**

Paul Stillwell: And probably the S-2.

Admiral Shelton: Oh, yes. Well, that was the conversation basically because we basically didn't have any S-2s left at that point.†† We were using C-2s and so forth. A

---

* Commander Charles B. Hunter, USN; Lieutenant Commander Lyle F. Bull, USN.
† Captain Wendell Boyd Muncie, USN.
‡ Captain James R. Foster, USN.
§ Captain Derrill P. Crosby, USN.
** The C-2 is a carrier on-board logistics plane; the E-2 is an electronic surveillance plane with look-down radar.
†† The S-2 was a carrier-based antisubmarine warfare aircraft.

lot of discussion at that point, the S-3A was coming along, and it was getting in its early flights, and there was a lot of consideration to making a COD out of it.* Part of the big problem with any COD was that with F-14s coming on you had to have a COD with enough legs that could ferry an engine from here to there with a fair amount of range. And as it turned out the S-3 really couldn't do that. The C-2 was the only one that could and still is the only one that can.

There were a lot of those kinds of discussions and at the same time putting out any fires that came to light with any kind of an airplane problem. For instance—and we didn't have this kind of a problem—but take the MD-80 problem that just came up in the civilian world here lately.† If you had some kind of a serious problem that happened on an airplane like that, why, it was between you and NavAirSysCom and other people. It was a job to put out the fire and get something done.

Paul Stillwell: Well, that as I remember was a horizontal stabilizer, and so they looked at all of them in that kind of airplane.

Admiral Shelton: Yes, that's right. And so, you know, there were always the discussions about grounding them or not grounding them. So you're in on a lot of that. Let's see. Steve De La Mater was OP-50B at that point; he'd had an LPH also.‡ Anyway, OP-506 was a good job, and as it turns out that's the job I made flag from. I got there in '69 and was selected for flag in April '71. My date of rank was November '71. So it was a good tour for me.

Paul Stillwell: Well, it turned out the LPH paid off after all, because a number of the CVA skippers didn't make flag.

---

* The S-3 Viking is a jet-powered, carrier-based antisubmarine aircraft with a four-person crew. Built by Lockheed, its first delivery to a fleet training squadron was in February 1974. The S-3A has a wingspan of 68 feet, 8 inches; length of 53 feet, 4 inches; maximum gross weight of 52,539 pounds, and a top speed of 514 miles per hour.
† The Boeing (originally McDonnell Douglas) MD-80, powered by two jet engines, was certified by the Federal Aviation Administration in August 1980 and entered airline service in October 1980.
‡ Captain Stephen T. De La Mater, USN, director, naval air weapons analysis staff, office of the DCNO (Air Warfare); he had previously commanded the amphibious assault ship Guam (LPH-9).

Admiral Shelton: Well, that's right. And you always have to have a certain amount of luck. You always have to have a certain amount of service reputation, I think, that goes along with all of this. I think service reputation really is one of the most important things, and nobody ever talks about it. I don't care how you spell it, everybody that's in this Navy has a certain amount of service reputation, good, bad, indifferent or outstanding or not. And that follows you. When you get before a selection board of any variety, service reputation, I think, is one of the more important things that anybody looks at.

Paul Stillwell: And sometimes it's a matter of luck that there are several people on that board who do know your reputation well.

Admiral Shelton: That's right, and there are those that consider that favoritism. I don't consider that favoritism at all. I think if you've done your job and you've been a performer and you go before a selection board, if there isn't somebody on there that knows what you've done, then you've missed the mark. So I never have thought that that was a part. I'm not saying that there haven't been incidences, and I'm sure you know SecNav and CNO and some of the others there, there are certain people they want to see get selected and they get selected. And that's going to happen. I don't care whether you're in the Navy or on the outside in some company or whatever, but in general terms I would still say that service reputation is the thing that you have going for you above all else.

Paul Stillwell: In that OP-05 tour do you have any specific comments about Admiral Connolly, his working style, his priorities, his personality?

Admiral Shelton: Yes. Admiral Connolly liked to think that he knew the English language better than anybody in the world, and he probably did. Bill Houser was there at the time, and I was given the job of writing a Distinguished Service Medal nomination for Houser for Admiral Connolly to send forward.* He didn't pick me by name. He just put out the word to 50B to get somebody to write up this award. Well, it was me. So I

---
* Rear Admiral William D. Houser, USN.

did like I'd done at OP-602C. I didn't have the benefit of a file, but I found a file that had good examples of what will sell and what won't sell and how you write them up and how you don't write them up, et cetera, et cetera. So I spent about a week or ten days, I guess, on that one. And knowing how Admiral Connolly was as far as the English language was concerned and putting things together, why, I was very persnickety with my own self to try to get it right. So at the end I sent up this proposed recommendation, and, lo and behold, I got it back. Admiral Connolly liked to use a blue pen or pencil, and he had put a little blue note on the top saying, "Who did this? This is very good." [Laughter]

Paul Stillwell: Made your day.

Admiral Shelton: Yes, made my day. And then he found out and he called me up there and said, "You know, you really did do a good job." And I said, "You probably don't remember, but I'm the guy that showed up at your desk down there at Patuxent one time and couldn't get in a certain class and later did."

He said, "Oh, yeah, I do remember that." But he was good to work for. He could chew ass with the best of them, but he could also put out the proper kind of praise at the right time with the best of them.

Paul Stillwell: And he was really the torchbearer for the F-14 program.

Admiral Shelton: Oh, amen. He was the torchbearer for a lot of things. Yes, he never hesitated to go where he needed to go to get support for what he sincerely thought needed to be done. And he was good. I thought he was great. I never did work for him in a squadron sense other than when I had VF-92 and he was the cardiv commander. But otherwise I was never in a squadron of course with him or anything like that, so it was strictly that kind of business there in OP-506. But, yes, he was good.

Paul Stillwell: What was your first flag job?

Admiral Shelton: Well, I got trapped in the OP-06 organization again. I say that lovingly, because I liked it, but I wasn't sure I wanted to go down there. Anyway, the flag selection list was hardly dry when I got a call from somebody telling me that I was going to go down to OP-61, which was political-military business. Good business. Not quite the same intensity as command relationships or anything like that, but it was a good job and one that everybody likes. So I went down to be OP-61B.

Admiral Small, a black shoe, was my boss, and he was a good boss.* I've had nothing but good bosses basically. That was, I think, one of the best things that has happened to me. Almost everybody that I ever worked for I thought was a good boss. But anyway he was a good boss, and this was basically taking care of Latin American affairs, and all the naval attachés in Washington came under that shop. So we went to a lot of attaché functions. I'd never been in that kind of line before and didn't know that I really wanted to be in that kind of line, but there I was.

I met some very interesting people. I remember Admiral Alvarez from Argentina that I thought was just one of the best guys I ever met. And every year at the Army-Navy game it was OP-61's job to get these guys to the Army-Navy game and back without too much damage. [Laughter]

It turned out to be a fascinating job in many respects. I got to know a lot of very fine naval attachés there in Washington. And my boss and myself were members of the Inter-American Defense Board there in Washington coming down from the OAS, Organization of American States. The Inter-American Defense Board would take a trip about once a year, and generally speaking the Air Force always provided transportation. But anyway we had several trips, because South America was where many of these people were from. We went to Brazil, Argentina, Uruguay, and Paraguay. At times we went other places down there, and that was fascinating. Got to see a lot of the countries that I'd heard of but never been to before and under the right circumstances. In other words, there was a lot of hospitality and we got to see the right places and the right people.

---

* Rear Admiral Walter L. Small, Jr., USN, Director, Politico-Military Policy Division, OpNav.

We happened to be in Buenos Aires when Peron came back from Spain.* That's the one occasion when we were asked to stay in our hotel rooms and watch it on TV instead of being anywhere else. As it turns out, they taxied his airplane out to the end of the airport and there was nothing going on, so late in the day they finally let us out of the hotel and we did other things.

Another trip we went up and did the Alaska and Canadian bit. We went to Yellowknife and went down in a gold mine 4,000 feet. Went up to Point Barrow and to Prudhoe and visited a couple of the radar stations across the way and at Churchill or Randolph. And went on over to the Air Force Base in Thule, Greenland. We went from there up to Point Alert, which is the northernmost point in Canada. We had some pretty sophisticated listening stations up there in those days. Strangely enough, that was in May, I think, and there wasn't a lot of snow around, but they had these little French tractors up there that looked like a combination between a Volkswagen and a Jeep and a tractor. I don't remember what they were, but they were pretty good little vehicles, and they ran on tracks like a tank. And without any snow up there you've never seen so much dust that far north in all your life. It was one dusty place. But that trip was interesting.

Paul Stillwell: Was the objective of all this—building hemispheric goodwill?

Admiral Shelton: Basically, and showing as much as you could of each other's capabilities and what was there and why it was there, et cetera, et cetera. So we had some very good trips.

As I said, one of the jobs that fell to us was to get all these fellows to the Army-Navy game every year, and that was quite an organizational task. We usually did it by Greyhound bus and usually stopped in Baltimore on the way back at a hotel for dinner. So we kept it pretty straightforward, and they all enjoyed it. I always did enjoy it.

About halfway through that tour, Admiral Small retired, and so I was elevated to OP-61. I thought, "Well, I've got another year and a half or so here enjoying this kind of

---

* Juan Domingo Peron was President of Argentina from 1945 to 1955, when he was ousted by a military revolt. He returned to the country in 1973, was again elected President that year, and served until his death in 1974.

thing." But that didn't last very long. I suddenly got a call one day to go up and see the VCNO, who was Admiral Weisner.[*] I'd never known Admiral Weisner before except by name and reputation, but he knew me. It turned out that there were some problems out in Subic Bay that needed to be rectified. Without going into all the details, Admiral Clarey had called Admiral Weisner and said, "This is an aviation problem. It's all your fault. You get an aviator out here that's going to fix it. I want him out here in ten days."[†] So there I was up in the VCNO's office, and he was telling me, "You're going to Subic and you have to be out there in ten days. If you want to get briefed on why you're going, why, you go over and see So-and-so, and he'll tell you."

So I said, "Does this have to be?" I said, "You know, I just moved up to OP-61, and I was kind of looking forward to being the head of that shed for about a year or so."

He said, "Well, that's not going to happen. You're going to Subic."

So I said, "Well, okay, ten days." I said, "You know, my dad back in Iowa is pretty ill. Could I at least extend it to 15 days so I can take a couple of days and go back there and see him?"

He said, "Yeah, you can do that." So I did. Well, in the meanwhile somewhere in there, why, I'd gone back down to the office and I was trying to digest all this. And one of the things about that office was that when Admiral Zumwalt who was CNO by then, had anybody like an ambassador in for a call, why, he generally had OP-61 come up unless it was some other problem.[‡] But generally OP-61 would go up and sit in on the office call and take notes for anything that was to be done as a result of the call or anything like that.

So I got this call to go up and sit it on the meeting between the ambassador to Iceland and Admiral Zumwalt. The problem was such that the ambassador to Iceland was telling Admiral Zumwalt that he wanted a new admiral in Iceland. I could see what was coming. [Laughter] Boy. So as soon as that meeting was over, I stopped back by the VCNO's office and I said, "You're going to get a call very shortly," because Admiral

---

[*] Admiral Maurice F. Weisner, USN, served as Vice Chief of Naval Operations from 1 September 1972 to 1 September 1973.
[†] Admiral Bernard A. Clarey, USN, served as Commander in Chief Pacific Fleet, 5 December 1970 to 30 September 1973.
[‡] Admiral Elmo R. Zumwalt, Jr., USN, served as Chief of Naval Operations from 1 July 1970 to 29 June 1974.

Zumwalt was not yet clued in on my going to Subic or what the problem was or anything else. So I went back and I asked to see Admiral Weisner, which I did, and I said, "You're going to get another call here in a few minutes about Iceland, and I don't want to go to Iceland."

Paul Stillwell: Subic was beginning to look better.

Admiral Shelton: Subic was beginning to look better already, although another classmate of mine ended up going up to Iceland. He thoroughly enjoyed the job, and I think I would have too. But I didn't want to go. And so he said, basically he said, "Never mind. I'll take care of that." And he did. So I went back to Iowa to see my dad for a few days. Came back to Washington, and this was in January I guess, first part of February in 1973.

Paul Stillwell: So the war in Vietnam was just about over at that point.

Admiral Shelton: Just about over. We'll get into that in a minute. But, anyway, this was so sudden, and the girls were in school. This is always a problem, of course, when these things happen, anything like this happens. We owned the townhouse that we were living in there in McLean, and so we decided that best thing was for Peggy to stay there with the girls until school was out and then she'd come out. So, sure enough, I went on out, and I eventually relieved.

Well, when I first got there, why, I was kind of sitting on my hands. I didn't really have anything to do until I relieved the guy that was there. Turned out to be John Dick, who I'd worked for in OP-602 and who I had a lot of respect for.[*] It turns out that's when the first POWs started coming back from Vietnam.

Paul Stillwell: What was the billet, ComNavPhil?

Admiral Shelton: It was ComUSNavPhil, Com U.S. Naval Forces, Philippines, CinCPac Rep Philippines, and one other hat. Those hats had originally been divided between the

---

[*] Rear Admiral John H. Dick, USN.

old commands up at Sangley and down at Subic. Then they brought both of those commands, two guys, down to Subic, and then they made it all one job, one guy. That's where it was when I got there. I had been there about a week when Admiral Gayler made his first trip out there to Clark to see the returning POWs.* And I requested permission to go up there and see some of the guys, because I knew most of the guys that were coming out. Ed Martin was one of them.† In particular I wanted to see Bill Lawrence because I'd known him quite well.‡ And so I did. I went up and got to see Bill Lawrence and the rest of the guys that were coming out at that time.

So then I finally took over from John Dick, and the big problem at that time was racial. They'd had a big problem on the Hassayampa, they'd had a big problem on the Kitty Hawk, and back in San Diego they'd had the problem on the Constellation.§ There at Subic there was a gang of people that had decided that they wanted to run through the chiefs' club there and tear it down basically, and they proceeded to do that. There were a group of people that wanted to call a section of Olongapo their own—the "Jungle"—and nobody else could come in there, and they did that. There were a group of people that wanted to beat up on their own shipmates coming back from the main gate down to the ships, and they were doing that. So my job was to put an end to that sort of thing.

So I got together with the COs of the eight commands there, even though I had direct command over none of them. They all had their own chain of command, but I wrote concurrent fitness reports on all of them, too, so they understood the situation. [Laughter] So I got them together, and I said, "You know this is nonsense." Whitey Weidman was CO of the naval station.** I had been through CinCPacFlt and had talked to the appropriate people there. I said to these COs, "Well, my idea of how to help this

---

* Admiral Noel A. M. Gayler, USN, served as Commander in Chief Pacific from 1 September 1972 to 30 August 1976. His oral history is in the Naval Institute collection. In February 1973 the first prisoners of war released by North Vietnam were flown to Clark Air Force Base in the Philippines to undergo medical evaluation and treatment before returning to the United States.
† Commander Edward H. Martin, USN. The oral history of Martin, who retired as a vice admiral, is in the Naval Institute collection.
‡ Captain William P. Lawrence, USN. The oral history of Lawrence, who retired as a vice admiral, is in the Naval Institute collection.
§ Racial disturbances broke out in the carrier Kitty Hawk (CVA-63) on 12 October 1972; in the oiler Hassayampa (AO-145) on 16 October 1972; and in the carrier Constellation (CVA-64) on 3 November 1972. See Captain Paul B. Ryan, USN (Ret.), "USS Constellation Flare-up: Was it Mutiny?" U.S. Naval Institute Proceedings, January 1976, pages 46-53.
** Captain Robert M. Weidman, Jr., USN.

situation initially is to put into effect something like the old armed guard that they used to have in Hawaii in the old days." They were a no-nonsense group, more or less like shore patrol, only they were a permanent group that had permanent people assigned and proper training and they knew how to handle a situation. In other words, they were like a good squad of police that knew how to handle a problem.

So the CO of the naval station found this big black chief whose name was Lloyd. One of the softest speaking people I ever saw in my life. He was about 6-7, and he was a black belt in karate. We decided that he was in charge of the newborn shore patrol. I got the blessings of CinCPacFlt, who was Admiral Clarey still. And got the blessings to task the ships to provide men. Normally when the ships would come in they would designate people to shore patrol, but it was just while they were in port. They didn't undergo any training basically. You were not going to get the kind of people that you needed in that circumstance, so when they got out in town they basically got run over by the guys that wanted to make trouble.

So I got the blessing of CinCPacFlt to task the ships to send a certain number of people there on temporary duty assignment. Well, the ships didn't like that, and I couldn't blame them for not liking it. But it was their people that were causing the problems, and so I felt it was partly their responsibility to help fix the situation. So I give them credit. They sent good people. Chief Lloyd took them in hand for about a month or so, and things started changing. We got public works to put up a whole series of floodlights, from the main gate down to the piers where the ships were. And we put out in legal form what the liberty path would be from the main gate back to the ships. Anybody outside of that path during certain hours was going to be apprehended and returned to his ship. Not arrested or anything like that, just returned to the ship. And there were a couple of other measures we set into motion.

But anyway basically Chief Lloyd went out in town with this group of newborn shore patrol that had some capability, and they went into the "Jungle" area where they'd been having trouble. A few people tried to take him on, and they learned right away that that was not a good idea. [Laughter] So the word started spreading. "Look out for this new guy that has this shore patrol. He's going to rack your ass." And rack it he did.

At the same time, I had gone out to the mayor of Olongapo and said, "You know, you and I are having the same kind of problems out here. Your bars are being torn up, and my sailors are getting beat up. Part of it is because neither you nor I can get a red light vehicle down some of these streets full of potholes, and they can't make it in time to do any good." I said, "I've got a cement plant on the base. You've got a lot of people out here that can handle it. I'll furnish all the material if you'll furnish the labor and we'll pave those streets and we'll make one-way traffic down here. We'll come out and help you make one-way traffic." So when you put that all together and the liberty corridor, so to speak, from the main gate down the ships and the word getting out that certain things weren't going to happen anymore, in about two months that situation really turned around.

Paul Stillwell: Great.

Admiral Shelton: And it was a pretty interesting evolution. So that was my start of the tour at Subic Bay. We had all kinds of interesting incidents out there, most of which I don't think we need to bother getting into. After school was out, why, Peggy and our younger daughter flew out to Manila, and we were able to fly them down from Manila down to Subic. So there they were, in a foreign land not of their making. Donna was a freshman in high school then. My other daughter, Deb, was already graduated, of course, and she was married. So we ended up there, and that's where the interesting shell collecting started.

My wife had known Mary Cousins, wife of Admiral Cousins.[*] She collected seashells. Peggy got interested, and I got interested, and so we sort of got addicted to shell collecting, so we have a pretty good collection of seashells. But beyond that we both enjoyed that tour at Subic. It was a full-time job. My wife never hesitated to go out in town whenever she wanted to. We visited a lot of different spots in the Philippines. Part of my job was CinCPac Rep Phil, and as that I was part of the country team up in

---

[*] Admiral Ralph Cousins, USN, had been Vice Chief of Naval Operations when Shelton was in the Pentagon; in 1972 he became Commander in Chief Atlantic Fleet.

Manila. So once a week I was up in Manila, at least once a week I was up at Manila and sat in on the country team meetings, which were always interesting.

Paul Stillwell: This was always the ambassador and who else?

Admiral Shelton: Well, all of his primary people. CIA and his political advisor, political officer I should say, and all that, and the ambassador at that time was William H. Sullivan, one grand guy if I've ever met one in the diplomatic corps.*

Paul Stillwell: He was the guy that was later out in Iran.

Admiral Shelton: Yes, that's right. And as I mentioned earlier in this whole thing Frank Maestrone was in the political part of the program. And it was always very enjoyable, because I could go up there by helicopter and we could land right there at the embassy and go and come as we needed to. The embassy compound, where they had a club and where some of the people lived and all that, was farther up the road two or three miles, but it was a very nice place where you could go, have dinner, have lunch. And because I was up there so much or whoever had my job was up there so much, why, we actually had a little Quonset hut up there that <u>Stars and Stripes</u> had one end of, and I had the other end as a real small apartment where I could change clothes and stay overnight if I needed to, that kind of thing.

Paul Stillwell: What kind of issues did the country team deal with when you were there?

Admiral Shelton: Well, they were all Philippine issues, and I would not be at liberty to discuss those because they didn't even discuss those outside the country team meetings. But every once in a while something would be in my bailiwick as well, and so they would want to know what I was going to do about it.

---

* William H. Sullivan, a Foreign Service officer, served as U.S. Ambassador to the Philippines from 6 August 1973 to 26 April 1977. He was subsequently ambassador to Iran from 26 May 1977 to 18 June 1977. He left after the Ayatollah Ruhollah Khomeini seized power and declared the nation to be an Islamic republic.

The biggest thing that came my way in that regard was when we started bringing Vietnamese refugees back later on. That was in April of '75.[*] The Philippines didn't want to agree to bring them back through Subic at all. But when they finally did agree to it they agreed that 14 days was the limit. Well, as it turned out, there were many cases when you just couldn't get anybody back out of there in 14 days so they were pretty understanding. They didn't make big noises about it. They'd made their case. Fourteen days was supposedly the limit, and they weren't going to make a big issue out of it.

Paul Stillwell: It became a goal rather than an absolute limit.

Admiral Shelton: A goal, yes. The only one that they ever really insisted on doing anything about was Nguyen Cao Ky when he came through.[†] I think he came back either on the Denver or the Ogden. And they said, "He cannot step foot on Philippine soil." And we lived up to that. We helicoptered him from either the Denver or the Ogden, whichever it was. We landed him over at Cubi Point. We stepped him down on a set of pallets [laughter] that led into the tail end of a C-130, and within three hours he was gone. [Laughter] So he literally did not step foot on Philippine soil, and he was not there more than about three hours.

Paul Stillwell: What was the big objection?

Admiral Shelton: I really don't know, and, you know, it wasn't my bailiwick to argue about that. But I was able to tell the ambassador, "Don't you sweat it. We've got this made." [Laughter] And he was glad about that.

Right in the mouth of Subic Bay there is a little island called Grande Island. It was more or less a recreation island, and so when we got the word initially that we were

---

[*] On 29-30 April 1975, as Saigon, the capital of South Vietnam, was being overrun by the North Vietnamese, U.S. Navy and Marine Corps helicopters evacuated almost 9,000 people. Included were 1,373 Americans, 6,422 of other nationalities, plus 989 Marines inserted to cover the operation. Graham Martin, U.S. ambassador to South Vietnam, was among the last to leave from the rooftop of the American embassy.
[†] Air Marshal Nguyen Cao Ky was the Vice President of the Republic of Vietnam.

going to be hosts to a lot of refugees coming from Vietnam, I told my people, "Well, go up to Clark. See what they plan on doing and come back."[*]

Well, Clark was a totally different situation from us, of course. They had a situation where they were going to have to use their gymnasiums, any building that had a living space where they could put up temporary cots or whatever, any kind. They came back to me and said, "Well, that's what they're going to do, and so probably we can do the same thing here."

I said, "No." We happened to be up at my quarters at the time when we had this meeting and we had an absolutely beautiful view of Grande Island from there so I pointed to Grande Island, and I said, "That's where we are going to put them." We had eight commands there, and they all dived in there and had C-5s bringing tents and cots and pallets and everything down there.[†] We had plenty of little boats like LCMs and that kind of stuff.[‡] A lot of them arrived by air. Some of them arrived by various kinds of ships, and I'll get into that a little bit if you want to. But anyway basically what we did was we went out there and we set up a chain link fence around the whole place. One of the facilities out there was in the old days what they called an old bathhouse where you could change clothes and go swimming and all that kind of stuff because the scuba diving was great right there.

We set it up so that when they got ashore at Grande Island they proceeded right into a corridor where they went through the bathhouse, had medical people inspect them. They turned over all their dirty clothes and everything to us. We gave them new clothes. We took all of their valuables so they wouldn't have any problem with them being stolen. And we had an armored tank that we set right under a big old tree out there right adjacent to the bathhouse, and we put armed Marines up in the tree 24 hours a day. And so we took all of the valuables that they had, and some of them had some pretty nice things. At the end of the day we gave them a receipt for what we got from them. When they were

---

[*] Clark Air Force Base was about 50 miles north of Manila, on the island of Luzon in the Philippines. It was closed as part of the U.S. military withdrawal from the nation in the early 1990s.
[†] The C-5 Galaxy is a jet-powered cargo plane, among the world's largest aircraft. Lockheed-Georgia Company delivered the first operational Galaxy to the 437th Airlift Wing, Charleston Air Force Base, South Carolina, in June 1970.
[‡] LCM—landing craft mechanized, a type of craft equipped with a bow ramp that can be lowered on a beach during an amphibious landing.

going to leave, why, we got their things out of the holding tank so to speak and gave them back to them and they were theirs.

We only had one complaint about valuables out of the whole business, and that was, as I recall, an older woman that complained that she did not get back some of her jewelry or whatever it was that she said had given us. We paid her $2,000, as I remember, right on the spot, and she was happy with that.

We set up medical and dental facilities out there, and in this group of refugees there were professionals, there were engineers, there were dentists, there were doctors. So we set up facilities for all of them and they set up a community. My wife went out there almost every day all day and she had a Vietnamese interpreter that had a large megaphone. And we had a bulletin board. Between the two of those we kept everybody informed of what was going on. We did all the food preparation over at Cubi Point. Helicoptered it by large vats and whatever over to Grande, and we had a great big tent set up there. We served all kinds of good food, and they were never hungry. At night we used the same tent to show movies.

The people out in Olongapo wanted to get involved, so they came in with their twinkling dance and showed the refugees how to do this. Twinkling is a dance where there are two bamboo poles at ground level with a person on each end and the dancer in the middle between the poles. The persons on the ends bang the poles together, and the person in the middle dances in and out between the poles. If unsuccessful, he or she gets a sore ankle or two.

You know, the Cambodians and the Vietnamese had never been big friends. So when the Cambodians first came through, we put them over on the Cubi side at a place we called Dungaree Beach, because we didn't want any fights going on or anything like that. So it wasn't very long before the head shed of the Cambodians requested to see me and he said, "You know, this is silly. We can handle this."

I said, "Okay." So we brought them all over and put them in right along with the Vietnamese.

Paul Stillwell: How much capacity did you have in that space?

Admiral Shelton: Well, we had 14,000 people in there at any one time, and that was loading it up pretty good. So the Cambodians got in there and sure enough, no troubles, and they became part of the basic organization. They were all living in Tent City, of course, and basically the thing that we feared the most was that was the rainy season. I kept saying over the telephone and sending messages one after the other reminding everybody back at CinCPac/CinCPacFlt that this was the rainy season, and we could expect a lot of rains. It turned out to be one of the lighter rainy seasons that we ever had, fortunately. But any way to forestall that, in the tents we put the pallets two deep, so they basically had a two-pallet floor in all the tents. And it did rain, and it got messy but not like it would have been otherwise.

Paul Stillwell: Where did the people go after they'd spent their two or three weeks or whatever in there?

Admiral Shelton: Some of them went through Guam. Others of them went direct to the United States. But they all went back to the United States one way or the other. I think it was 91,000 people that we put through there from April to August. The only person that died while they were there was an older lady who was very dehydrated when she got there; she just couldn't overcome it. We had a couple or three babies born there that managed to survive everything quite well. It really was a pretty good deal.

I've often said to anybody that wanted to listen it was one of the best Navy operations I ever saw. Everything went right, and it was for a good cause. And everybody chipped in. We took the kids from school, including my daughter, out there to, not every day certainly but periodically to make friends and let them know they were welcome.

Paul Stillwell: Did you give any orientation in American ways to these people to prepare them for going to the States?

Admiral Shelton: Not a whole lot. We were able to tell them pretty much where they were going. And of course a lot of them had been separated from some of their families who were refugees also, so there was a system set up and it worked quite well. But we could take anybody's name and who they were looking for and put it in the system and get back if we could find them, and they generally did, could tell them, "Well, they're at Guam now," or "They're at Fort Chaffee now," or wherever they were. And, "You will get back together," and they did. So they thought that was pretty outstanding. So did I. But, no, we did not spend a whole lot of time trying to indoctrinate them into the ways of the United States. I think most of them knew by then. They'd all been associated with all the service people over in Vietnam, so I don't think there was a whole lot to tell them.

Paul Stillwell: You were just providing hotel services.

Admiral Shelton: Well, that and medical and everything else. But it worked out quite well. As a matter of fact, after I retired and moved here to Del Mar, I found out that up in Solano Beach there's a little tailor and beauty shop set up by a Vietnamese man and his wife. I was talking to him one day about this whole thing. He said, "Oh, I came through Subic."

He was in the Navy, and that's a whole other thing that we could talk about that forever. He had come in there on a Vietnamese Navy ship. And so I said, "Well, I've got a book at home that you'd like to see." There are two books that we put together, and they have all this information on what we did. And so he was looking through there, and sure enough there he was, right up on the bridge of this Navy ship. Phang Trang is his name. We do all of our tailor work with him. So here he is over here in the United States doing well. Loves it. He and his wife are putting their son through UCLA.

Paul Stillwell: Did you get some of kind of budgetary supplement, because this must have cost you a bunch you hadn't budgeted for?

Admiral Shelton: Per se I didn't, but all the commands did. I didn't own that part of it or anything like that. I didn't have to worry about the transportation. The naval station had the boats and Cubi had the airport and the naval station had Grande Island, so it wasn't anything. But, yeah, we had to get augmentation. Everybody did. But they got it and we never had a halt. C-5s were flying in and out of there like you wouldn't believe bringing tents and cots and everything we needed.

Paul Stillwell: Were they all airlifted out?

Admiral Shelton: I believe they were. I believe all of them were airlifted out.

Paul Stillwell: What had been the importance that was put on the idea of sending you as an aviator to that job? You said that had been one of the specifications.

Admiral Shelton: I'd better not get into that. I don't mind talking about it, but I don't think it's something that needs to be aired basically.

Paul Stillwell: Well, your judgment on that one.

Admiral Shelton: Let's just say that Admiral Clarey considered the problem out there to be a naval aviators' problem, and he wanted to see a naval aviator out there to correct it. And right away. [Laughter] I never knew Admiral Clarey before, but there are people that do and he was a taskmaster. There's no question about that. He spoke with one voice, and that was authority. But he gave me all the support I needed, and I did the job that he wanted done, I think. So I got along fine with him.

Paul Stillwell: Well, one inference that we might draw is that because there had been incidents in aircraft carriers that that brought it higher to his attention.

Admiral Shelton: Well, without getting into the details that was the bag of worms. By the time of the refugee operation, Admiral Weisner was CinCPacFlt and then moved up to CinCPac later.* Almost all the time I was there Admiral Gayler was CinCPac. And so I saw quite a bit of him coming and going.

---

* Admiral Maurice F. Weisner, USN, served as Commander in Chief Pacific Fleet, 30 September 1973 to 12 August 1976. He later served as Commander in Chief Pacific from 30 August 1976 to 31 October 1979.

Paul Stillwell: Any impressions on him?

Admiral Shelton: None I want to talk about. [Laughter] He and I were not in the same ballpark whatsoever. I never worked for him except in that job. And I never was in a squadron or an air group with him or anything like that, so it would be out of place for me to say anything about Admiral Gayler one way or the other. My relationships with him in the job out there were good. I didn't have a problem.

Paul Stillwell: Well, one of the phenomena of that period was the flood of Z-grams and initiatives that Admiral Zumwalt was putting out.* What impact did you see, say, at your level out in the Philippines?

Admiral Shelton: I didn't have any problem with it at all except what problems the ships had, and I made those my problems when they were in Subic. I put out the word to the ships before they ever came in, and they adopted the habit of briefing everybody before they got to the Philippines, on the way across from the West Coast. And every time they came in if there was anything new, why, I made sure the COs knew what it was about. Once we got this big initial situation corrected, why, we didn't have a problem.

Cubi was a little different situation. Cubi Point O-club was a little different situation than the O-club over on the Subic side because Cubi was where the aviators gathered to have a place to let down their hair when they came in off the line. And I tolerated that. I got some complaints from some of the civilians we had working on the base, but I told them in a nice sort of way that they had their nice shore base place here, that they didn't have to worry about whether they were safe or not. These guys were over there fighting the war, and they needed a place to let down their hair. I said, "As far as I'm concerned, they're going to have that place," so they did. I'm not saying they weren't loud and raucous because they were, but I said, "We've got another O-club over

---

* Z-grams were consecutively numbered policy directives from Chief of Naval Operations Zumwalt that attempted to deal with such issues as enlisted rights and privileges, equal opportunity, and Navy families. Junior personnel viewed them much more favorably than did their seniors. See U.S. Naval Institute Proceedings, May 1971, pages 293-298.

there on the Subic side, and if you want to be that quiet, why, be my guest. Come on over."

Paul Stillwell: And I've heard that the contents of that Cubi O-club have been transported somewhere to the states.

Admiral Shelton: They're down at the National Naval Air Museum in Pensacola—bar and all. A supply officer that had the vision of an aviator when Subic was turned back over to the Philippines bundled all that stuff up and sent it down to the National Naval Air Museum in Pensacola, and there it is, a nice place to go have lunch.[*] [Laughter]

Well, I was going to get back to the Z-gram bit a little bit. We weren't too concerned with it out there. We were out in Subic Bay, and there were elements of morale that had been a problem. They were not a problem now, and I wasn't going to let them be a problem. So the uniform was what I said it was, and haircuts were what I said they were. Shoeshines were what I said they were, and what you wore in the O-club after 6:00 o'clock in the evening was what I said it was. I found that if you're fair and square in that sort of thing and let it be known quite adequately that this is the way it is, why, generally speaking, people respect that.

Paul Stillwell: Did you get any complaints?

Admiral Shelton: A few, and so when I got a complaint I invited him up to my office the next morning. And we sat and had a chat. [Laughter]

Paul Stillwell: Kind of a one-way chat.

Admiral Shelton: [Laughter] No, it wasn't quite like that; I listened to them. And, you know, sometimes I'd take a couple of hours with some of these people. I wouldn't say they went away happy, but they went away understanding. I can think of probably about

---

[*] Because of the Philippine Government's unwillingness to extend basing rights, the U.S. Air Force vacated Clark Air Force Base in November 1991, and the U.S. Navy left Subic Bay in the autumn of 1992.

six times I did that where somebody had a complaint they thought they really wanted to talk to somebody like me about. And so I said, "Okay. Come up and talk." And we did.

Paul Stillwell: What was life like for your family in that environment?

Admiral Shelton: Oh, my wife loved it. I have to say that my younger daughter didn't care that much for it then. She has good thoughts about it now. I think there were a total of 27 people in her high school class. And the kids in schools mostly stayed on base except when they went up to Baguio or on a trip someplace, and those were organized trips, but they didn't go out in town on a regular basis.[*] So life was a little different for them. We had fine schoolteachers on the base, and all the schoolteachers took an interest in all the kids. But it was not like being back in high school in Del Mar or in McLean, and she let me know that quite regularly. [Laughter] Yes, we had our little arguments. I would say that of all the people that I had to talk to out there I was probably least successful talking to her. [Laughter]

There was a drug problem, both on the ships and on the base, so I got together with the CO of the naval station, Whitey Weidman. This was about halfway through the tour, I guess, and I had pretty big hammer authority out there in that respect. If there were people on the base that were civilians that were a drug problem, I could send them back to the States without even blinking an eye. And I did that on a few occasions, not many but a few.

Basically the CO of the naval station and I set up a drug rehab course over there in the personnel center. I required all the civilians on the base and all the kids up through, not in junior high, but in high school to go through this, including my wife. She and my daughter went through that. It was two weeks, and they learned all of the things that we wanted to tell them about drugs, et cetera, et cetera, et cetera. They met a lot of service people that were on drugs, had been on drugs. Some of them would go back to being on drugs, and some of them wouldn't. But it was a requirement. And if they didn't want to do that, then I got them a set of orders back to the States. That happened a couple

---

[*] Baguio is the site a summer resort about 130 miles north of Manila on the island of Luzon in the Philippines.

of times, and the reason it happened was because they knew they had a drug problem and they didn't want to do anything about it. So they went back to the States post haste.

But it worked out pretty good. There was a lot of noise about it, a lot of objections to it when it was first started. They said it was an inconvenience, and it was. Nobody wanted to spend two weeks over there doing it, and I can understand that. But I also understood that there was a problem, and that was one the ways I got at that problem. I couldn't do anything about the ships necessarily except for the people that they sent there.

Paul Stillwell: Did you have some medical people running this program?

Admiral Shelton: We did have medical people there. They weren't running it. It was really more of a personnel accounting type of program, and the medical people ran the lectures, the indoctrinations, that kind of thing. If there was a brig aspect to it they didn't run that part of it. We ran that. But they ran the program as far as lectures, demonstrations, all this kind of thing.

[Interruption]

Paul Stillwell: We've just had a short break here and your wife reminded you that you had to sleep in your office or chose to during that time of the refugee operation.

Admiral Shelton: Yes, it was sort of the only answer because most of my conversations over the phone or the message traffic with CinCPac or CinCPacFlt, as the case may be, was usually anywhere between 2:00 and 4:00 o'clock in the morning. The issues were always things that had to be decided right then and not anything that you were going to wait a half a day or a day for an answer either on their end or my end. And so it was a pretty simple requirement. I just stayed there right there where the communications were. I brought all my shaving gear down there, and I'd get back up to the quarters every once in a while to get a change of uniform or something like that. But basically I stayed down there from April until August.

Tom Kilcline came out to relieve me in August, and so the operation was essentially just about over at that time when I left.* So I had the pleasure of doing the whole thing, the whole operation there. Over on the Cubi side they had a good place where I could hold a little conference every now and then. So periodically, not every day but once a week or so, why, I would hold a little public announcement kind of thing and sit before the microphone and take questions from the locals or from the Filipinos or whomever. But basically I'd have to say that the Filipinos were very understanding about it. They laid down a set of regulations--as you said, as goals—but they didn't pursue them as a mandate. And we didn't have any trouble, so there wasn't any aspect of it that caused them to say, "Well, you're having nothing but trouble with them down there." They sent some people down to look it over every once in a while, which we welcomed.

We had a lot of visitors come through there. Dorothy Parker, who was a big— I've forgotten what her job was, but she looked into all these kinds of things where you take care of refugees and all this sort of thing. Admiral Weisner came out a couple of times, as you would expect, to look it over. The ambassador came down from Manila to look it over. We had a lot of people that came down there to look it over. And, by and large, I think they all liked what they saw. I had eight commands there that were doing their best, and their best was pretty good. It flowed like clockwork. We just didn't have any problems.

Paul Stillwell: Well, there were really two substantial achievements from that tour. One is getting the racial situation squared away, and the other is the refugee care and feeding.

Admiral Shelton: That's right. In between times I enjoyed myself. [Laughter] I enjoyed it anyway. You know, if you go back to when I got orders to go out there and I didn't exactly really want to go out there. As it turned out after I was there and got back, I thought, "Man, that was kind of like when I dragged my heels going to the war college." When I looked back on it a year later, it was a pretty good deal. That's what I thought about Subic, and I have nothing but great fond thoughts about Subic at this point.

---

* Rear Admiral Thomas J. Kilcline, USN, also an aviator, became Commander Naval Base Subic Bay.

Paul Stillwell: Well, where did you move on from there?

Admiral Shelton: Now, that brings up what I was going to talk about. During the time that I was there was also a time for renegotiating the bases agreement out there. That generally comes about with the ambassador as the head of the team and the head of the Philippine armed forces on their side and me on my side basically. If we can't get it ironed out, why, then it goes to some other level. But we got it renegotiated once while I was there, and then just as I was leaving or right after I left, the next set of negotiations were supposedly five years apart, but the Philippines had requested to get back into it again.

Basically there were a number of Philippine senators in Manila that had gotten on the kick again of getting us out of Subic. So we were trying to solve that situation and renegotiate the bases agreement right along with it. So even though I left Subic and went back to Washington, D.C. to OP-07 as my next tour of duty, the ambassador and Admiral Weisner requested that I go back out to Subic to be the head military member on that negotiation team, which I did. I was able to take Peggy back out there with me for part of that trip. We started out up in Baguio, and that wasn't working too well. The Filipinos on the armed services part were having to fly back and forth all the time to Manila, so they got tired of that. So we moved everything down to Manila, and basically we were doing the negotiations partly in their bailiwick and as far as buildings are concerned and partly at the embassy as far as we were concerned. We got that partly settled, of course, and then as history will say, it didn't really solve the problem, I guess, because later on those same senators managed to make enough noise that we eventually lost the bases agreement entirely and were moved out of the Philippines. But anyway when I left Subic, and I was out there for about four months on that tour, came back to OP-07.

Paul Stillwell: This is now still 1975?

Admiral Shelton: This was now into '76. So then I left. I was OP-07B. Vice Admiral Parker Armstrong was my boss.* He was OP-07. And so then, let's see, I left there and Admiral Weisner, he had moved up to CinCPac.

Paul Stillwell: Is there anything to say about the OP-07 job?

Admiral Shelton: No. I wasn't there long enough; I was mostly out in the Philippines during that whole time.

Paul Stillwell: I see.

Admiral Shelton: So there really wasn't much to say about that job. We did get into two little things and whatever, but basically I was gone most of that time. Admiral Weisner wanted me to come out and replace Bill McClendon as J-5, and so I finally agreed to do that.†

Once again we loaded everybody up and moved out of McLean and made our way out to Hawaii this time and spent three nice years there. I was the J-5. I traveled with Admiral Weisner on a lot of trips when he was making his official visits to various places. And I made a lot of trips myself to various places myself. The deputy J-5 job at that time was an Army brigadier job and that was Jack Sadler. He was a fine guy. And he wasn't there very long before he was relieved by a fellow named Norm Schwarzkopf, who was a brand-new caught brigadier general.‡ I don't think Norm really wanted to be there, but I tried to tell him that the Army thought that was a really good job for an Army guy to have, and I certainly thought so. I told him that to get oriented in that job, he would take an initial orientation trip to the various places where we did business with, Japan, Australia, et cetera, et cetera.

---

* Vice Admiral Parker B. Armstrong, USN, Director, Research, Development, Test, and Evaluation, OpNav.
† Rear Admiral William R. McClendon, USN, Assistant Chief of Staff for Plans, U.S. Pacific Command.
‡ On 23 November 1988, General H. Norman Schwarzkopf, USA, became Commander in Chief, U.S. Central Command. He was in that position during the successful Persian Gulf War of 1991. He held the billet until 9 August 1991.

Basically his job was to run the staff and ride herd on the planning. The outgrowth of his work would be things that I would go to Japan with an aide and talk to the Japanese Self-Defense Force about and down to New Zealand, the same reason, and Australia, and Korea. So I had a fairly busy travel schedule. I was gone some, not tremendous amounts. But if you add in the times that I also went to those same places with Admiral Weisner on official visits, why, I was gone quite a bit. Norm had a lot to do with staying there and running the shop.

Paul Stillwell: What can you tell me about Admiral Weisner's style?

Admiral Shelton: His style is pretty direct. [Laughter] He doesn't have any problem letting you know right away what it is that he wants done, and he's very good at keeping track of whether or not you get it done, and he's equally very good at letting you know if he thinks you did a good job. I don't think there's too much you can ask for beyond that. I enjoyed working for him. We played a lot of golf together. He always took my money one way or another. [Laughter] But we enjoyed it, and I enjoyed working for him. I don't know that I ever worked for anybody better.

Paul Stillwell: That's an accolade.

Admiral Shelton: My only disappointment in him was that he wasn't CNO, and I've said that to him personally. Why he didn't put his name in the hat, I don't know, but for whatever the reasons he decided he didn't want to put his name in the hat so he didn't. But I would have been really happy anywhere along the line if he had put his hat in the ring for CNO, and I think he would have been a great one.

Paul Stillwell: Was this essentially a political-military type role that you were filling?

Admiral Shelton: Yes. It's to a large extent the same thing as OP-06; we talked to our people back in OpNav whenever we needed to. We didn't really do that very much because we were a unified command, so we talked to CinCPacFlt and PacAF more than anybody else, but when we did need to talk to anybody back in Washington about various problems including the Philippine bases, why, OP-06 was who we talked to.[*] And Admiral Crowe was OP-06 at that time.[†] But, yes, it was political-military, plans and policy. And I enjoyed it. We made some headway with the Japanese. If you've read the books, you know that the Japanese very adamant about not exceeding nine-tenths of one percent for money committed to defense.

Paul Stillwell: Of their gross national product.

Admiral Shelton: Of their gross national product. And we made some headway on that. We finally got them to spend more than that, and that was quite an accomplishment. We had good relations with South Korea. Enjoyed going there. General Vessey was Commander U.S. Forces Korea at the time, and I never met a guy in another service that I thought as much of as General Vessey. I just thought he was absolutely super.

Paul Stillwell: He was later Chairman of the JCS.[‡]

Admiral Shelton: Yes, that's who it was. And I'm sure Admiral Weisner felt the same way about him. And I think General Vessey felt the same way about Admiral Weisner, so it was a good relationship, good working relationship, good personal relationship for them, and made life easier for all of us down in the next echelon.

Paul Stillwell: Did you have any ties with the People's Republic of China?

---

[*] PacAF—U.S. Air Force Pacific.
[†] Vice Admiral William F. Crowe, Jr., USN, served as Deputy Chief of Naval Operations (Plans, Policy and Operations) from August 1977 to March 1980.
[‡] General John W. Vessey, Jr., USA, served as Chairman of the Joint Chiefs of Staff from 18 June 1982 to 30 September 1985. He had served as Commander-in-Chief, Republic of Korea-United States Combined Forces Command; United Nations Command; Commander, U.S. Forces, Korea, Commanding General, Eighth U.S. Army, 1976-1979.

Admiral Shelton: Not the PRC. I went to Taiwan several times and had the opportunity to be hosted by their CNO, and I had a lot of good Chinese food and lot of good Chinese rice wine. Didn't go there that often. I went there more often with Admiral Weisner than I did by myself.

Paul Stillwell: What about the mainland people?

Admiral Shelton: No. I had absolutely zero contact with anybody in the PRC at that time. Went down to New Zealand and Australia roughly once every six months. Always enjoyed that. I would have liked to have gone down there every day, but I couldn't quite manage that. I went down to their war college so to speak down south of Canberra there a few miles several times and always had a good visit down there.

Paul Stillwell: Was New Zealand raising the issue of nuclear weapons they became so hot about?

Admiral Shelton: Yes, they were. It hadn't become that hot at that time, but their government hadn't changed yet so that's what happened. One of our most far-flung trips really was to New Guinea with Admiral Weisner. He tried and did succeed in making the circuit out there with everybody that was in his realm. And he was very good about it. The Japanese loved to have Admiral Weisner come and visit, and I forget who the one was, I ought to know. But Admiral Weisner is one of the few military people that I know of that was ever invited into a Japanese home. You know, it just doesn't happen, but it did for Admiral Weisner. They always liked to see him come out there.

Paul Stillwell: Was there ever any offer or consideration for an afloat job for you during this period?

Admiral Shelton: No. When I left Subic I expressed my desire to get a command at sea, preferably again back in the carrier world, and that didn't sell. I guess the Zumwalt era had promoted a situation that designated certain flag people that would get shore-based jobs and certain people that would go get at sea jobs, and I was not one of those that was going to get an at-sea job, I guess. I made my desires known, but I didn't succeed in getting it.

Paul Stillwell: Well, at least you had a good alternative then, working for somebody that you liked and respected so much.

Admiral Shelton: Yes, and I can't complain about the jobs. They were fine jobs, so there it was. I'll think of some more things, but basically when time came to retire, why, I came back to San Diego. Admiral Weisner wanted to give me a retirement ceremony out there at CinCPac, and I said, "No, I'd rather go back to San Diego at NTC," so I did. Came back to NTC.*

Paul Stillwell: Which is where you'd started.

Admiral Shelton: Started the whole thing.

Paul Stillwell: When was that?

Admiral Shelton: That was October 1, 1979, so it adds up to 40 years, 2 months, 27 days and 3 hours, [laughter] almost exactly. Yes, and of course Peggy and Donna. Came back with Donna, the youngest daughter, who had a little boy, Robbie, by that time. He was just about a year old, I guess, if that old. Came out to visit us in Hawaii, and then she came back to San Diego with us and was at the retirement ceremony. My oldest daughter, Deb, is an artist, and she's got more art coming out of her little finger than I know what to do with. I can't draw a straight line or a curve, but she knows how to do it, and she knows how to do a lot of things. That's not an eagle, that's a hawk up there. That's one of hers. Those are all vertical lines in there and that's all India ink. So she

---

* NTC—Naval Training Center, which was where Shelton had gone through recruit training in 1939.

does that sort of thing and she also does silver jewelry at this point. She makes it and I'll show you a piece of my wife's jewelry that she made.

Deb married a man who had been in the Army in Vietnam in the military police. Didn't like the Army. Got out and looked around for a while and decided to look at the services again, and he picked the Coast Guard. He was the most competitive guy that I've known in a long, long time. He came back in as an E-3, and he made chief in about seven or eight years. He ended up making WO-4 and he retired on 27 years last April. They're still up in Anchorage, Alaska. He had one tour at old Otis Air Force Base in Massachusetts. From there he went up to Kodiak for his first tour. Left Kodiak and came down to Washington, D.C., at National Airport, and was the head chief under the maintenance officer for the Commandant's airplanes. Went back to Kodiak for another tour. When he left Kodiak again he came right back to Washington, D.C., same job except he was the maintenance officer. And then went back to Kodiak for his final tour. He loves Kodiak.

Paul Stillwell: Evidently.

Admiral Shelton: He loves to hunt and fish. And, as I said, he was very competitive. All the way up through all of this, he always stood number one or two in every exam he ever took. And so they're retired. They live in Anchorage right now, and he's trying to make his way in the civilian investment world, and I don't know whether he's going to enjoy that or not.

Meanwhile, Deb at present works for the Alaskan Museum of History and Art in downtown Anchorage, and in her spare time she does Alaskan silver jewelry at this point, and she's very good at it. Their daughter, Megan, lives and works in Virginia and has presented us with our only great-grandchild so far, a fine little boy named Marc.

Paul Stillwell: What are the highlights for you in the last 20 years since retirement?

Admiral Shelton: Lots of golf. Haven't shot my age yet. I manage to hang onto about a 10 or 12 handicap. When I get over this back surgery I intend to get back, and I hope to get lower than that. But when I retired I decided I'd look into doing something for the community, so I volunteered for the board of the San Diego County Mental Health Association. I did that for four and a half years, and I finally decided that I'd done as much as I could do to help them, if I had done anything at all, and I'm not sure I did. But I learned a lot about civilian charity organizations, more than I really wanted to know. And so after that I didn't do anything more.

I didn't try to go to work in the industry. I didn't want to. If I had wanted to do that, I would have gone back to Washington, D.C. and tried to do it big time, but I didn't want to do that. I did get a call from retired Vice Admiral Howie Greer one day to come down to Convair, and he had something he wanted to talk to me about.* It turned out that he—along with a friend named Cal Swanson, Charles Albert Lindbergh Swanson—wanted to talk to me about the Tomahawk.† It was on paper at that point, and they needed to put together a brochure, if you want to call it that, to go back to OP-03 to sell the program.

Cal and I sat down, and I said, "Yeah, I'll try to help you out." So Cal and I sat down, and our job was to pick out the places in the world where we thought the Tomahawk could be utilized. Both of us being carrier aviators, we didn't want to sell that down the drain either, so we were trying to be a little bit careful there. But we did pick out about, it was either 10 or 12 or 14 places where we felt the Tomahawk could be used and wrote scenarios about how it could be used in those places. Well, it turned out to be a pretty decent brochure. We didn't put the brochure together. All we did was that part of it. But it turned out to be a pretty decent brochure I guess, because the admiral who was OP-03 at the time used that to go to Congress to sell the Tomahawk. So it turned out pretty well, and as it turns out of the 10 or 12 or 14 locales that Cal Swanson and I had picked out and laid it out there's been about five or six of them where it has been used.

Paul Stillwell: It has become the weapon of choice now.

---

* Vice Admiral Howard E. Greer, USN (Ret.).
† Tomahawk is a long-range cruise missile that entered the fleet in the early 1980s, capable of delivering either conventional or nuclear warheads.

Admiral Shelton: Become the weapon of choice and logically so. So that about sums up my professional involvement since I retired.

I've got to say a couple of words about my youngest daughter, Donna. As I said, she didn't enjoy high school out at Subic, and when we all came back to the United States and she began to regroup, why, she did not have a college degree, but she got into the technical end of computer business. At this point she is a junior executive and runs an office back in Reston, Virginia. So she's doing quite well too.

Paul Stillwell: And what's her husband doing?

Admiral Shelton: Her husband is the staff journalist and photographer for Loudon County Times, which is the political newspaper in Northern Virginia. He gets all kinds of awards every year for his journalistic efforts in the photography world, so they're doing quite well. Donna's oldest child, Robbie, is a young man in his third year at Virginia Tech and doing quite well towards getting two degrees in four and a half years. Donna has a daughter, Tiffany, that's just 14, so she's still to pick out which guy she's going to marry and what she's going to do. But she's coming along just fine. All of them are.

Paul Stillwell: As we come near the end, are there any other thoughts that you'd like to offer?

Admiral Shelton: Yes. The one disappointment I have about the Navy is its failure to provide proper family medical care for retirees. Perhaps I should blame the DoD rather than the Navy. In any case, I, along with most retirees, feel that Navy has let us down—and not very gently. The problem isn't with the medical talent or capability but with the poor administration, policies, and lack of commitment to do the job.

Paul Stillwell: Well, I showed up here three days ago just to reminisce about our mutual background in Springfield, Missouri, and it has turned out to be far more beneficial than that. You've given us a lot of wonderful material for history from your own experience.

Your service to the Navy and the nation is one legacy, and what you've said in the last couple of days is another, so I'm most grateful.

Admiral Shelton: I appreciate that.

Paul Stillwell: Thank you very much also for your hospitality and that of your wife over the last two days.

Admiral Shelton: My wife has put up with me this long [laughter] so it must have been pretty good.

Paul Stillwell: And may it continue for many more.

Admiral Shelton: Right. May it do so. Thank you. I appreciate the opportunity.

Paul Stillwell: Thank you.

Index to the Oral History of
Rear Admiral Doniphan B. Shelton
U.S. Navy (Retired)

A-6 Intruder
    Was developed in the 1960s to have all-weather capability, 174-175

AD/A-1 Skyraider
    Operations in Korea in 1951, 168
    In the mid-1960s operated from the carrier Bon Homme Richard (CVA-31), 192, 194

Air Force, U.S.
    Discussion in the mid-1960s on the service's role in amphibious doctrine, 203-204

Air Group One
    See: Carrier Air Group One

Air Warfare
    Pioneering night flight work during World War II, 95-98, 114-115
    In the late 1940s in Fighter Squadron One Easy, 96-100, 108-109
    In the late 1940s in Night Composite Squadron One, 109-112
    In the Korean War the F4U-5N flew night missions from carriers, 117-122, 168-170
    The Korean War did much to further night flight operations, 147, 173-174
    During the late 1950s VF-124 flew the F3H Demon at night, 144-145
    In the early 1960s VF-92 flew the F3H at night, 165-166

Air Wing 19
    See: Carrier Air Wing 19 (CVW-19)

Alaska
    In July 1967 the ammunition ship Paricutin (AE-18) visited Ketchikan, 206-208

Alcohol
    Served in 1944 at Ulithi Atoll in the Carolines, 63-64
    In August 1945 a bottle of rye whiskey was a useful bribe, 85-86

Ambrose, Lieutenant Commander Robert W., USN
    In the early 1960s served as executive officer of VF-92, 162-163

Ammunition
    In the spring of 1945 a merchant ship supplied ammunition to the cruiser St. Louis (CL-49), 73-74
    In 1967-68 the ammunition ship Paricutin (AE-18) replenished combatants off Vietnam, 210-219

Amphibious Warfare
    Discussion in OpNav in the mid-1960s on amphibious doctrine, 203-204
    In the late 1960s, off Vietnam, Marine helos operated from the assault ship Tripoli (LPH-10), 224-225

Antiair Warfare
    Cruiser St. Louis (CL-49) antiaircraft fire against kamikazes in November 1944, 65
    Use of smoke screens against kamikazes in 1945, 77-78

Antisubmarine Warfare
    In the late 1940s hunter-killer groups used escort carriers in night ASW exercises, 96-97

Argentina
    In 1973 the Inter-American Defense Board visited Buenos Aires when President Juan Peron returned to the country, 235-236

Armed Forces Staff College, Norfolk, Virginia
    In the late 1950s provided officers an opportunity to learn about each others' services, 154, 157

Army, U.S.
    Army transport that operated in the Pacific in 1944, 61-63
    In the early 1960s sent officers as students at the Naval War College, 179, 181

Astronauts
    In the early 1950s the F7F was tested for possible astronaut accommodation, 131
    In the late 1950s several future astronauts were at the Test Pilot School, 157-160

Attack Squadron One Easy (VA-1E)
    In the late 1940s used TBM Avengers in antisubmarine exercises, 96-97

Aurand, Lieutenant Commander Evan P., USN (USNA, 1938)
    In the 1940s was a pioneer in Navy night fighter operations, 96, 110
    Lost a tailhook when flying an FJ-1 Fury in the late 1940s, 148

Austin, Vice Admiral Bernard L., USN (USNA, 1924)
    In the early 1960s was president of the Naval War College, 180

Badoeng Strait, USS (CVE-116)
    Used in the late 1940s for pilots' carrier qualifications, 95-96, 99

Bairoko, USS (CVE-115)
    Used in the late 1940s for pilots' carrier qualifications, 95-96, 99

Baldwin, Vice Admiral Robert B., USN (USNA, 1945)
    As a Naval Academy midshipman in the early 1940s, 60
    In the late 1950s served in the Bureau of Naval Personnel, 153
    In 1969, while in BuPers, arranged for Shelton to go to the OpNav staff, 230

Barbers Point Naval Air Station, Hawaii
    In the late 1940s was the base for Night Composite Squadron One, 98-99, 109-116
    Living conditions, 114-116

Barton, USS (DD-722)
    In 1945 took part in the Okinawa operation, 80-81

Battson, Captain Arthur L., Jr., USN (USNA, 1944)
    In the late 1960s commanded an amphibious ready group off Vietnam, 221, 223

Bennett, Midshipman Walker Gardner II, USN (USNA, 1945)
    At the Naval Academy in the early 1940s, 61

Bombs/Bombing
    In August 1945 atomic bombs hit Japan, 83-85
    Japanese hit the aircraft carrier Franklin (CV-13) in March 1945, 84
    By the F4U-5N Corsairs of VC-3 during the Korean War, 119-120, 168-170

Bon Homme Richard, USS (CVA-31)
    Made an Indian Ocean cruise in 1964, 188-193
    Operation in 1964-65 of Carrier Air Wing 19, 190-193
    Nuclear weapons on board, 191-192
    Stops in Japan and Hong Kong on the way home, 194-195
    Provided air cover for Secretary of Defense Robert McNamara's Vietnam visit in 1964, 195

Boot Camp
    See: Recruit Training

Bringle, Vice Admiral William F., USN, (USNA, 1937)
    In 1948-49 commanded Air Group One during an around-the-world cruise, 98, 100-102
    In 1968, as Com7thFlt, attended a change of command on the assault ship Tripoli (LPH-10), 220

Bureau of Naval Personnel (BuPers)
    Difficulty for a Filipino steward converting to electrician's mate in the late 1960s, 208-209
    In 1968 assigned Shelton to an LPH instead of a CVA, 227-229

Bureau of Ordnance
    During the Korean War, a representative from the bureau helped solve a problem with 20-millimeter guns, 44-45

BuPers
    See: Bureau of Naval Personnel (BuPers)

C-2 Greyhound
    Role from the 1970s onward in supporting F-14s on carriers, 231-232

CVW-19
    See: Carrier Air Wing 19 (CVW-19)

Cabot, USS (CVL-28)
    In the summer of 1945 returned Shelton to the United States, 86-87

California, USS (BB-44)
    In 1940 as flagship for Commander Battle Force, 27
    Commander Robert B. Carney as executive officer, 27-28

Cambodia
    In the spring of 1975 Cambodian refugees were housed at Subic Bay in the Philippines, 245-246

Canada
    Visited in the early 1970s by members of the Inter-American Defense Board, 236

Carney, Commander Robert B., USN (USNA, 1916)
    In 1940 as executive officer of the battleship California (BB-44), 27-28

Carrier Air Group One
    In 1948-49 made an around-the-world cruise on board the carrier Tarawa (CV-40), 98, 100-101

Carrier Air Wing 19 (CVW-19)
    Makeup of the air wing in 1964-65, 188
    Indian Ocean cruise in 1964, 188-193
    Operations in 1964-65 from the Bon Homme Richard (CVA-31), 190-193, 195
    Provided air cover for Secretary of Defense Robert McNamara's Vietnam visit in 1964, 195

Chance-Vought
    In late 1945 destroyed many new P-51 fighters because the war was over, 92
    In the mid-1950s had to deal with problems in the F7U, 139

Chandeleur, USS (AV-10)
    In the spring of 1945 operated in support of the Okinawa campaign, 74, 82

China
    In 1948 the carrier Tarawa (CV-40) visited Tsingtao, 102-103

Clarey, Admiral Bernard A., USN (USNA, 1934)
    As CinCPacFlt in 1973, sought a solution to problems at Subic Bay in the Philippines, 237, 240, 248

Clark Air Force Base, Philippines
    In early 1973 U.S. prisoners of war arrived at Clark after being released by North Vietnam, 238-239
    In 1975 temporarily housed refugees from South Vietnam, 244

Commercial Ships
    In the spring of 1945 a merchant ship supplied ammunition to the cruiser St. Louis (CL-49), 73-74
    In the late 1960s had some near collisions with the ammunition ship Paricutin (AE-18), 211

Composite Squadron Three (VC-3)
    In the Korean War a night detachment flew F4U-5N Corsairs, 116-122, 168-170
    The Bureau of Ordnance helped solve a problem with 20-millimeter guns, 44-45
    In the early 1950s was based at Moffett Field, 112, 123-125, 129, 133
    Ran a transitional training unit for the F7U Cutlass in the mid-1950s, 134, 137-140

Congress, U.S.
    In the early 1940s, Reuben T. Wood helped with a Naval Academy appointment, 8, 27

Connolly, Vice Admiral Thomas F., USN (USNA, 1933)
    In the early 1950s was director of the Test Pilot School, 123, 135
    In 1961-62 was ComCarDiv 7 during Sparrow missile tests, 163, 166-167
    From 1966 to 1971 served as OP-05, involved with various aircraft, 135-136, 230-231, 233-234

Cooper, Lieutenant Commander Damon W., USN (USNA, 1941)
    During the Korean War served on a carrier division staff based on the Princeton (CV-37), 169

Corpus Christi, Texas, Naval Air Station
    In the mid-1940s was the site of flight training, 92-93

Cubi Point Naval Air Station, Philippines
    In 1964 a pilot made a long bingo flight from the Bon Homme Richard (CVA-31), 193
    In 1973 was used for evacuating South Vietnamese refugees, 243, 245
    In the early 1970s the officers' club was a place for aviators to let down their hair, 249-250
    Contents of the club are now at the National Museum of Naval Aviation, 250

Dallas Naval Air Station
    Site of flight training in 1945, 88-92
    Dismissal of an officer in the mid-1940s for fraternization, 90-91

Del Mar Target
    Deployed in the early 1960s on F3Hs as a Sparrow missile target, 162-163, 166

Dexter, Commander Edwin B., USN (USNA, 1928)
    In 1945 commanded the destroyer Barton (DD-722) at Okinawa, 80-81

Dick, Rear Admiral John, USN
    Headed OP-602C in the mid-1960s in the area of command relations, 198-199
    In the early 1970s was Commander U.S. Naval Forces Philippines, 238-239

Diego Suarez
    Visited in 1964 by the carrier Bon Homme Richard (CVA-31), 190

Disciplinary Problems
    Dismissal of an officer in the mid-1940s for fraternization with an enlisted woman, 90-91
    In the early 1970s Subic Bay in the Philippines had problems of racial unrest on the base, 237-241
    Drug abuse at Subic Bay in the early 1970s, 251-252

Doudiet, Lieutenant (junior grade) Norman W., USN (USNA, 1939)
    In 1939-40, as division officer on board the battleship New Mexico (BB-40), 16-17
    Died on board the light cruiser Juneau (CL-52) in 1942, 38

Drug Abuse
    Dealing with drug problems at Subic Bay in the Philippines in the mid-1970s, 251-252

Edmonston, Commander Lilburn A., USNR
    Aviator who served in Corpus Christi and other locales in the 1940s, 92-93

Elder, Commander Robert M., USN
    Commanded Air Group 12 from March 1956 to November 1957, 137, 144, 147-150, 165
    Treated with reverence by fellow aviators, 148

Enlisted Personnel
    Recruit training in late 1939 at San Diego, 10-15
    Promising fleet sailors in 1939-40 were prepared for Naval Academy entrance exams, 16-17
    Tough boatswain's mate on board the battleship New Mexico (BB-40) in early 1940s, 17-19
    Most enlisted crewmen in the early 1940s were not married, 19-20
    Dismissal of an officer in the mid-1940s for fraternization with an enlisted woman, 90-91
    Difficulty for a Filipino steward converting to electrician's mate in the late 1960s, 208-209

Enterprise, USS (CV-6)
    Did pioneering work in night flight operations in World War II, 96, 109, 111-112

Ewing, Lieutenant Commander James W., USN
    Pilot who had to retire in the late 1950s because of an aircraft accident, 137, 143

F2H Banshee
    Service tests in the early 1950s at the Naval Air Test Center, 128, 136
    In that period posed a problem on straight-deck carriers, 130

F3D Skyknight
    Jet that flew in the early 1950s, not a good carrier plane, 129

F3H Demon
    In the late 1940s VF-124 was the first Demon squadron on the West Coast, 137, 143-146
    Description of, 143, 144-, 152
    In the late 1950s an F3H shot down a Regulus missile with a Sidewinder, 145, 151-152
    Near accident in 1962 because of an engine failure, 162
    Operations in the early 1960s in VF-92, 162-166

F4U Corsair
 In the Korean War the F4U-5N flew missions from carriers, 117-122, 168-170
 Engine problems in cold weather, 121-122

F6F Hellcat
 In the late 1940s the F6F-5N version was used for both day and night operations, 95-98, 108-109

F7F Tigercat
 Tests in the early 1950s for accommodating astronauts, 131

F7U Cutlass
 Service tests in the early 1950s at the Naval Air Test Center, 131-132, 136
 Description of, 132-133, 143
 Fleet introduction team in the mid-1950s at Moffett Field, 132-133, 138-142
 Sustained many accidents, 132-135, 141-142

F8F Bearcat
 Unsuccessful night fighter version in the late 1940s, 113

F8U/F-8 Crusader
 In the mid-1960s operated from the carrier Bon Homme Richard (CVA-31), 191, 193

F9F Panther/Cougar
 Service tests in the early 1950s at the Naval Air Test Center, 131, 134, 136

F-14 Tomcat
 Work of OpNav and Naval Air Systems Command in the late 1960s and early 1970s, 230-231

FJ-1 Fury
 In the late 1940s had problems with tailhooks pulling out, 148

FR-1 Fireball
 Flown by the Navy in the 1940s but not a good fleet airplane, 94-95

FAWTUPAC
 See: Night Composite Squadron One (VCN-1)

Fighter Squadron One Easy (VF-1E)
 In the late 1940s flew various types of airplanes, 93-97
 Antisubmarine warfare exercises, 96-97
 In 1948-49 made an around-the-world cruise on the Tarawa (CV-40), 98-101

Fighter Squadron 51 Able (VF-51A)
 In the early 1950s was flying FJ-1 Furies, 148

Fighter Squadron 92 (VF-92)
 Operated the F3H in the early 1960s, including a Western Pacific deployment, 160-167
 In the early 1960s the squadron used Del Mar targets for work with Sparrow missiles, 162-163, 166

Fighter Squadron 124 (VF-124)
 Operated the F3H in the late 1950s, including a Western Pacific deployment, 124, 137, 143-150

Fitzpatrick, Rear Admiral Francis John (USNA, 1939)
 In 1939-40 was a division officer of the battleship New Mexico (BB-40), 16-17
 Career communication specialist, 38

Fleet All-Weather Training Unit Pacific (FAWTUPAC)
 See: Night Composite Squadron One (VCN-1)

Flight Training
 In 1945-47 in Texas and Florida, 88-92

Food
 Meals in 1939-40 on board the battleship New Mexico (BB-40), 22-23
 In 1967 an Alaska cannery provided fish to the ammunition ship Paricutin (AE-18), 207-208

Franklin, USS (CV-13)
 In March 1945 hit by Japanese bombs, 84

Fuhrman, Robert A.
 Civilian engineer at the Naval Air Test Center, 1946-53, 128

Gambling
 In the summer of 1945 on board the light carrier Cabot (CVL-28), 86-87

Gayler, Admiral Noel A. M., USN (Ret.) (USNA, 1935)
 In the early 1970s was Commander in Chief Pacific as the Vietnam War wound down, 239, 248-249

George Washington University, Washington, D.C.
 In 1962-63 provided a master's degree program for Naval War College students, 176-177, 181, 184

Gilruth, Robert R.
 In the late 1950s became director of NASA's Project Mercury, 158

Godfrey, Arthur
 For Navy Day 1940 did a radio interview with Shelton, 32-33

Gunnery, Naval
 Practice fired in 1939-40 by the battleship New Mexico (BB-40), 22
 Was a subject studied at the Naval Academy in the early 1940s, 51
 Cruiser St. Louis (CL-49) firing in 1944-45, 65, 67-70, 78-79

Guns
 A Bureau of Ordnance representative helped Composite Squadron Three solve a problem with 20-millimeter guns during the Korean War, 44-45

Habitability
 Messing and berthing in 1939-40 on board the battleship New Mexico (BB-40), 20-22

Harmer, Lieutenant Commander Richard E., USN (USNA, 1935)
 In the 1940s was a pioneer in night fighter operations, 95-96, 109-112, 115, 125, 166
 During the Korean War, 117, 123-125, 129

Hawaii
 In the late 1940s Honolulu provided recreation for off-duty naval aviators, 114-116
 In the late 1950s an F3H Demon shot down a Regulus missile with a Sidewinder at Barking Sands, 145, 151-152

Helicopters
 In the late 1960s, off Vietnam, Marine CH-46s and CH-53s operated from the amphibious assault ship Tripoli (LPH-10), 224-225

Hille, Midshipman Warren R., USN (USNA, 1945)
    Bilged out of the Naval Academy in the early 1940s and later joined the Army, 48

Hong Kong, British Crown Colony
    Visited in the late 1950s by the aircraft carrier Lexington (CVA-16), 165
    Visited in the late 1960s by the amphibious assault ship Tripoli (LPH-10), 226-227

Honolulu, Hawaii
    In the late 1940s provided recreation for off-duty naval aviators, 114-116

Hoover, Ensign William H., USN (USNA, 1945)
    In the late 1940s flew in Fighter Squadron One, 95

Inter-American Defense Board
    Work of the board in the early 1970s, 235-236

Iran
    In May 1964 received a visit from the carrier Bon Homme Richard (CVA-31), 189

Istanbul, Turkey
    In the late 1940s the carrier Tarawa (CV-40) visited Istanbul, 105-106

Jackson, Vice Admiral Andrew M., Jr., USN (USNA, 1930)
    In the mid-1960s served as Deputy CNO (Plans and Policy), 199

Japan
    Surrendered in August 1945 after being hit with atomic bombs, 83-85
    Visited by the carrier Ranger (CVA-61) in the early 1960s, 164-165
    The Bon Homme Richard (CVA-31) was repaired at Yokosuka in 1964, 194
    The amphibious assault ship Tripoli (LPH-10) stopped at Yokosuka in the late 1960s, 223, 226-227
    Limited defense spending in the late 1970s, 257

Japanese Navy
    Torpedoed the battleship Pennsylvania (BB-38) at Okinawa in 1945, 79-80

Jarrett, Lieutenant Commander Harry B., USN (USNA, 1922)
    In the early 1940s in the Naval Academy executive department, 55

Jet Engines
    Unreliable engine in the FR-1 in the late 1940s, 94-95
    VC-3 ran a transitional training unit for jet aircraft in the mid-1950s, 134, 137-140
    J-71 and J-46 engines in the F7U Cutlass in the mid-1950s, 132
    J-71 in the F3H Demon in the late 1950s, 138, 144-145, 163

Jidda, Saudi Arabia
    In the late 1940s the carrier Tarawa (CV-40) visited Jidda, 103-105

Kamikazes
    Suicide attacks against U.S. ships near the Philippines in late 1944, 64-66
    Attacks on U.S. ships at Okinawa in 1945, 74, 76-78

Kasten, Lieutenant Robert I., USN (USNA, 1945)
    In 1955, while at Alameda, introduced Shelton and his future wife, 155

Kennedy, President John F.
    Visits to Newport, Rhode Island, in the early 1960s dislocated service families, 182-183

Kenya
    Visited in 1964 by the carrier Bon Homme Richard (CVA-31), 190

Kerr, Ensign Alex A., USN (USNA, 1945)
    Grew up in Australia, entered the U.S. Naval Academy, and graduated in 1944, 39-40

Ketchikan, Alaska
    In July 1967 the ammunition ship Paricutin (AE-18) visited Ketchikan, 206-208

Kilgariff, Lieutenant (junior grade) Thomas G., USN
    Attended Test Pilot School in the early 1950s, later joined McDonnell, 127

King, Rear Admiral Ernest J., USN (USNA, 1901)
    In October 1940, while on the General Board, had a brief meeting with Shelton, 33

King, Midshipman Louis N., USN (USNA, 1940)
    Served as an enlisted man in the 1930s before attending the Naval Academy, 7-8

King, Lieutenant Commander Richard D., USN (USNA, 1942)
    In the late 1940s flew into Saudi Arabia while attached to the carrier Tarawa (CV-40), 103

Kiper, Lieutenant William D., USN
    In 1964, in an F-8, made a long bingo flight from the Bon Homme Richard (CVA-31), 193

Korean War
    F4U-5N Corsairs of VC-3 flew missions from the carrier Princeton (CV-37), 117-122, 168-170
    The war did much to further night flight operations, 147, 173-174
    BuOrd helped VC-3 solve a problem with 20-millimeter guns, 44-45

Kullberg, Lieutenant Cecil L., USN
    In the 1940s was a pioneer in Navy night fighter operations, 96, 110-111

Ky, Nguyen Cao
    Former Vice President of South Vietnam, evacuated through the Philippines in 1975, 243

Laboon, Midshipman John F., Jr., USN (USNA, 1944)
    As a Naval Academy midshipman in the early 1940s, hazed plebes, 41-42

Lamoreaux, Captain Lewis Scott, USN
    In the early 1970s was detail officer on the F-14 fighter project, 230-231

Leave and Liberty
    In San Diego in the late 1930s, 13
    Long Beach area in 1939-40, 25-26
    Norfolk in the early 1940s was not hospitable to sailors, 32
    In the late 1940s in Tsingtao, China, 102-103
    In the late 1940s Honolulu provided recreation for off-duty naval aviators, 114-116
    Hong Kong was an attraction in the late 1950s, 165
    In the late 1960s in Hong Kong and Yokosuka, Japan, 226-227

Lemoore, California, Naval Air Station
    In 1964 was the site of nuclear weapons targeting sessions, 192

Leonard, Captain William N., USN (USNA, 1938)
    In the early 1960s commanded the carrier Ranger (CVA-61), 161-163, 167

Lewis, Midshipman Albert Clayton, USN (USNA, 1945)
    Boot camp at San Diego in 1939, then served in the battleship New Mexico (BB-40), 12, 17
    In 1940-41 attended the Naval Academy prep school, 32

Lexington, USS (CVA-16)
    In the late 1950s made a Western Pacific deployment, 145-146, 150

Livingston, Commander William H., USN
    In the mid-1950s observed tests of an F7U Cutlass, 139
    In the late 1950s was director of the Test Pilot School, 153, 157-158

Loheed, Commander Hubert B., USN (USNA, 1948)
    In the mid-1960s was shot down and lost in Vietnam, 197-198

Long Beach/San Pedro, California
    Repairs in 1944-45 to the damaged cruiser St. Louis (CL-49), 68-69

Luosey, Lieutenant Commander Michael J., USN (USNA, 1933)
    During World War II was a company officer at the Naval Academy, 54

Maestrone, Ambassador Frank E.
    Foreign Service officer who was a student in the early 1960s at the Naval War College, 179, 181
    In the early 1970s was stationed in the Philippines, 242

Magda, Lieutenant Commander John J., USN
    Served in the late 1940s in fighter squadrons, 98, 125
    Killed in March 1951 while commanding Fighter Squadron 191, 124

Manila, Philippines
    Operation of the U.S. Embassy in the early 1970s, 241-242, 254

Marine Corps, U.S.
    In the late 1960s, off Vietnam, Marine helos operated from the amphibious assault ship Tripoli (LPH-10), 224-225

Martin, Vice Admiral Harold M., USN (USNA, 1919)
    During the Korean War opposed recognition for naval aviators who flew at night, 174

Martin, Commander William I., USN (USNA, 1934)
    In the 1940s was a pioneer in Navy night attack operations, 96, 110-111, 114-115, 167
    Served in the late 1940s as exec of VCN-1/FAWTUPAC at Barbers Point, 112, 114

Mayfield, Lieutenant (junior grade) Harley D., USN
    During the Korean War was in a detachment of Composite Squadron Three, 121-122

McClench, Lieutenant Commander Donald, USN
    In the early 1940s taught at the Naval Academy prep school, then at the academy itself, 45

McCrary, Lieutenant Commander Shannon W., USN
    Killed in the late 1950s while in command of VF-124, 137, 143

McDonald, Admiral David L., USN (USNA, 1928)
    As CNO in the mid-1960s was involved in discussion on amphibious doctrine, 203-204

McNamara, Robert S.
    During his visit to Vietnam in 1964, Carrier Air Wing 19 provided cover, 195
    Proposal in the mid-1960s concerning command relations in Vietnam, 198, 200-202, 204-206

Medical Problems
    In 1941, prospective Naval Academy midshipmen had trouble passing physical exams, 39
    In the late 1960s a crew member on board the ammunition ship Paricutin (AE-18) hurt a leg, 214-215
    In 1968-69, off Vietnam, the assault ship Tripoli (LPH-10) treated wounded Marines, 224-225
    Shelton's view on medical care for military retirees, 262

Military Academy, West Point, New York
    Honor system in the early 1940s, 57

Missiles
    In the late 1950s an F3H Demon shot down a Regulus missile with a Sidewinder, 145, 151-152
    In the early 1960s F3H used Del Mar targets for work with Sparrow missiles, 162-163, 166
    Development of the long-range Tomahawk in the 1980s, 261-262

Moffett Field Naval Air Station, Sunnyvale, California
    In the early 1950s was a base for Composite Squadron Three, 112, 123-125, 129, 133
    Site of F7U Cutlass fleet introduction work in the mid-1950s, 132-133, 138-142
    VC-3 ran a transitional training unit for jet aircraft in the mid-1950s, 134, 137-140

Moorer, Captain Joseph P., USN (USNA, 1945)
    In 1951-52 attended Test Pilot School, 126-128
    In the late 1960s commanded the replenishment ship Camden (AOE-2), 217

Morrison, Captain George Stephen (USNA, 1941)
    In the early 1960s commanded the carrier Bon Homme Richard (CVA-31), 193-194

Music
    High school program in Springfield, Missouri in the 1930s 3, 170-171
    Shelton's friends joined service bands in 1939
    Band on board the battleship New Mexico (BB-40) in 1940, 26

N2S Kaydet
    Used in 1945 at Dallas for primary flight training, 88-89, 92

NASA
    See: National Aeronautics and Space Administration

National Aeronautics and Space Administration
    In the late 1950s did various tests to prepare for the space program, 158

Naval Academy, Annapolis, Maryland
    In the late 1930s in movies and the news media, 7-8
    Preparation in 1939-40 of promising enlisted men in the fleet for academy entrance exams, 16-17
    Hazing of plebes in 1941, 40-42
    News of the attack on Pearl Harbor, 42-43
    World War II combat heroes talked to the midshipmen, 43-44
    Academics in the early 1940s, 44-49, 51, 59
    Practical training, 46, 51-52

Athletics, 49-50
Marching and drilling, 50-51
Social life and etiquette training for midshipmen, 53-54
Role of the executive department, 54-55
Informal honor system, 55-57
Aviation exposure for midshipmen, 58-59
Chapel services, 60-61

Naval Academy Preparatory School, Norfolk, Virginia
In the early 1940s prepared prospective midshipmen for academy entrance exams, 29-31, 35-38
In October 1940 Shelton visited Washington, D.C., and met Rear Admiral Ernest King, 32-33

Naval Air Systems Command
Role in the late 1960s and early 1970s with the F-14 fighter, 230-231

Naval Air Test Center, Patuxent River, Maryland
Service test of aircraft in the early 1950s, 131-135

Naval Reserve
In 1940-41 reserve officers were the instructors at the Naval Academy Prep School in Norfolk, 30-31

Naval Ship Systems Command
Attempts in the late 1960s to fix throttle problems in the assault ship Tripoli (LPH-10), 222
In the late 1960s received complaints about the stabilization system in LPHs, 222-224

Naval War College, Newport, Rhode Island
Program for students in the early 1960s, 176-181

New Mexico, USS (BB-40)
In 1925 visited Australia, 39-40
In 1939-40 preparation of crewmen for Naval Academy entrance exams, 16-17
Tough boatswain's mate directed work on deck, 17-19
Most enlisted crewmen were unmarried, 19-20
Messing and berthing arrangements, 20-22
In 1939-40 operated out of Long Beach, California, including gunnery practice, 22
Meals for the crew, 22-23
Liberty in Southern California, 25-26
Handling in heavy weather in 1940 en route to Bremerton, 23-24
Installation of radar, 23-24
In the spring of 1940 moved to Hawaii, 24-25
Ship's band, 26

Newman, Lieutenant Gene, USNR
In 1945 served as a flight instructor in Dallas, 88, 90

Newport, Rhode Island
Housing available in the early 1960s for Naval War College students, 175-176, 182-183
Visits by President John Kennedy in the early 1960s dislocated service families, 182-183

Newport News, USS (CA-148)
In 1968 replenished from the ammunition ship Paricutin (AE-18) off Vietnam, 213-214, 216

Night Composite Squadron One (VCN-1)
Operations out of Barbers Point, Hawaii, in the late 1940s, 109-116
Stable of aircraft used, 109

Night Operations
    Pioneering night flight work during World War II, 95-98, 114-115
    In the late 1940s in Fighter Squadron One Easy, 96-100, 108-109
    In the late 1940s in Night Composite Squadron One, 109-112
    In the Korean War the F4U-5N flew night missions from carriers, 117-122, 168-170
    The Korean War did much to further night flight operations, 147, 173-174
    During the late 1950s VF-124 flew the F3H Demon at night, 144-145
    In the early 1960s VF-92 flew the F3H at night, 165-166

Norfolk, Virginia
    In the early 1940s was not hospitable to sailors, 32

Nuclear Weapons
    In August 1945 Japan was hit by atomic bombs, 83-85
    Targeting sessions in 1964 at Lemoore Naval Air Station, 192
    Early 1960s survival training for those who would be involved with nuclear weapons, 185-188
    On board the carrier Bon Homme Richard (CVA-31) in the mid-1960s, 191-192

O'Hare, Lieutenant (junior grade) Edward H., USN (USNA, 1937)
    In 1942 talked to Naval Academy midshipmen as an aviation role model, 43-44

Okinawa
    Participation of the cruiser St. Louis (CL-49) and other ships in the 1945 operation, 73-74, 76-82

Olongapo, Philippines
    Problems in the early 1970s of racial unrest among U.S. servicemen, 239-241
    In 1975 residents helped deal with South Vietnamese refugees, 245

O'Neill, Lieutenant Commander Hugh Daniel, USN
    During World War II, shot down a Japanese bomber while test-firing his guns, 125
    In the Korean War headed a detachment from Composite Squadron Three, 116, 125

OpNav Staff
    Work of OP-602C in the mid-1960s in the area of command relations, 198-206
    Long hours in the Pentagon in that era, 203
    Work on amphibious doctrine, 203-204
    Role of OP-506 in 1969-71 in naval aviation requirements, 230-235
    Role of OP-61 in the early 1970s in politico-military affairs, 235-237

Organization of American States
    Work in the early 1970s of the Inter-American Defense Board, 235-236

Osborn, Midshipman James B., USN (USNA, 1942)
    At the Naval Academy in the early 1940s, 40-43, 59

P-51 Mustang
    In 1945 many were destroyed at Dallas because the war was over, 92

PBY Catalina
    During World War II based at Annapolis, Maryland, for midshipmen, 58-59

Pacific Command, U.S.
    Role of the plans shop in the late 1970s, 255-259

Pahlavi, Mohammad Reza
    In May 1964 the Shah of Iran visited the carrier Bon Homme Richard (CVA-31), 189

Paricutin, USS (AE-18)
    In July 1967 visited Ketchikan, Alaska, 206-208
    Difficulty for a Filipino steward converting to electrician's mate, 208-209
    The ship was plagued by old equipment, 209-210, 218-219
    Deployment to the Western Pacific in 1967-68 in support of the Vietnam War, 210-219
    Quality of the crew in the late 1960s, 218

Patuxent River, Maryland, Naval Air Station
    In the early 1950s operated the Test Pilot School and Naval Air Test Center, 126-130

Payne, Captain Paul E., USN
    In the late 1950s commanded VF-124, the first West Coast F3H squadron, 137, 144-146, 151-152
    In the late 1960s commanded the amphibious assault ship Princeton (LPH-5) off Vietnam, 214

Pensacola, Florida, Naval Air Station
    In the mid-1940s was the site of flight training, 93

Pennsylvania, USS (BB-38)
    Torpedoed at Okinawa in August 1945, 79-80

Perry, Commander Donald W., USN
    In the late 1960s served as executive officer of the amphibious assault ship Tripoli (LPH-10), 223

Petersen, Vice Admiral Forrest S., USN (USNA, 1945)
    A Naval Academy midshipman in the 1940s, later an outstanding aviator, 45, 47, 59

Philippine Islands
    Japanese kamikaze operations in the vicinity in late 1944, 64-65
    Difficulty for a Filipino steward converting to electrician's mate in the late 1960s, 208-209
    In the late 1960s Subic Bay was a support base for ships in the Vietnam War, 210-211, 215, 222
    In the early 1970s had problems of racial unrest on the base at Subic Bay, 237-241
    In early 1973 U.S. POWs arrived at Clark Air Force Base after release from North Vietnam, 238-239
    In the 1970s the U.S. country team had both military and Foreign Service personnel, 241-242, 254
    In the spring of 1975 South Vietnamese refugees were housed at Subic Bay, 243-248, 253
    Dealing with Navy drug problems at Subic in the mid-1970s, 251-252
    Base agreement renegotiations in the mid-1970s, 254

Philippine Sea, USS (CV-47)
    Operations during the Korean War, 123-124

Phillips, Commander Billy, USN
    In the mid-1960s commanded VF-194 on board the Bon Homme Richard (CVA-31), 188, 191, 193

Pirie, Vice Admiral Robert B., USN (USNA, 1926)
    In the late 1950s and early 1960s served as OP-05, 159, 174

Porter, Lieutenant Edward M., USN
    In the late 1950s flew an F3H Demon as part of VF-124, 144, 146

Princeton, USS (CV-37/LPH-5)
    Reactivated in 1950 and served off Korea, 117-125, 168-170
    Replenished from the ammunition ship Paricutin (AE-18) off Vietnam in the late 1960s, 214

Prisoners of War
    In early 1973 U.S. prisoners of war arrived at Clark Air Force Base in the Philippines after being released by North Vietnam, 238-239

Promotion of Officers
    Consideration of factors for selection of flag officers in the early 1970s, 232-233

Propulsion Plants
    Repairs to a turbine on board the Bon Homme Richard (CVA-31) in 1964, 194
    Problems in the late 1960s with the throttle mechanism on the assault ship Tripoli (LPH-10), 221-222

Racial Issues
    In the 1930s-1950s Springfield, Missouri, was a segregated city, 33-35
    Difficulty for a Filipino steward converting to electrician's mate in the late 1960s, 208-209
    In the early 1970s Subic Bay in the Philippines had problems of racial unrest on the base, 237-241

Radar
    In 1940 was installed in the battleship New Mexico (BB-40), 23-24
    Use of during World War II on board the cruiser St. Louis (CL-49), 72-73
    In the late 1940s the F6F-5N night fighter had the APS-6 radar, 98, 108-109
    In the late 1940s on board the carrier Tarawa (CV-40), 108
    In the Korean War the F4U-5N flew with the APS-19 radar, 117-122, 169
    Use of in the late 1960 for underway replenishments off Vietnam, 213, 219

Radio
    For Navy Day in October 1940 Arthur Godfrey interviewed Shelton, 32-33

Ramage, Commander James D., USN (USNA, 1939)
    In the mid-1950s set up a transitional training unit at Moffett Field for the F7U Cutlass, 138, 140, 142

Ramsey, Captain Paul H., USN (USNA, 1927)
    In the late 1940s commanded VCN-1/FAWTUPAC at Barbers Point, 110, 112

Ranger, USS (CVA-61)
    In the early 1960s made a deployment to the Western Pacific, 161-167

Recruit Training
    In the latter part of 1939 at San Diego, 10-15

Reed, Midshipman John Hull, USN (USNA, 1945)
    At the Naval Academy in the early 1940s did well in academics, 47

Regulus Missile
    In the late 1950s an F3H Demon shot down a Regulus missile with a Sidewinder, 145, 151-152

Religion
    Naval Academy chapel services in the early 1940s, 60

Replenishment at Sea
    In the late 1960s the ammunition ship Paricutin (AE-18) replenished combatants off Vietnam, 210-219

Rich, Lieutenant Clarence E., USN
    In the late 1940s provided training in night fighter operations, 99, 110

Rockets
    LSMRs used them in 1945 for shore bombardment at Okinawa, 76-77

Roberts, Captain Ralph H., USN (USNA, 1919)
    During World War II commanded the cruiser St. Louis (CL-49), 71

SC-1 Seahawk
    In World War II operated from the cruiser St. Louis (CL-49), 172-173

SNJ Texan
    In the mid-1940s used for naval flight training, 93
    Used in the late 1940s for instrument training, 97

SOC Seagull
    In World War II operated from the cruiser St. Louis (CL-49), 171-173

Sacramento (AOE-1)-Class Replenishment Ships
    Capable new ships that went into service in the 1960s, 213, 216-217

St. Louis, USS (CL-49)
    Operations in the Pacific in late 1944, including a kamikaze hit, 63-66
    Main battery of 6-inch guns, 67, 69-70, 73, 79
    Operation of catapults for aircraft, 171-173
    Repairs at Manus and Long Beach in 1944-45, 66, 68-69
    Bridge watches, 70-73
    Okinawa campaign in the spring of 1945, 73-74, 76-83
    Junior officers were not encouraged to go into aviation, 75-76
    Went to the Philippines shortly after war ended in 1945, 75-76, 83, 85
    Near the carrier Franklin (CV-13) in March 1945 when she was hit, 84
    At Formosa for Japanese surrender there in August 1945, 76, 85

San Diego Naval Training Station/Center
    Site of recruit training in the latter part of 1939, 10-15
    Site of Shelton's retirement in 1979, 259

Sarver, Rear Admiral Ben W., Jr., USN (USNA, 1935)
    During World War II was gunnery officer of the cruiser St. Louis (CL-49), 70-71, 153
    In early 1958 was at the Armed Forces Staff College, 153

Saudi Arabia
    In the late 1940s the carrier Tarawa (CV-40) visited Jidda, 103-105

Schirra, Lieutenant Walter M., Jr., USN (USNA, 1946)
    In the mid-1950s was part of the F7U fleet introduction team, 137-138, 140
    In the late 1950s was part of VF-124, an F3H Demon squadron, 145-146

Schwarzkopf, General H. Norman, USA (USMA, 1956)
    In the late 1970s served in the plans shop of the CinCPac staff, 255-256

Sedaker, Lieutenant Commander Thomas S., USN
    Received his flight training as an aviation cadet, 149
    In 1948 joined Fighter Squadron 51 Able, 98

Shah of Iran
    See: Pahlavi, Mohammad Reza

Shelton, Rear Admiral Doniphan B., USN (Ret.) (USNA, 1945)
    Boyhood in the 1920s and 1930s in Missouri, 1-9, 33-34, 170-171
    Parents of, 1-2, 4-5, 8, 34, 48-49, 60, 237-238
    Siblings of, 3-5, 68, 74, 82
    Wife Peggy, 59, 91, 154-156, 161, 165, 175, 184, 238, 241, 245, 251, 254, 259, 263
    Daughters Deborah and Donna, 154-156, 161, 165, 188, 238, 241, 246, 251, 259-260, 262
    Education of, 2-3, 8, 44-47
    Recruit training in 1939, 9-15
    In 1939-40 as a seaman on board the battleship New Mexico (BB-40), 16-26
    In 1940 in the band of the battleship California (BB-44), 26-28
    In 1940-41 attended Naval Academy prep school at Norfolk, Virginia, 28-33, 35-38
    Naval Academy midshipman, 1941-44, 38-61
    Junior officer in 1944-45 in the light cruiser St. Louis (CL-49), 62-85, 149, 171-172
    Return to the United States in 1945, 85-88
    From 1945 to 1947 took flight training in various locations, 88-93
    Served in 1947-48 in Fighter Squadron One Easy, 93-108
    Served in 1948-49 in Night Composite Squadron One, 109-116
    During the Korean War was in a detachment of Composite Squadron Three, 116-126, 168-170
    In 1951-52 attended Test Pilot School, 126-131, 135
    In 1952-53 was a test pilot at the Naval Air Test Center, 131, 134
    Part of the F7U fleet introduction team in 1953-54, 132-136, 138-141
    In 1954-56 was a team leader for the jet transitional training unit, 134, 137-140
    In 1956-58 was ops officer and XO of Fighter Squadron 124, 137, 143-152, 165
    Attended the Armed Forces Staff College in early 1958, 152-157
    Served 1958-61 as admin officer at the Test Pilot School, 157-158
    In the late 1950s was a candidate to become an astronaut, 158-160
    In 1961-62 commanded Fighter Squadron 92, 160
    Was a student in 1962-63 at the Naval War College, 175-184
    Went through survival school en route air wing command, 185-188
    In 1964-65 commanded Carrier Air Wing 19 on the Bon Homme Richard (CVA-31), 188-198
    From 1965 to 1967 served in OP-602C1 on the OpNav staff, 198-206
    In 1967-68 commanded the ammunition ship Paricutin (AE-18), 206-220, 228-229
    In 1968-69 commanded the amphibious assault ship Tripoli (LPH-10), 220-229
    From 1969 to 1971 served in OP-506 on the OpNav staff, 230-235
    Served in 1971-73 in OP-61, dealing with politico-military affairs, 235-237
    From 1973 to 1975 was Commander U.S. Naval Forces Philippines, 238-254
    Served 1977-79 as J-5 (Director for Plans) on the CinCPac staff, 255-259
    Post-retirement activities since 1979, 260-263

Shelton, Lieutenant (junior grade) Robert F., Jr., USNR
    In 1945, in Patrol Squadron 21, flew a PBM, 74, 82

Shepard, Commander Alan B., USN (USNA, 1945)
    Future astronaut who attended Test Pilot School in the 1950s, 125-126, 159

Shepherd, Rear Admiral Burton H., USN (Ret.)
    In the mid-1950s was part of the F7U fleet introduction team, 138, 140-141
    Became a minister after he retired from the Navy, 141

Ship Handling
    In the late 1960s the ammunition ship Paricutin (AE-18) replenished combatants off Vietnam, 210-219

Shore Patrol
    Use of at Subic Bay in the early 1970s to deal with racial unrest, 239-241

Sickel, Lieutenant Commander Horatio G. IV, USN (USNA, 1944)
Was at Moffett Field in the mid-1950s as part of the F7U program, 132-133, 141-143

Sidewinder Missile
In the late 1950s an F3H Demon shot down a Regulus missile with a Sidewinder, 145, 151-152

Smith, Commander Andrew Jackson, USN (USNA, 1931)
In 1945 was executive officer of the cruiser St. Louis (CL-49), 75-76

Smith, Vice Admiral John Victor, USN (USNA, 1934)
In the mid-1960s served in the OP-06 organization in OpNav, 200
In the late 1960s was Commander Amphibious Force Pacific Fleet, 229

Smith, Senator Margaret Chase
In the mid-1960s asked OpNav for a study on command relations in Vietnam, 198, 200-202, 204-206

Snyder, Captain Edwin K., USN (USNA, 1944)
In the late 1960s commanded the heavy cruiser Newport News (CA-148) off Vietnam, 213-214

Snyder, Commander Jack L., USN
In the mid-1960s commanded VF-191 on board the Bon Homme Richard (CVA-31), 188, 191

South America
Work in the early 1970s of the Inter-American Defense Board, 235-236

Space Program
In the early 1950s the F7F was tested at for possible astronaut accommodation, 131
In the late 1950s NASA did various tests and screen potential astronauts, 158-160

Spangler, Midshipman Eugene H., USN (USNA, 1945)
Former enlisted man at the Naval Academy in the early 1940s, 48-49, 53
Shortly after World War II went through flight training, 93

Sparrow Missile
In the early 1960s the F3H used Del Mar targets for work with Sparrow missiles, 162-163, 166

Spell, Lieutenant Billie C., USN
During the Korean War was landing signal officer for the carrier Princeton (CV-37), 122

Steele, Vice Admiral George P. II, USN (USNA, 1945)
As a midshipman in the early 1940s at the Naval Academy, 36-37

Stockdale, Commander James B., USN (USNA, 1947)
In 1965 was rerouted from command of Air Wing 19 to Air Wing 16, 196-197

Streeper, Commander Harold P., USN
In the early 1960s went through survival training in California, 186

Subic Bay, Philippines
In the late 1960s was a support base for ships in the Vietnam War, 210-211, 215, 222
In the early 1970s had problems of racial unrest on the base, 237-241
In the spring of 1975 South Vietnamese refugees were housed at Subic, 243-248, 253
Dealing with Navy drug problems in the mid-1970s, 251-252

Suez Canal
    Transit by the carrier Tarawa (CV-40) in the late 1940s, 105

Survival Training
    Conducted in the early 1960s in California for aviators involved with nuclear weapons, 185-188
    Discussed by Commander James Stockdale in 1965 in command turnover briefings, 196-197

TBM Avenger
    In the late 1940s was used in antisubmarine warfare exercises, 96-97

TV Seastar
    Used in the late 1950s for inverted spin tests, 157

Tarawa, USS (CV-40)
    In 1948-49 made an around-the-world cruise with Air Group One, 98-106, 108-109
    Description of the ship, 107

Test Pilot School, Patuxent River, Maryland
    In the early 1950s Commander Thomas Connolly was director, 123, 135
    During that time trained some of the Navy's top pilots, 126-131
    In the late 1950s future astronauts were at the school, 157-158
    Curriculum had improved by that time, 157-158

Tierney, Commander John M., USN (USNA, 1946)
    In 1965 took command of Carrier Air Wing 19, 197

Tomahawk Missile
    Development of in the 1980s, 261-262

Torpedoes
    The Japanese torpedoed the battleship Pennsylvania (BB-38) at Okinawa in 1945, 79-80

Training
    Boot camp in the latter part of 1939 at San Diego, 10-15
    Naval Academy summer cruises in YPs during World War II, 51-52
    Flight Training in 1945-47 in Texas and Florida, 88-92
    Instrument training for aviators in the late 1940s, 97
    In the early 1950s Test Pilot School trained some of the Navy's top pilots, 126-131
    Survival training was conducted in the early 1960s in California, 185-188

Transitional Training Unit
    In the mid-1950s VC-3 trained pilots to move from propeller planes to jets, 134, 137, 139-140

Tripoli, USS (LPH-10)
    In 1968-69 the supported amphibious operations off Vietnam, 220-222, 224-226
    Problems with the engineering plant, 221-222
    The stabilization system was faulty, 222-224
    Medical treatment of Marines wounded in combat in Vietnam, 224-225
    Port visits to Hong Kong and Yokosuka, Japan, in the late 1960s, 226-227

Trout, Lieutenant Commander R. L., USN
    In the late 1940s commanded the night fighter detachment on board the Tarawa (CV-40), 99-100

Tsingtao, China
    In 1948 the carrier Tarawa (CV-40) visited Tsingtao, 102-103

Turkey
    In the late 1940s the carrier Tarawa (CV-40) visited Istanbul, 105-106

Ulithi Atoll, Caroline Islands
    Fleet anchorage and recreational spot in 1944, 63

Uniforms—Naval
    Training in 1939 at boot camp in San Diego about stowage of uniforms, 10-11

VA-1
    See: Attack Squadron One (VA-1)

VC-3
    See: Composite Squadron Three (VC-3)

VCN-1
    See: Night Composite Squadron One (VCN-1)

VF-1
    See: Fighter Squadron One Easy (VF-1E)

VF-51
    See: Fighter Squadron 51

VF-92
    See: Fighter Squadron 92 (VF-92)

VF-124
    See: Fighter Squadron 124 (VF-124)

Vessey, General John W., Jr., USA
    Service as Commander in Chief of U.N. forces in Korea in the late 1970s, 257

Vietnam War
    Survival training was conducted in the early 1960s in California, 185-188
    Air Wing 19 provided cover for Secretary of Defense Robert McNamara's Vietnam visit in 1964, 195
    Aviators shot down in Vietnam in the mid-1960s, 196-198
    Proposal in the mid-1960s concerning command relations in Vietnam, 198, 200-202, 204-206
    In 1967-68 the ammunition ship Paricutin (AE-18) replenished combatants off Vietnam, 210-219
    In 1968-69 the assault ship Tripoli (LPH-10) supported operations off Vietnam, 220-222, 224-226
    In early 1973 U.S. POWs arrived in the Philippines after being released by North Vietnam, 238-239
    In the spring of 1975 South Vietnamese refugees were housed at Subic Bay, 243-248, 253

Ward, Captain J D, USN
    In the mid-1950s was part of the F7U fleet introduction team, 138, 141

Washington, D.C.
    For Navy Day 1940 Arthur Godfrey did a radio interview with Shelton, 32-33

Way, Lieutenant (junior grade) H. R., USNR
    In 1945 served as a flight instructor in Dallas, 88-90, 122

Weather
    The battleship New Mexico (BB-40) rolled during heavy weather in 1940, 23-24
    Wintertime aircraft carrier operations in the Korean War, 118-122

Weidman, Captain Robert M., Jr., USN (USNA, 1948)
    In the early 1970s commanded the naval station at Subic Bay, 239-240, 251

Weisner, Admiral Maurice F., USN (USNA, 1941)
    As VCNO in 1973, sent Shelton to deal with problems in Subic Bay, Philippines, 236-238
    In the mid-1970s was Commander in Chief Pacific Fleet, 248, 253-254
    In the late 1970s was Commander in Chief Pacific Command, 255-258
    Assessment of style and capability, 256

Wells, Lieutenant Commander Aaron Lee, USN
    In the late 1960s served as exec of the ammunition ship Paricutin (AE-18), 211, 215, 218-219

Wendt, Vice Admiral Waldemar F. A., USN (USNA, 1933)
    In the late 1960s served as Deputy CNO (Plans and Policy), 199-200

Weymouth, Commander Ralph, USN (USNA, 1938)
    As air group commander in the Philippine Sea (CV-47) during the Korean War, 123-124

Widhelm, Commander William J., USN (USNA, 1932)
    In the 1940s was a pioneer in Navy night fighter operations, 110-111

Williams, Commander David T., USN
    In the late 1940s flew night fighter planes, 99-100, 102-104, 110, 127, 148-149
    In the 1950s was on the staff at Test Pilot School, 127

Wilson, Midshipman Edward P., Jr., USN (USNA, 1945)
    At the Naval Academy in the early 1940s, 51, 61

Women in the Navy
    Dismissal of an officer in the mid-1940s for fraternization with an enlisted woman, 90-91

Wood, Representative Reuben T.
    In the early 1940s, assisted Shelton in getting a Naval Academy appointment, 8, 27

Yokosuka, Japan
    Repaired the carrier Bon Homme Richard (CVA-31) in 1964, 194
    Port visit for the amphibious assault ship Tripoli (LPH-10) in the late 1960s, 223, 226-227

Zumwalt, Admiral Elmo R., Jr., USN (USNA, 1943)
    In the early 1970s served as Chief of Naval Operations, 237-238, 249, 250, 258-259

www.ingramcontent.com/pod-product-compliance
Lightning Source LLC
Chambersburg PA
CBHW080616170426
43209CB00007B/1446